CANADIAN EDITION

Cornerstone

BUILDING ON YOUR BEST

RHONDA J. MONTGOMERY

The University of Nevada, Las Vegas

PATRICIA G. MOODY

The University of South Carolina

ROBERT M. SHERFIELD

Community College of Southern Nevada

DON FRASER

Durham College

LISA FRASER

LDF Publishing Inc.

ALLYN AND BACON CANADA

Canadian Cataloguing in Publication Data

Main entry under title:

Cornerstone: building on your best

1st Canadian ed.

ISBN 0–205–26874–9

1. College student orientation.   I. Montgomery, Rhoda J.

LB2343.3.C676 1997   378.1'98   C96–932034–5

© 1997 Prentice-Hall Canada Inc., Scarborough, Ontario
A Division of Simon & Schuster/A Viacom Company

Allyn and Bacon, Inc., Needham Heights, Massachusetts
Prentice-Hall, Inc., Upper Saddle River, New Jersey
Prentice-Hall International (UK) Limited, London
Prentice-Hall of Australia, Pty. Limited, Sydney
Prentice-Hall Hispanoamericana, S.A., Mexico City
Prentice-Hall of India Private Limited, New Delhi
Prentice-Hall of Japan, Inc., Tokyo
Simon & Schuster Southeast Asia Private Limited, Singapore
Editora Prentice-Hall do Brasil, Ltda., Rio de Janeiro

ISBN 0-205-26874-9

Vice President, Editorial Director: Laura Pearson
Acquisitions Editor: Cliff Newman
Signing Representative: Kris Begic
Developmental Editor: Imogen Brian
Production Editor: Amber Wallace
Copy Editor: Ann McInnis
Editorial Assistant: Ivetka Vasil
Production Coordinator: Sharon Houston
Permissions/Photo Research: Marijke Leupen
Cover Design: Julia Hall
Cover Image: © Sibley Peteet Design. Courtesy Jaqueline Dedell Artist Representative.
Character Illustrator: Christian O'Brien
Page Layout: Gail Ferreira Ng-A-Kien

Original English Language edition published by Allyn and Bacon, Inc., Needham Heights, MA. Copyright © 1997.

1 2 3 4 5   CC   01 00 99 98 97

Printed and bound in United States.

Visit the Prentice Hall Canada web site! Send us your comments, browse our catalogues, and more. **www.phcanada.com**
Or reach us through e-mail at **phabinfo_pubcanada@prenhall.com**

CONTENTS

UNIT II SHARPENING THE TOOLS OF LIFE   108

An Insider's View: Raymond Barnes

An Insider's View: Peter Keech

So Much to Do, So Little Time to Do It: Priority Management   110

I Heard You! I Heard You! What Did You Say?: The Art of Active Listening   140

Will This Be on the Test?: The Essentials of Note-Taking   164

Avoiding the "All-Nighter:" Studying for Success   184

The Proving Ground: Strategies for Test Taking   210

UNIT IV   THE NUTS AND BOLTS OF COLLEGE LIFE   *318*

To Join or Not to Join—That Is the Question: Campus Activities   320

What Are You Doing for the Rest of Your Life: Career Planning   334

APPENDIX

Things You Need to Know but Probably Will Never Ask   360

CORNERSTONE was born out of our desire to help new college and university students develop the skills that would enable them to be successful in their post-secondary education. Seldom will you read a textbook as honest and straightforward as we have tried to make this one. The words that you read and the activities provided in this worktext have not come easily to us. They are the result of our collective experiences over our many years of teaching and administration in higher education. We hope our words will provide you insight that will enable you to make it to graduation and beyond.

> Education is not preparation for life, education is life itself.
>
> John Dewey, educator

This worktext is designed to help you make the most of your college and university experience. If you already know what you want to get out of your higher education and you've got a concrete plan for getting there, that's great! Hopefully this worktext will give you some new ideas on how to improve your academic work habits and enhance your personal growth.

If you're not certain of why you're here or if you haven't got a great track record, this worktext can help you make a brand new start. We've got a section on how to set goals that are right for you, and how to get motivated so that you see a good reason for putting in hard work. We've got some suggestions on how to work smart so that you make it academically, yet still have time for life outside the classroom. We have some information on personal development to make your years at college and university and your life after graduation as fulfilling as possible.

Within the pages of this worktext you will find many activities such as *At This Moment* and *The One Minute Journal,* which will help you explore where you are and where you are going. Each unit begins with stories from students across Canada discussing issues found within the unit. Each unit ends with an *Internet Activity* that will both help you explore issues and actively learn to use one of the most powerful technological tools available today.

Cornerstone contains many activities and questions for you to answer. We hope that our words will teach you and challenge you. It is also our hope that you'll be open and willing to participate. With your participation, this worktext holds unlimited possibilities for bringing change, improving skills, and setting you off on a lifetime of success.

Available with your book is a double entry journal, in which you are asked to respond to a variety of questions. When used properly, this journal can be a valuable communication tool between you, your peers, and your instructor. Take your time to reflect honestly and openly on the questions asked. Only through your own soul-searching and self-revelation will the features of this book help you improve your skills as a student and assist you in becoming a productive citizen.

We wish you luck in building your future on the cornerstones that will carry you for the rest of your life.

Rhonda J. Montgomery

Rhonda Montgomery is the Assistant Dean of Student Affairs for the William F. Harrah College of Hotel Administration at the University of Nevada, Las Vegas and has been teaching in higher education for 10 years. Rhonda has been responsible for developing and incorporating first-year orientation/study skills curricula into existing introductory courses and programs.

Rhonda is the co-author of five texts including two student success texts, *Cornerstone* and *365 Things I Learned in College* (Allyn & Bacon, 1996). She has also presented at The National Conference on the Freshman Year Experience and spoken extensively to first-year students and educators about building success into their curriculum.

Patricia G. Moody

Patricia G. Moody is a Professor and Chairman of the Department in Business and Marketing Education at the University of South Carolina, where she has been a faculty member for over twenty years. An award-winning educator, Pat has been honored as Distinguished Educator of the Year at her college, Collegiate Teacher of the Year by the National Business Education Association, and has been a top-five finalist for the Amoco Teaching Award at the University of South Carolina. In 1994, she was awarded the prestigious John Robert Gregg Award, the highest honor in her field of over 100,000 educators.

Pat frequently speaks to multiple sections of first-year students, incorporating personal development content from her trademark speech, "Fly Like an Eagle," as well as numerous strategies for building self-esteem and for achieving success in college. She also works with first-year classes on subjects such as goal setting, priority management, and diversity.

Robert M. Sherfield

Robert Sherfield has been teaching public speaking, theater, and study skills and working with first-year orientation programs for over 13 years. Currently, he is a full-time faculty member at the Community College of Southern Nevada, teaching both study skills and orientation courses.

Robb's extensive work with student success programs includes experience with the design and implementation of these programs— including one program that was presented at the International Conference on the Freshman Year Experience in Newcastle upon Tyne, England.

In addition to his coauthorship of *Cornerstone: Building on Your Best,* he has also coauthored *Roadways to Success* (Allyn & Bacon, 1997) and the trade book, *365 Things I Learned in College* (Allyn & Bacon, 1996).

Don Fraser

Don Fraser has been a professor at Durham College for the past 22 years. He co-designed and implemented Durham's student success program 10 years ago, and has been working in this area ever since. Don has done a great deal of research on student success and retention, and has done first year experience consulting with many colleges and universities internationally. Don won a National Institute for Staff and Organizational Development award for his contribution to Durham College's student success program in 1988.

Lisa Fraser

Lisa Fraser owns LDF Publishing Inc. and has authored *Making Your Mark,* a college success book that has sold over 100,000 copies. Prior to this she was a professional proposal writer, securing funding and grants for community college projects.

CORNERSTONE

UNIT

Laying a Strong Foundation

■ AN INSIDER'S VIEW

Scholastica Whitney
Age 30
Camosun College
Victoria, British Columbia

I've had to deal with a lot of change in my life. In 1990, I came to Canada from Nigeria. Adapting to a totally new culture was quite difficult; one of the most difficult things to adjust to was the pace of life here. Everything was so much faster! People spoke faster, worked faster — I was used to a much more relaxed lifestyle.

Though I'd taken English in school, I found that I wasn't easily understood because of my heavy accent. It was important to me to fit into my new culture, and it was extremely frustrating when people couldn't make out what I was saying. Determined to make the most of my new experience in Canada, I enrolled in Camosun College's English as a Second Language (ESL) program.

I was fortunate to have as classmates people who were well-educated in their native countries. It helped to keep me motivated; I thought that if they could work through the difficult adjustments they were facing, I could too. One of the things that made me successful was how I developed my academic work habits. I took a lot of notes, and I never missed a class. I worked really hard, and I found it easier to do well because I made friends with other students who were as committed to succeeding as I was.

When I graduated from the ESL program, I took an 8-week career options course. We went out to interview people working in career areas that interested us. The course really changed my life. I decided that working in an office appealed to me, and I identified the skills I'd need to get an office job. This led me to the Office Administration program at Camosun. It was more difficult than the ESL program because I was the only one whose first language wasn't English, but I applied the same work habits that I'd used in my previous courses, and I graduated from the program. I am now working in the ESL office at Camosun College.

It was a long process, but I've now got a good job that I really enjoy. I'd like to say, particularly to new Canadians, to take the time that's required to get an education and develop a career. Polish your English skills, research which career you'd like to have, and be patient while you're going through the learning end of it. Sometimes you may feel like quitting, like it's all too long and difficult, but make the most of the changes in your life. You've been given a great opportunity now that you're at college. Set goals for your life, and follow them up with the education you need to get there. It's worth the effort.

■ AN INSIDER'S VIEW

Devin Smith
Age 24
Durham College
Oshawa, Ontario

When I was in high school, I didn't think too much about the future. In retrospect, I guess I was too interested in socializing, and I didn't pay enough attention to what I wanted to do with my life. As a result, when it was time for university, I took history because that was what my father and brother had done. I thought I'd become a teacher and follow in their footsteps. I got average marks, and I kind of drifted through my university years.

I had always enjoyed sports, and had spent my summers running hockey clinics; one year I went to New York City to work for a sports agent. That summer, I realized that I wanted a career in sports. I set the specific goal of working in professional hockey, and I decided to apply to Durham College's sports administration program. I met with one of the professors to convince him that I should be accepted into the program. I told him that my average marks were a thing of the past, that I would work my hardest because I now had a clear-cut career goal. My background in sports and my determined attitude demonstrated my commitment to succeed in this field.

As a result, I was accepted into the program. While I was at college, I volunteered at as many sporting events as possible with the goal of making job contacts and gaining relevant job experience. I also wanted to do well academically, so I decided to aim for an A average. Since I had set my sights on getting good grades, I got them—I made the dean's list. I'm convinced that if I'd

Since I had set my sights on getting good grades, I got them—I made the dean's list.

approached my studies without a set goal, my marks wouldn't have been as high.

I am now working with the Vancouver Canucks Hockey Club as the Manager of Media Relations and Hockey Information. I'm here to say that if you want anything badly enough, and you set a goal to get there, you will.

Life is its own journey, it presupposes its own change and movement, and one who tries to arrest change does so at his eternal peril.

Van der Post

Nothing Stays the Same: Preparing for and Dealing with Change

Diane was an honours high school student. She was accepted at the three universities she applied to, and she decided to go to the one located in the city in which she lived. She wanted to pursue a career in the health sciences field, and decided on a course of studies that included mostly sciences. Diane arrived on campus the first day of classes, and was surprised to find that there were 250 fellow students in her psychology class. She had a hard time following the lecture, and was disconcerted to find that she was expected to get the majority of her notes from a cassette tape recorder in a lab setting. She experienced much of the same in her other classes, and by the end of her first week, she was feeling pretty disappointed with her initial university experience. But because she had a history of doing well in high school, she was determined to do the same at university. It was difficult, though, because she lived off campus, and didn't really have a chance to meet new friends. The impersonal setting, the competition for high

marks that was rampant among students vying for a medical career, and eventual career indecision took their toll, and Diane eventually dropped out at the end of the first semester.

Diane worked for six years before she returned to post secondary education. She worked at a bank, took French and Spanish courses at night, went on a French immersion program for a summer in Quebec, travelled to Europe, and worked for a government office during that time. She made sure that even though she wasn't enrolled in a full time educational institution, she was constantly upgrading her basic skills and improving her

workplace skills.

After much reflection, Diane decided that she wanted to take a business administration program at a community college. She applied as a mature, nontraditional

Change is a constant in life.

student, and enrolled at a college that was located 100 miles from her hometown. She wanted to live away from home and make the most of her college experience.

Diane approached her education with the same intensity and commitment that she applied to everything else she did. She tried never to miss a class, listened carefully to everything the professors said, took a complete set of notes, and studied hard for each test and exam. She worked hard on her assignments—probably too hard—but throughout her time at college she was on the honour roll and made the dean's list. She won two scholarships, and graduated with the highest standing in her division. Diane was hired as the business manager for a small company upon graduation, where she worked for four years. She is now running her own business, and has used the experience she gained in the workforce and the knowledge acquired at college to become a successful entrepreneur.

Diane's story is significant because it shows that change is a constant in life, and that regardless of your path to post secondary education, it is never too late to be successful. Diane's career path changed several times, her jobs changed, her skill base changed, her goals changed, and to this day, she is changing with each new experience. College was one of the most significant changes in her life; it shaped her career and her life. It is a wonderful opportunity to make a new start.

Regardless of your path to post secondary education, it is never too late to be successful.

Why Address Change?

Take a minute and think about your life so far. You've already faced some major changes. For some of you, graduating from high school recently was a big change. For others, returning to school after being out for five or ten years is a monumental change. For still others, the loss of your job or changing job requirements have caused you to return to college. In the days, weeks, and months to come, you'll be faced with many more changes, changes that you perhaps did not or could not have expected. You will meet people whose religion, race, national origin, age, or sexual orientation differs from your own. You'll be asked to sit in groups with people who do not have the same values, morals, judgments, and actions as you. You'll be told and shown things by professors and peers that you never imagined possible. Some of these events will be positive, some shocking, some disturbing, some elevating, and some life altering. You are embarking on one of the most exciting rides of your life—so get ready!

In many of the situations that will arise in the coming days, you may not have to be involved or take any action, you may be only an observer. In some situations you will need to take immediate action. In other cases you'll have time to ponder and reflect on the appropriate action. This chapter will help you cope with change and make wise and healthy decisions. After completing this chapter, you will be able to

- Determine how important college is to you

- Identify reasons for attending college

- Discuss how college changes people

- Analyze recent changes in your personal life

- Prepare for changes in the coming days

- Prepare for life changes

- Discuss the premises of change

- Recognize and deal with the physical and emotional effects of change

- Incorporate into your life the cornerstones for dealing with change

Why Cornerstone?

What Can This Book Do for You?

This book is intended to change you. We hope that this book will help you see more clearly the possibilities the future holds; that the activities included here will help you anticipate and cope with the many new situations you will face; that in the days and weeks to come you will use this book as a guide to help you contend with change, discover more about yourself, develop study and prioritizing skills, master the terminology of college life, develop a system for personal wellness, learn more about careers, cope with stress, and develop an appreciation for diversity. We hope that our words together—yours and ours—will help you make your goals and dreams come true. This book is primarily about decisions: decisions

> Life is about change, and about movement, and about becoming something other than what you are at this very moment.
>
> Unknown

List the major reasons that you are in college or university today. Be honest with yourself!

1. _____

2. _____

3. _____

4. _____

Were all four blanks easy to fill? Did you do it quickly? As you discuss these reasons in class, you will find that many of your classmates are attending college for many of the same reasons you listed. If your class holds true to form, most of your classmates responded "to get a better job and make more money." In a poll conducted by *The Chronicle of Higher Education* (August 25, 1993) 78.5 percent of first-year students polled responded to this question with the answer "to be able to get a better job."

Depending on how you approach it, college can, and should be, one of the most exciting times of your life. Certainly college brings stressful times, party times, happy times, tearful times, and life-altering times. And yes, college can lead to a more lucrative future. In 1992, Statistics Canada reported that 83.6 percent of those with less than grade eight education earned less than $20,000 per year, while 56.5 percent of those with a post secondary diploma made more than $20,000 per year. Of those with a university degree, 54.2 percent made more than $30 000 per year.

The average salary of a college graduate was $26 395; a university graduate earned on average $36 650. The following table provides a more detailed overview of differences in earning power based on educational level. There are even more compelling reasons to pursue a post secondary education. "In 1994, 145 000 jobs in Canada disappeared for people with high school education or less, while 422 000 jobs were created for workers with post secondary education" (Foote, 1996).

We do not mean to suggest that the only reason for attending college is to get a better job or to make more money. Many other considerations may be at least as important as money to a person's decision to attend college, among them knowledge, spiritual development, sports, socialization, peer or parental pressure, and job training. Some of these reasons are practical, and some have a more altruistic appeal. Were any of these items listed as one of *your* reasons for attending college?

Percentage Distribution of Individuals by Income Groups and Education

	Grade 8	Some High School	High School Diploma	Some Post Secondary	Post Secondary Diploma/Cert.	University Degree
Income Group	%	%	%	%	%	%
$0–9,999	20.3	22.6	17.8	29.2	14.8	12.7
$10–14,999	48.3	29.0	20.6	19.4	15.5	9.2
$15–19,999	15.0	16.3	13.7	12.1	13.1	8.9
$20–24,999	5.6	7.6	9.9	6.8	10.8	7.5
$25–29,999	4.6	7.3	8.8	7.3	9.1	7.4
$30–39,999	3.2	9.8	14.5	10.9	16.8	15.1
$40–49,999	1.5	4.1	7.9	8.0	10.1	15.2
$50,000+	1.5	3.3	6.7	6.5	9.7	23.9
Total %	100	100	99.9	100.2	99.9	99.9
Average Income	$15 246.00	$18 903.00	$23 762.00	$21 371.00	$26 395.00	$36 650.00
Median Income	$13 041.00	$14 751.00	$18 917.00	$15 529.00	$22 641.00	$32 812.00

Source: Statistics Canada, 1994.

thoughts

Change is certain to happen during your college years.

One response you probably won't find on your list of reasons for attending college or university—or on the lists of your classmates—is "I want to change." Although most people do not come to college for the express purpose of changing, change is certain to happen during your college years. The key to dealing with change is to realize that change is the only thing in this world that is assured, short of death and taxes.

Whatever your reasons for attending college and university, if you embrace the notion that change is going to occur and respond to change by guiding it along, nurturing your new relationships with peers and professors, learning to study effectively, becoming involved in campus activities, and opening your mind to different views and ideologies, this will be a "moment in time" that you can carry with you for the rest of your life. You will be building on your best.

The Significance of Your College Experience

In your lifetime many events, people, places, and things will alter your views, personality, goals, and livelihood. Few decisions, people, or travels will have a greater influence on the rest of your life than your decision to attend college and the years you spend in structured higher learning. College and university can mean hopes realized, dreams fulfilled, and the breaking down of social and economic walls that may be holding you captive.

Before reading any further, jot down some thoughts about college and university life, what you value about being there, and what you expect from your institution.

While in post-secondary school, I want to achieve…

1. _____
2. _____
3. _____
4. _____

I feel this education is significant to my life because…

1. _____
2. _____
3. _____
4. _____

From my school I expect…

1. _____
2. _____
3. _____
4. _____

My school expects from me…

1. _____
2. _____
3. _____
4. _____

Noted authors and experts on the first-year student experience John Gardner and Jerome Jewler (1995) suggest that students undergo several life-altering changes and developments during their college or university years. Some of the changes they cite are

- Self-esteem grows
- Political sophistication increases
- The need for control or power declines
- Autonomy or independence grows
- Appreciation of beauty deepens

Our observations of students reveal these changes also. If your professor were to make a video of you as first-year students and allow you to view it as graduates, you would be astounded at the changes in you. Beyond changes in appearance you would see development in attitudes, values, judgment, and character. Generally, college tends to teach students to be more gentle, more accepting, more open, and more willing to get involved in their community and to share their resources; often, college creates in students the desire to continue to learn.

No one, not all the researchers in the world, not your authors, not your professors, not even your friends, can put a real value on the experience that college provides or the degree of change you will undergo. The value differs for each student, and it is private. You may share with others the benefits of your higher education, but fundamentally, the results of these years are quietly consumed by your character, your actions, and your values. Some people will change a little, some people will change a lot. For all, however, change is coming.

What Do You Want?

Thinking about Your Choices

Today, you face many decisions. Some of them will affect the rest of your life. Some changes and decisions will be of your own making; others will be beyond your control. Some will be easily altered; others will hold for the long run.

Before you read further, think about where you are at this very moment and where you want to be in the coming years. Remember the quotation, "If you don't know where you are going, that's probably where you'll end up." The following activity is one of the first cornerstones of this book. It requires you to look at your current status, your peers, your past, and your aspirations and is intended to guide you in evaluating your life, attitudes, and thoughts. Take your time, be honest with yourself, and think in terms of realistic goals.

1. *Define success.* _____

_____

_____

2. *Name one person whom you deem successful. Why is that person successful?*

_____

_____

3. *List the one accomplishment that you want to achieve more than any other in your life.* _____

_____

_____

4. *How do you plan to achieve this accomplishment?* _____

_____

_____

5. *What part will your college/university experience and education play in helping you reach this accomplishment?* _____

_____

_____

6. *In what way have you changed the most in the past six months?* _____

_____

_____

7. *Was this change peaceful? Why or why not?* _____

_____

_____

8. *Describe the most stressful change you have undergone to date.* _____

_____

_____

9. Describe the least stressful change you have undergone to date. _____

_____

_____

_____

10. Describe the most important change in your life to date. _____

_____

_____

_____

11. What do you hope to change in yourself over the next 12 months? _____

_____

_____

_____

12. What will you have to change about yourself to achieve success as you defined it in question 1? _____

_____

_____

Changes in the Days to Come

One of the first changes you will notice about college is the degree of freedom you are given. There are no late slips to be sent to the principal's office, no mandates from your school board regarding attendance, and, usually, no parent telling you to get up and get ready for school. You may have only one or two classes in a day. "Great!!" you say, and maybe you're right. This freedom can be wonderful, but it can also be dangerous. Many people do their best when they are busy and have a limited amount of time to accomplish a task. College can give you more freedom than you are used to. You need to learn how to handle it quickly, before the freedom that is intended to liberate you destroys you. Chapter 5 will help you with priority management.

Another change coming your way involves the workload for your courses. The workload is likely to be greater than what you are used to. You may be assigned a significant amount of reading as homework.

> You gain strength, experience and confidence by every experience where you really stop to look fear in the face . . . . You must do the thing you think you cannot.
>
> Eleanor Roosevelt

Although you may have only two classes in one day, it has been said that for every hour spent in class, a minimum of 2 hours should be spent in review and preparation for the next class. Quick math: if you are taking five classes and are in class for 15 hours per week, you need to spend 30 hours studying; this makes a 45-hour week— 5 hours more than a normal work week for most people! Not I, you may say, and you may be right. It all depends on how wisely you use your time and how difficult the work is. However tempting, don't make the mistake of putting off assignments for very long. Waiting until the last minute may cause serious problems for you sooner or later, probably sooner. And, think about your schedule before you register to make sure that you have enough time to deal with the demands of the courses you have selected. Talk to friends, professors, and returning students about your schedule; see what they think about it. Although you may have to register for your first semester without benefit of these resources, thereafter be sure to make good use of them.

You have probably already noticed a difference between your college professors and your high school teachers in terms of teaching style and relationship with students. You may have encountered a teaching assistant, usually a graduate student who serves as an instructor in first-year and second-year classes. Unlike teaching assistants, professors take on many different roles. They are involved in research, community and college service, teaching, and committee work.

A significant change you may face in the days and weeks to come is the amount of diversity in the people around you. You may have come from a high school with a fairly homogeneous student body. If you went to school in a metropolitan area such as Vancouver, Calgary, Toronto, Montreal, or Halifax, you may be used to a diverse student body. Regardless of your background, you will meet students, peers, and classmates whose views, values, customs, language, sexual orientation, race, ethnicity, and origin are 100 percent different from yours. You will encounter people who are atheistic and people who are ultra religious; people who are pro-life and people who are pro-choice; people who are against the death penalty and people who support capital punishment; people who disagree with interracial relationships and people to whom race does not matter. If you come from a region or from a family in which these positions are not openly expressed, you must prepare yourself for change and realize how much you can learn from diversity. Chapter 4 is dedicated to understanding diversity.

Remember, the most healthy way to deal with change is to realize that it happens daily and to prepare for it.

Premises about Change

The author and speaker Eric Olesen (1993) suggests that a person undergoes three stages when change occurs:

> The real voyage of discovery consists not in seeing new lands, but in seeing with new eyes.
> M. Proust

- Letting go
- Making the transition
- Starting over

Letting go means simply agreeing that change is coming. **Making the transition** entails being in the middle of change, dealing with new ideas, new methods, and new information. **Starting over** means accepting that change has occurred. Starting over requires persistence and determination; it brings with it problems, frustrations, pain, and yes, beauty. Yet starting over can be easier than letting go. Sometimes, to let go it helps to remember the old saying, "every time a door closes, a window opens."

Several characteristics are common to any change, regardless of its cause.

CHANGE IS NEVER EASY

Even the best changes in our lives, such as earning a promotion, having a baby, getting married, or buying a home, come with a degree of stress and anxiety. To deal effectively with change, we need to realize that even good change is often hard.

CHANGE IS ALMOST ALWAYS MET WITH RESISTANCE

Human beings are creatures of habit. We tend to resist change, especially if the change affects a security that has been enjoyed for a long period of time.

THE PERSON WHO INITIATES CHANGE IS ALMOST ALWAYS UNPOPULAR

The person who initiates change, the change agent, frequently is an outsider or is relatively new to a situation. By suggesting that change could improve a situation, this person threatens the status quo. Olesen (1993) suggests that when change occurs, everyone begins at zero, everyone begins anew. Thus, people who have been secure for years fear losing that security, and the person proposing change often becomes the subject of rumour and innuendo.

CHANGE CREATES UNFAMILIAR GROUND

We are more comfortable with what is familiar to us; the unfamiliar can be scary and sometimes dangerous. We may be inclined to shy away from change because it creates unfamiliar ground. It may be helpful to recognize that every new step is basically unfamiliar—for you and everyone around you. Not to take the step only limits your possibilities and weakens your opportunities. It is important to learn how to move out of the comfort zone, where you feel secure and warm. A ship may be safe in the harbour, but that is not what ships are made for.

CHANGE TAKES COURAGE

Often, because of the resistance and negative reactions of others, a change agent will remain quiet. It takes courage to initiate change. Even if a change will eventually benefit others, you sometimes have to risk unpopularity and ridicule to initiate change.

Physical and Emotional Reactions to Change

By the time you've read this far, you've probably gone through a few changes. Were they exciting? Were they stressful? When you experience change, your body typically goes through a process of physical and emotional change as well. Learning to recognize these symptoms in order to control them can help you control the stress that can accompany change. You may already have experienced some of these emotional and physical changes since arriving at your college. Take a moment now to reflect on your first few days in your new surroundings.

1. How did you feel on entering your first class in college? _____

_____

_____

2. If you are married or have children, how did you feel when you had to leave your family today? _____

_____

_____

3. How did you feel when you received your first syllabus outlining the content of a course? _____

_____

_____

4. If you are living away from home, how did you feel during your first week in a new town? _____

_____

_____

   For most of you, these events caused a degree of stress and anxiety because you were experiencing change. Chapter 11 will help you learn to deal with the stress associated with college and everyday events.

   Don't be shocked if your body and spirit begin to feel

- Nervousness

- Stress

- A sense of being on the edge

- Fear

- Fatigue

- Guilt

- Homesickness

- Denial

- Anger

- Depression

These feelings are normal when you go through a powerful change, but they are temporary. If any of these feelings are becoming overwhelming or life threatening, seek counselling, talk to your friends, go to your advisor, or speak with your instructors. These people are your support group; use them. Don't wait until it is too late to ask for help. Don't hide your feelings and pretend that nothing is wrong. Change is not easy. One of the most crucial steps in successfully dealing with change is realizing that it can cause problems.

Change Anxiety Scale

This table lists ten changes known to cause anxiety in students. Rate each change situation according to the amount of anxiety that this situation has caused (or might cause) you. After you circle the appropriate response, plot the number on the graph that follows.

Change Anxiety Scale

1= low anxiety   10 = high anxiety

1. Leaving home	1	2	3	4	5	6	7	8	9	10
2. Moving away from longtime friends	1	2	3	4	5	6	7	8	9	10
3. Choosing your academic program	1	2	3	4	5	6	7	8	9	10
4. Living away from home	1	2	3	4	5	6	7	8	9	10
5. Starting classes	1	2	3	4	5	6	7	8	9	10
6. Dealing with conflicting points of view and values	1	2	3	4	5	6	7	8	9	10
7. Assuming responsibility for decisions	1	2	3	4	5	6	7	8	9	10
8. Adjusting to professors	1	2	3	4	5	6	7	8	9	10
9. Making new friends	1	2	3	4	5	6	7	8	9	10
10. Balancing school, work, friends, and extracurricular activities	1	2	3	4	5	6	7	8	9	10

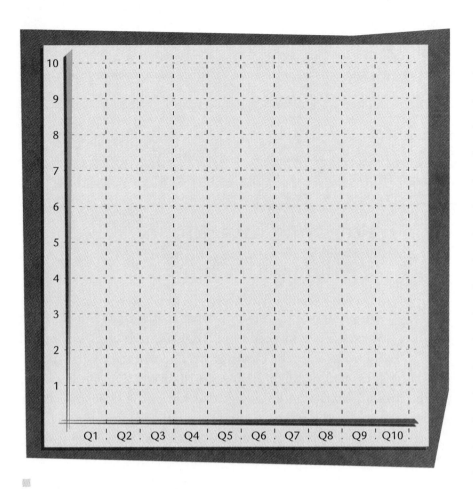

Plot Your Responses

After you have charted your response to the anxiety scale, select the three situations you rated as causing the most anxiety and complete the next section.

Number 1 anxiety-causing change: _____

How can you reduce anxiety and prepare for future change in this area?

_____

_____

_____

Number 2 anxiety-causing change: _____

How can you reduce anxiety and prepare for future change in this area?

_____

_____

_____

_____

Number 3 anxiety-causing change: _____

How can you reduce anxiety and prepare for future change in this area? _____

_____

_____

_____

Preparing for and Dealing with Change

Take a moment to reflect on what changes you might expect to experience this semester. Then list each change in one of the wedges on the change wheel: record the change that you consider most stressful or the biggest change in the largest wedge; put the smallest change or the change that causes the least stress in the smallest wedge. As the semester continues, reflect on this wheel to see if you were correct in your assumptions about the change and stress you face in college.

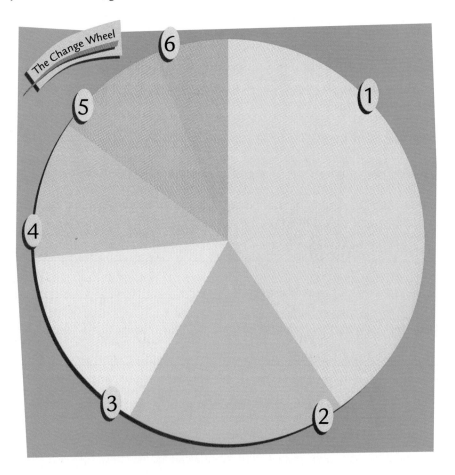

The Change Wheel

Your world is different now that you are in college. People are different, attitudes are different, and classes are different. List some of the most obvious differences between your high school and your present institution.

1. _____

2. _____

3. _____

4. _____

5. _____

Beyond the changes just listed, what changes have taken place in your personal life?

1. _____

2. _____

3. _____

4. _____

5. _____

Take a moment to think about where you want to be in one year, two years, or when you graduate. What changes will have to take place for this to happen?

_____

_____

_____

_____

_____

Successful people in general, and successful students in particular, know how to deal with change and embrace the positive effects that change brings. A study of people who were more than 100 years old revealed that these centenarians had two common traits: they accepted death as a part of life, and they knew how to deal with change.

ATTITUDES THAT HINDER CHANGE

You can develop attitudes that hinder change and stop growth. Such attitudes are dangerous because they rob you of opportunity, happiness, growth, and goals. These attitudes include

■ The "I can't" syndrome

■ Apathy, or the "I don't care" syndrome

- Closed mindedness

- Unfounded anxiety

- Fear of taking chances

- Loss of motivation

- The "let someone else deal with it" syndrome

If you can learn to control and watch out for these negative attitudes, you will begin to view change as a wonderful and positive life-long event.

 **for dealing with change**

The successful student prepares for change. The cornerstones for dealing with change will help you create a healthy attitude about change. You may wish to refer to these cornerstones on a daily basis in the coming weeks.

 GET INVOLVED IN THE CHANGE

Most people let change happen to their lives; they don't try to direct the focus or the outcome of the change. Successful students get involved in the change that is happening in their lives and try to direct it toward a desirable outcome.

 LET GO

The successful student knows how to let go of past events, places, and people who are not assisting in creating the desired future outcome.

HOLD ON

Holding on to people, memories, trinkets, and dreams that make you feel good and help you see today and tomorrow more clearly is healthy. The successful student knows when to hold on and when to let go. Both actions may be difficult, but both are necessary for dealing with change.

ASK FOR HELP

One of the most effective ways to deal with change is to ask for help, so don't be afraid or ashamed to do so. Many people will be having experiences similar to yours. Asking for help is the first step in finding a person to whom you can relate and with whom you feel comfortable.

DEVELOP A SENSE OF HUMOUR

Laughter is one of the most powerful medicines available. Remember to laugh, smile, lounge around outside, admire the maple trees in the fall or flowers in the spring, eat a pizza, go to the movies. Too often, we forget to nourish our souls; we forget to feed our spirit a daily diet of beauty, and it grows tired and weary. Laughing and refusing to take life too seriously can provide the shot in the arm you need to make it through the week. (Chapter 11 addresses personal wellness.)

FOCUS ON THE OUTCOME

To deal effectively with change you need to look beyond the moment of fright or anxiety, to develop the ability to see the outcome. There has to be rain before there can be a rainbow. Moving beyond immediate gratification and realizing the potential long-term gain is a positive way to approach change.

SEARCH FOR TRUTH

Successful students know that they do not possess all the answers to every question; no one does. If you can look at change as a way of searching for the truth and deeper meaning, change will become less frightening, even though the truth can sometimes be unsettling.

TAKE RISKS

Although it does not come easily, learning to take calculated risks can be a tool for positive and steady growth.

HAVE AN OPEN MIND

Some of the most successful students deal with change by being open-minded, unbiased, and ready to listen to all sides.

VIEW CHANGE AS GROWTH

If your life is peaceful all the time, you are probably not growing or changing. Of course, everyone experiences times when things go according to plan and there is little change or anxiety; this is normal. But, if nothing has changed in your life in the past five years, you are most likely stagnating. Change means growth and as such, it is healthy; without change, there can be no progress.

COMMUNICATE WITH PEOPLE

One of the most effective and healthy ways to deal with change is to talk with others about it. Tell your friends and family what you're going through. Seek out people who may be going through, or may have recently gone through, the same changes.

MAINTAIN PERSPECTIVE

"This, too, shall pass." You may have to rely on this motto for a while to help you realize that change will not always be this stressful or this painful. Think clearly. Think about all the changes you've experienced in the past and how small they seem now compared with what they felt like when you were going through them. Keep things in perspective and deal with them accordingly. Enjoy the ride—"you shall pass this way but once."

The transition from one place to another is never easy, even when it is what you want. Entering college has forced you to assume new roles, develop new friendships, meet new people, work under different circumstances, and perhaps adjust your lifestyle. These changes form the very essence of the university experience; they create wonderful new experiences. Now is the time for you to seek new truths, associate with new and different people, read books that you will never have time to hold in your hands again, develop a solid philosophy of life, explore new religions, go to plays, attend varsity games, join a club, read a book of poetry, go on a picnic with friends, sing, laugh, cry, write home, and love much. The winds of change are coming—fly!

The one minute journal

I n a minute or less, jot down one major idea you learned from this chapter.

Planning Your Dreams: Motivation and Goal Setting

From adversity comes greatness.

Winston Churchill

This story began about ten years ago, when I met Leah, a shy, sullen, withdrawn young woman, the daughter of an acquaintance. I had met Leah's mother, a hotel housekeeper, while conducting training for the hotel staff, and knew that Leah's mother had high hopes for her daughter. I thus took an interest in Leah.

Leah's family lived under difficult circumstances. Her father had abandoned the family when

Leah was a small child; her mother had supported the seven of them by working as a housecleaner. Leah's mother was concerned for her daughter's future. Leah had had few opportunities, little direction, and little encouragement—almost everything was working against her.

I asked Leah about her plans after graduation from high school. Leah responded that she would like to go to university but could not afford it. I asked to see Leah's transcript, and learned that she was ranked very high in her graduating class. Leah had more opportunities to go to university than she could imagine.

I helped Leah apply for grants and scholarships and gave her a job as a work study student. It soon became obvious that Leah was a serious student. She studied at every opportunity; she read voraciously, from classics to current events; she asked questions; and she observed everything. She was like a sponge, literally soaking up knowledge. Gradually, she began to change. She became more friendly and outgoing, her confidence seemed to increase, and she smiled more often. Leah was becoming a classic example of the powerful difference that education plus motivation and goal setting can make in a person's life.

Leah matured rapidly and began to take on more responsibility.

Although she had been awarded a scholarship that provided full tuition and room and board, she worked two jobs. She upgraded her

She began to realize what she could become.

wardrobe, bought a car, and became totally independent. She still conferred with me occasionally, but Leah made most of her own decisions. She was growing quickly and positively, and she was beginning to know who she was and what she wanted. More important, she began to realize what she could become. All her professors quietly marvelled at the dramatic changes in her.

When Leah took my class in her third year, she was introduced to goal setting, motivation strategies, and using adversity as a strength. She listened quietly, asked questions, and quickly designed her own blueprint for success. Leah was on her way because she had a clearly defined plan and she was willing to pay the price to reach her goals.

Prior to graduation, Leah applied to several prestigious graduate schools and was accepted at every one. She graduated with honours and was awarded several scholarships for graduate school. She continued to work two jobs during the summer; she wanted to save money for her expenses so that she would not have to work during the semester and could concentrate on her studies. Leah was highly motivated, goal directed, and focused on her plans.

Several years later, Leah stopped by my office. She had earned her CA credentials and was a full-fledged accountant working for an international accounting firm. Dressed in a classic suit and carrying a briefcase, Leah stood up straight, smiled with confidence, and spoke assertively. I was struck with the awesome difference between this Leah and the one I had met those many years ago.

Today, Leah owns her own accounting firm, and several CAs work for her. She is a great example of the power of motivation and goal setting.

You Are on Your Own

The great thing about going to college or university as a traditional student is that you get to be your own boss. For the first time in your life, you will be free to make your own decisions, choose your own friends, and determine your own destiny. There will be no one to tell you to go to bed, to get out of bed, to wear a jacket, to comb your hair, to clean up your room, or to watch out for strangers. You have the freedom to party at all hours, eat whenever you want, and ignore your homework—that's the good news.

On the other hand, you will probably not have teachers who take a close interest in you. Instead, you will have professors who expect you to take responsibility for your own learning. To many of them, you will be just another face in a big sea of faces. You probably won't know many people when you arrive on campus, and you will meet people who are very different from those you have known. The competition will be tough; many professors will be more demanding and less empathetic than the teachers you may be used to, and their directions and information may not be as specific.

If you are a nontraditional student, you will be able to explore new career choices, learn from traditional students, expand your opportunities, and broaden your personal and professional network—all exciting possibilities. However, you will be juggling schedules, racing back and forth between work and school, readjusting to the demands of completing assignments and writing papers, and, at the same time, helping your family adjust to your new schedule.

Your classmates may hail from all over the country and perhaps from all over the world. People of many races and religions will share your college campus. You will attend classes with people of all ages—35-year-old businesspeople, 40-year-old homemakers, and 60-year-old retirees, as well as the traditional students, aged 18 to 23. Some of these people will expose you to ideas unlike any you have experienced. You will associate with highly motivated, scholarly students, students committed to various campus organizations, varsity athletes, and students whose focus is partying and having a good time. Welcome to college life and all the excitement and challenges it will bring you!

When you finish this chapter, you will be well ahead of the average student because you will have learned to put direction in your life, to plan for success, and to focus on what you want. After completing this chapter, you will be able to

■ Discuss the importance of motivation in your life

■ Discuss the potential role of adversity in your success

■ List the common characteristics of peak performers

■ Discuss the role of fear and desire in motivation

■ Use visualization of your goals to help you achieve them

■ Differentiate between short-term goals and long-term goals

■ Write goals, objectives, and action steps for accomplishing your own personal strategic plan

You should know up front that all first-year students don't go on to a second year. According to a recent study of Ontario community colleges, it was found that between 22 and 26 percent of first year students did not make it to second year, and that between 38 and 46 percent of students dropped out in their second or third years (*Strategies for Student Success: Targeting Excellence and Efficiency,* Ministry of Education, 1994). On a national level, only 50 percent of students attending a Canadian post secondary institution actually graduate (Colin Campbell, 1994). But you should also know that you have the ability to graduate from college or you would not have been admitted. If you truly want to graduate from college and at the same time enjoy a full social life, you can do it.

Before looking at the motivation process, take a minute to assess your level of motivation as it is now.

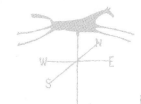

5 = Strongly Agree

4 = Agree

3 = Don't Know

2 = Disagree

1 = Strongly Disagree

1. I am a highly motivated person at this time.
   1 2 3 4 5

2. Adversity causes me to give up. *1 2 3 4 5*

3. I depend on other people to motivate me. *1 2 3 4 5*

4. I have a winning attitude.
   1 2 3 4 5

5. I prepare every day for success. *1 2 3 4 5*

6. I choose friends who are goal oriented and directed.
   1 2 3 4 5

7. I avoid letting my fears stand in my way.
   1 2 3 4 5

8. I visualize myself succeeding when I try something new.
   1 2 3 4 5

9. I know how to write goals with measurable objectives, deadlines, and action steps.
   1 2 3 4 5

10. I have an updated written set of goals to which I often refer.
    1 2 3 4 5

A SELF-ASSESSMENT Total your points from these ten questions. Refer to the following rating scale to determine where you stand in relation to motivation and goal setting.

0–10   *Your motivational level is low. You do not spend a lot of time thinking about your future plans; you probably do not write your goals down or review them daily.*

11–20   *Your motivational level is somewhat low. You may have goals, but you do not write them down and you do not review them on a regular basis.*

21–30   *Your motivational level is average. You may write down your goals, but you probably do not have them posted and you do not review them regularly.*

31–40   *Your motivational level and goal-setting skills are above average. You probably write down your goals, post them, and refer to them frequently.*

41–50   *Your motivational level and goal-setting skills are excellent. You write down your goals, post them, refer to them consistently, establish time lines for their completion, and update them often.*

Now, refer to your journal and respond in writing to your findings. Consider the following questions when writing in your journal:

1. Do you feel that you are a motivated person?

2. What motivates you?

3. Is motivation important in your college career? Why or why not?

Motivation Comes from Within

The first thing you need to know about motivation is that it comes from within—no one else can give it to you. Someone may pump you up or temporarily inspire you, but on a daily basis you must reach down inside and find the will to motivate yourself. Your college experience will make hundreds of unique, life-changing opportunities available to you, but no one will force you to take advantage of these gifts. Keep your eyes open, desire to achieve, and be willing to pay the price; college will open the door for you to make your dreams come true.

DECIDING WHAT YOU REALLY WANT IN LIFE

You are much more likely to be motivated if you are working for something that you really want. If you don't know what you want in life, you may wander aimlessly from one idea to another.

Once you've determined exactly what you want, you are ready to design a personal strategic plan. The best way to maintain motivation is to focus your energy, time, and emotion on reaching your goals.

Although you may not be sure what you want at this time, you need to start thinking about it. As your college experience changes you, some of your goals will change; this is not only perfectly acceptable, but it's desirable as well. In fact, changing a goal may be a sign of growth and maturity.

In an ideal world, students would arrive at college knowing exactly what careers they wanted to pursue. But since nothing in life is ideal, many students don't make up their minds until they've been at college for several semesters. Perhaps you dropped out of school years ago or maybe you never attended college because you didn't know what you wanted to do with your life. Perhaps you are 18 and never gave a great deal of thought to what you wanted to do with your life. If you haven't decided on a career, goal setting may be difficult at this time. Even so, you can work on several important areas as you determine your career goals.

One goal could be to study the different job markets available and to decide on one that appeals to you. Though it is not urgent, set a deadline for choosing a career path. You

should have a good idea of what you want to do with your life by the time you have completed your first-year courses. Remember, you have to want something in order to be motivated; being motivated is difficult unless there is something you want to accomplish, to have, or to become.

In your double-entry journal, make a list of everything you want. Don't give the items much thought at this time—just list them as they come to mind. If you are a traditional student, your list might include a college diploma or university degree, a good part-time job, a special person with whom to share your life, a ski trip, a new outfit, an A on your first exam. If you are a nontraditional student, your list might include a promotion, a special event with your family, or the purchase of a home. Later, you will use this list to help you design a personal strategic plan.

BECOMING A PEAK PERFORMER

If you are highly motivated and have direction in your life, you have a great chance of becoming a peak performer. Did someone once tell you that you "didn't work up to your potential"? Put it behind you. You are starting a new chapter in your life, and you can begin now to become a peak performer.

Peak performance is an attitude and a habit. Beginning now, you need to accept responsibility for your own destiny. It's a cop-out to lay blame on your teachers, parents, or siblings—what you become is entirely up to you, your own personal motivation, and the price you are willing to pay. Peak performers have in common several characteristics. Study them carefully as you begin your own quest for peak performance.

> Extraordinary people are just ordinary people who believe in themselves and get a little better every day.
> Patricia G. Moody, professor and author

Peak Performers

- Focus on results, not activities
- Know where they are going
- Demonstrate persistence and consistency
- Are flexible
- Don't give up easily
- Are creative and innovative
- Adapt to change
- Take responsibility for themselves
- Share generously with others
- Enjoy all aspects of life
- Are committed to success and quality
- Choose their own mission
- Forgive themselves when they fail

In your double-entry journal, discuss two characteristics of peak performers that you think you are practising already. Then consider two other areas on which you think you need significant work. When you design your own personal strategic plan, you may want to include goals relating to these items.

Attitude—The First Step in Getting What You Want

How many people have you met who turned you off immediately with their negative attitudes? They whine about the weather or their parents; they verbally attack people who differ from them; they degrade themselves with negative remarks. Listen for the negative comments people make and the messages they send out about themselves. When people continually feed their brains negative messages, their bodies respond accordingly.

When a man's willing and eager, the gods join in.
Aeschylus, Greek playwright

To be successful at anything, you have to develop a winning attitude, you have to eliminate negative thinking. Begin today: tell yourself only positive things about yourself; build on those positives; focus on the good things; work constantly to improve.

Thought for every morning: This is going to be a great day for me!

Winners get up early with an with an attitude of "I can't wait for this day to start so I can have another good day." You may not get up early, but you can get up with a positive attitude. Tell yourself things that will put you in the right frame of mind to succeed. When you are talking to yourself—and everybody does—feed your brain positive thoughts. Think of your brain as a powerful computer; you program it with your words, and your body carries out the program.

Pay attention to the messages you send out to others as well. What kinds of remarks do you make about you and about others when you are with your friends? Do you sound positive or negative? Do you hear yourself saying positive things such as

Oliver is such a great guy!

My parents are really cool.

I'm making great progress on my exercise program.

I had a long talk with Professor Wang, and he really does care about his students.

My computer skills have really improved.

Jane is teaching me to line dance, and I'm having a blast.

List some positive statements you say to yourself. _____

_____

_____

_____

Now list some negative statements you say to yourself. _____

_____

_____

_____

You have spent time preparing for college—you have gotten your clothes ready, bought supplies, adjusted to roommates. Now you need to spend time preparing your mental attitude to succeed. You will have a great advantage over most other entering students, indeed, over most other people, if you have a winning attitude. Start developing it today! Use the following steps today and every day.

PREPARING FOR SUCCESS

1. Prepare for success the evening before—organize your clothes and books and make a list of things you need to do the next day. (You'll read more about this in Chapter 5.)

2. Eat properly, get enough rest, and exercise. Winners know that a fit mind requires a fit body. (You'll read about this in Chapter 11.)

3. Get up early (at least occasionally), sing in the shower, think about positive outcomes.

4. Talk to yourself using positive "I" statements: "I will have a good day today;" "I will perform well today because I have prepared to do well;" "I will be happy and positive and outgoing." (Chapter 3 on self-esteem addresses this subject.)

5. Read motivational books as well as biographies of famous people who overcame adversity to reach their goals. Reading will help keep you motivated while expanding your knowledge!

6. Stay connected to your positive support system and seek spiritual wellness.

CHOOSE YOUR FRIENDS CAREFULLY

Although your motivation and attitude belong to you and are uniquely yours, they can be greatly influenced by the people with whom you associate. People do tend to become like the people with whom they spend time.

As a new student, you have a clean slate where friends are concerned. You need to choose your very best friends carefully. Of course you want to spend time with people who have interests in common with yours. That's a given. But you also want your friends to have ambition, good work habits, positive attitudes, and high ethical standards. Seek out people who read good books, watch educational television programs, are goal oriented, and don't mind taking a stand when they believe strongly about something. Find friends who will work out with you, go to the library with you, attend plays and concerts with you. One of the best ways to make the most of your post secondary education is to befriend people who have interests and hobbies that are new to you. Staying focused is much easier if you surround yourself with positive, motivated, goal-oriented people.

Read, Read, Read

Reading a variety of books is an excellent way to improve yourself. Make a habit of reading books and articles that you *want* to read, not just those that you *have* to read, on a regular basis. If you read an average of 5 to 10 books a year while in college, your overall abilities will improve significantly: you'll have more creative ideas, you'll broaden your vocabulary, you may become a more interesting conversationalist, and you'll gain valuable insights into numerous topics.

Although any reading you do in addition to reading textbooks will be beneficial, you'll gain the most if you read a variety of fiction and nonfiction materials. Read books as well as periodicals such as *Maclean's, Canadian Business, Time,* the *Globe and Mail* and computer/ technology magazines. This practice will keep you informed on what is happening right now in society, government, politics, and the international arena. As a result of what you read, you may want to alter your goals. You'll be exposed to ideas that will have an impact on your thinking, creativity, and direction. Once you see the value in reading just for fun and knowledge, you might want to try reading classics and great philosophers.

Name at least one book or article you have read within the last three months that taught you useful information, provided entertainment, or inspired you to improve yourself. _____

_____

_____

Name two ideas you learned and are now using from this book or an article that you recently read. _____

_____

_____

If you had trouble completing this exercise, consider adjusting your schedule and goals so that you can read books other than textbooks on a regular basis. You may also want to try talking about these books with a group of friends.

Reading Assignment. Buy or borrow a nonfiction, self-help book on motivation and goal setting. Read it, then make a list of important ideas you can use to improve your own motivation.

WORK HARD, WORK SMART

To succeed in college or university, as in life, you must be prepared to work hard; you must be prepared to do whatever it takes to get the job done. Hard work with direction is key. Start building a work ethic by exhorting yourself to do your best every day. Push yourself to do more than simply get by.

Remember, though, that hard work alone will not make you successful. If you look around you, you will see hundreds of people who have worked hard all their lives but have not maximized their potential. Working smart is equally important.

Working smart means acquiring all the knowledge you can, making wise decisions, thinking creatively, applying what you have learned, organizing your time, setting priorities, and working toward accomplishing a written set of goals.

Learning to work smart is not easy; it comes with practice. You can start learning how to work smart by watching other people. When you see someone doing something that impresses you, ask questions. If there is an outstanding business executive in your hometown, ask how he or she became so successful. If one of your professors is writing a book, find out how he or she researched the book. If you meet a classmate who spends every summer working in a resort area, ask how that person gets these jobs. If you overhear a student talking about a personal interest, such as the Internet, ask how he or she got started. Decide if any part of what someone else is doing is right for you.

Reading can help you work smart, too. Read with the idea of learning how to improve what you are doing now. For example, if you have always been a procrastinator, find a book that might help you improve your time management habits.

Ask yourself questions. As you make decisions about studying ask, "Is this the best thing for me to be doing right now?" If you are working ask, "Is this the best way to accomplish this task, or could I be more effective if I tried a new way?"

Many other questions can lead to your working smart as well: "How can I be more creative in my career planning?" "What kinds of volunteer experiences can I be getting now that will make me more attractive to an employer when I'm being interviewed?" "How could I arrange my work hours to allow for more study time and personal time?"

If you are a nontraditional, working student you might want to examine ways in which you can progress more rapidly up the career ladder. You might ask, "What subjects can I take now that will prepare me to get the promotion I want?" Both traditional and nontraditional students can work smart by taking specific courses to accumulate knowledge that can lead to more success on the job, a lucrative hobby on the side, or an interesting personal pursuit.

If your field of study is not likely to lead directly to a viable career, you could work smart by taking subjects or night school courses that complement your career objective. For example, if you are majoring in a foreign language and you don't plan to teach, you could have trouble finding a well-paying job. But taking courses in business or hospitality may enable you effectively to combine your major and a career. Once you start practicing working smart, you will find ways to improve every day.

> They who have conquered doubt and fear have conquered failure.
>
> James Allen

Overcoming Doubts and Fears

Fear is a great motivator; it probably motivates more people than anything else. Unfortunately, it motivates most people to hold back, to doubt themselves, to accomplish much less than they could, and to hide the person they really are.

One of the biggest obstacles to reaching your potential may be your own personal fears. If you are afraid, you are not alone; everyone has fears. However, our fears are learned. As a baby, you had two fears: a fear of falling and a fear of loud noises. As you got older, you probably added to your list of fears. And, if you are like most people, you let your fears dominate parts of your life, saying things to yourself like: "What if I try and fail?" "What if people laugh at me for thinking I can do this?" "What if someone finds out that this is my dream?"

You have two choices where fear is concerned. You can let fear dominate your life, or you can focus on those things you really want to accomplish, put your fears behind you, and go for it. The people most successful in their fields will tell you that they are afraid, but that they overcome their fear because their desire to achieve is greater. Barbra Streisand, recording artist and stage performer, becomes

physically nauseated with stage fright when she performs, yet she faces these fears and maintains her position as one of the most popular entertainers of our time.

Name one of the smallest fears you have now. What can you do to overcome it?

_____

_____

_____

_____

What is your greatest fear? Why do you think you have this fear? _____

_____

_____

_____

_____

What steps do you think you can take to overcome this fear? _____

_____

_____

_____

_____

MOVING OUT OF YOUR COMFORT ZONE

Successful people face their fears because their motivation and ambition force them out of their comfort zones. Your comfort zone is where you know you are good, you feel confident, and you don't have to stretch your talents far to be successful. If you stay in your comfort zone, you will never reach your potential and you will deny yourself the opportunity of knowing how it feels to overcome your fears.

Deciding to go to college probably caused you some level of discomfort and raised many fears: "What if I can't get good marks?" "What if I flunk out?" "What if I can't make the team?" "What if I can't keep up with the kids just out of high school?" "What if I can't do my job, go to school, and manage a family at the same time?" The mere fact that you are here is a step outside your comfort zone—a very important step that can change your life dramatically.

Everyone has a comfort zone. When you are doing something that you do well, and you feel comfortable and confident, you are in your comfort zone. When you are nervous and afraid, you are stepping outside it. When you realize you are outside your comfort zone, you should feel good about yourself because you are learning and growing and improving. You may not progress unless you step outside your comfort zone.

The circle shown represents your comfort zone. Think of several activities in which you feel confident and comfortable and write them in the circle.

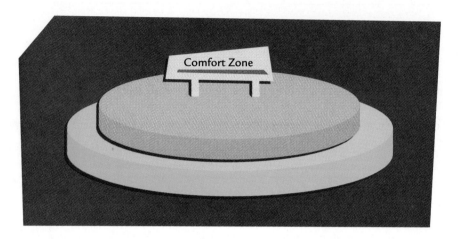

Now look at the illustration that shows the same comfort zone circle with three larger circles around it. The larger circles represent taking small steps to move out of your comfort zone.

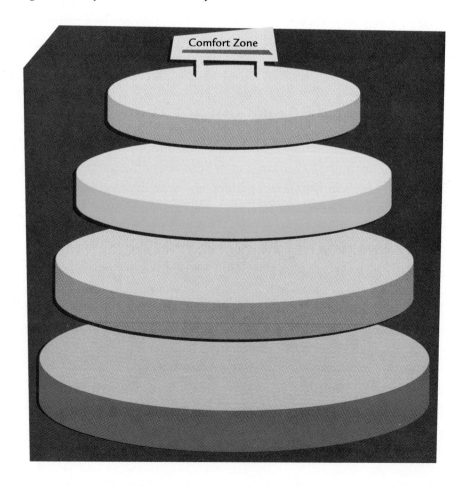

In each of the three larger circles write something that you would like to do, to experience, to be, to take a risk on—something that would take you out of your comfort zone. Work on taking the first step outside your comfort zone by tomorrow. When you are at ease with that one, move to the next circle. Say to yourself, "A little better every day."

Incorporate this practice into the habits that you want to form. Plan to take one step outside your comfort zone every day. Soon your comfort zone will be greatly expanded, and you will become more confident and able to move on to the next steps more quickly.

DEALING WITH ADVERSITY AND FAILURE

To be motivated, you have to learn to deal with failure. Have you ever given up on something too quickly, or gotten discouraged and quit? Can you think of a time when you were unfair to yourself because you didn't stay with something long enough? Did you ever stop doing something you wanted to do because somebody laughed at you or teased you? Overcoming failure makes victory much more rewarding. Motivated people know that losing is a part of winning: the difference between being a winner and being a loser is the ability to try again.

If you reflect on your life, you may well discover that you gained your greatest strengths through adversity. Difficult situations make you tougher and more capable of developing your potential. Overcoming adversity is an essential part of success in college and in life.

Think of a time in your life when you faced difficulties but persisted and became stronger as a result. Perhaps you failed a course, didn't make an athletic team, lost a school election, had a serious illness, broke up with a long-term boyfriend or girlfriend, or experienced your parents' divorce. If you are a nontraditional student you may have been fired from a job or passed over for a promotion, suffered through a divorce, or experienced a death in the family.

Describe your experience of adversity. _____

_____

_____

_____

What did you learn from this experience? _____

_____

_____

_____

_____

_____

How can you use this experience as a reminder that you can overcome adversity,
learn to grow from it, and become a better person as a result of it? _____

_____

_____

_____

_____

If you study the lives of the people we consider our greatest heroes
—national leaders, executives, movie stars, authors, athletes—you will
discover that they all share the ability to persist in the face of adversity.

Stephen Leacock, one of Canada's best-loved authors, became a
success story despite tremendous odds. Leacock had an unhappy
childhood, with an alcoholic father who abandoned his family. After
he won an academic scholarship and enrolled at university, Leacock
had to quit school to support his mother and seven younger siblings.
He decided to pursue teaching, and took a three-month teacher training course before securing a teaching position at a high school. While
teaching, he completed his Bachelor of Arts degree, and wrote many
short stories. He endured the rejection of his more serious works, but
he found success selling his humorous stories. His wife died when
their only child was still young, yet he still found it in him to continue
his writing career. Few people are aware of Leacock's personal difficulties, but the world knows of his literary successes.

Shania Twain, the popular country singer, was raised with four
brothers and sisters in Timmins, Ontario. Her family was extremely
poor. While growing up, she worked part time to help support her
family, and at 22 was faced with a major tragedy when her parents
were killed in a car accident. Shania raised her three younger siblings
while taking on singing engagements to earn the money her family
needed to survive. When her brothers and sisters were old enough to
take care of themselves, she went to Nashville, where she has become
a country music star. The secret to Shania's success was that she had a
dream and she never took her eyes off this dream, she persisted even
when the odds were against her, she paid the price, and she overcame
adversity. Shania Twain has talent; yet many talented people are never
successful because they fail to persist in the face of adversity.

STEPS IN REACHING YOUR GOALS

- **Turn adversity into stepping stones.** When you have a setback, stop and analyze the situation. How can you learn from it? What can you do next time to avoid a similar situation? Use positive self-talk: "This is an opportunity for me to learn from my mistakes and to grow stronger." Don't fall into self-pity.

- **Overcome negative people.** When other people doubt you, find the strength and determination to go on. Many successful people were told by guidance counsellors that they wouldn't make it to college. Arsenio Hall's high school counsellor told him he was not college material. In spite of his counsellor's predictions, he attended college, became a television talk-show host and actor, and now has millions of fans. After failing his first year of engineering at university, Canadian actor Donald Sutherland transferred to English. He spent as much time as possible studying acting, pursuing a career he had dreamed of since childhood. Sutherland had taken engineering because his father had wanted him to, and consequently did not do well. What other people think does not matter as long as you believe in yourself and are prepared to work hard.

- **Persist even if you are losing.** When you are down on the mat and want to give up, will yourself to renew your commitment never to give up. One of the most revered heroes of this century, Winston Churchill, was sent home from school as a boy because he was such a poor student. Years later Churchill, prime minister of Great Britian and an international hero, was invited to return to that school to deliver the commencement address. His entire speech was "Never give up! Never give up! Never give up! Never, never, never give up!" Make up your mind that you will not allow yourself to quit. Always try to improve a little every day, to move toward your goals, and you will succeed.

WORRY ACCOMPLISHES NOTHING

Studies show that 60 percent of what we worry about has absolutely no basis, another 20 percent of our fears are related to things that have already happened and are out of our control, and 10 percent of our worries and fears concern petty matters that don't deserve our time and attention. Only 4 to 5 percent of our fears are real, and there's very little we can do about half of them. What this boils down to is that only about 2 to 3 percent of our fears should be given any attention at all. The best way to deal with that small percentage is to quit worrying and start moving. If you sit and worry, your fears will stay with you. If you start working toward a goal, you might leave your fears behind.

Everyone going to college or university for the first time is afraid. If you think you are the only one who is anxious, think again. No matter how cool some of your classmates may seem on the outside, you can count on the fact that they are just as uneasy as you are on the inside. And, no matter how afraid or worried you are, you have one emotion that is much stronger than either fear or worry—hope—and another intangible that takes you beyond your fears—faith in yourself. The powerful combination of faith and hope almost always overcomes fear and worry.

As long as you are growing, learning, stretching, and becoming, you will be on unfamiliar ground. You can choose to be comfortable and bored or to overcome your fears and live your life to the maximum.

If you put into practice the ideas in this chapter, you will be well on your way to success. Incorporate these ideas into your daily life so that they become as natural as breathing. If you can stick to a technique for 21 days, it will become a habit and will be much easier to maintain. Success is an attitude!

The soul never thinks without a picture.
Aristotle, Greek philosopher

Visualize Your Success

Another way of stating Aristotle's idea is in order to be able to do something, you must be able to visualize yourself doing it. Many people have dreams of excellence when they are young but settle for mediocrity somewhere along the way. Instead of living, they begin to die. Merely existing, even if you are comfortable, is not living. Real living requires a certain amount of discomfort. Real living also requires that you have dreams and that you actively pursue those dreams. Once you focus on your dreams, your mind and body will work much more effectively to make those dreams happen. To succeed in spite of adversity, you need to be passionate about your goals and dreams.

Passion will carry you through a lot; disappointment, pain, the worst of times and the best of times.
Eva Marie Saint, Academy Award– and Emmy Award–winning actress

Everyone is born to win, but many people are conditioned to lose by others who have no vision and who have never learned to dream. If you have dreams and don't pursue them, you are allowing other people to put boundaries on your comfort zone. You owe it to yourself to expand the walls of your comfort zone further and further every day.

Can you think of something you have a passion for, something you want to accomplish or to become or a place you want to visit? If you have a specific dream, find a picture (or several pictures) that represents your dream and place it where you will see it often. Focus on how you are going to attain that dream. Develop a passion for achieving whatever it is you most want out of life. Passions in life drive us and help us reach our goals.

Every great athlete knows the necessity of concentration. Regardless of what the fans are doing or how much the competition may be harassing them, great athletes stay focused on their goals and desires. They *see* themselves playing the perfect game. You, too, must *see* yourself accomplishing your dreams. Keep positive pictures in your mind. If you want to lose weight, focus on how you will look when you lose ten pounds, not on how you look now. If you want to improve your golf swing, picture the perfect golf swing in your mind. If your greatest desire is a sports car, visualize yourself driving that car. Be so familiar with your dream car that you can describe it in great detail—the color, the interior, the tires—and don't forget to visualize yourself in the driver's seat.

No matter how positive you are or how well you visualize your goals, once in a while you will get kicked in the teeth. When you face difficult times, don't whine or complain; take action immediately, and deal with the problem before it grows bigger. When obstacles last longer than a few days, remind yourself that they will not last forever.

You have had the opportunity to think about motivation, dreams, and accomplishments; now it's time for you to do something. The wisest person in the world will not be successful if that wisdom is not put into action.

 **CORNERSTONES** for motivation

- ■ Tap your own wellspring of motivation and turn it on.
- ■ Know what you want and focus on it.
- ■ Embrace a winning attitude.
- ■ Adopt the habits of successful people whom you admire.
- ■ Read good books and associate with upbeat, motivated people.
- ■ Learn to accept the fact that sometimes you will fail.

- Face your fears—step outside your comfort zone every day.
- Use adversity to get stronger.
- Focus on your goals.
- Dream big dreams.
- Use the power of positive mental thoughts and mental pictures.
- Picture yourself succeeding and accomplishing all your goals.

Remember the Formula for Success:

Attitude + Determination + Discipline + Direction = Success

To help you stay focused while you are working to spell out your goals, write this formula on several sheets of paper and place the papers where you will see them often—on your desk, on the wall above your desk, in your notebook, by your bed. A + D + D + D = S: if you have the right attitude, if you are determined to succeed, if you demonstrate discipline, and if you know where you want to go, you will succeed.

Assess yourself relative to each component of this formula to determine where best to focus your efforts for improvement.

Attitude _____

_____

_____

_____

_____

Determination _____

_____

_____

_____

_____

Discipline _____

_____

_____

_____

_____

_____

Direction _____

_____

_____

_____

_____

The Goal-Setting Process

Goal setting itself is relatively easy. Many people make goals, but fail to make the commitment to accomplish those goals. Instead of defining their goals in concrete, measurable terms, they think of them occasionally and have vague, unclear ideas about how to attain them. The first step toward reaching a goal is the commitment to pay the price to achieve it. Opportunities abound everywhere; commitment is a scarce commodity.

When you are ready to make a commitment to achieve your goals, write them down, along with steps for accomplishing deadlines that must be honoured. These goals are your targets. Now you are ready to act, to begin accomplishing your goals, and you need to do so without delay. Be prepared to fail, because you surely will fail some of the time, but you must be equally committed to getting up and trying again. Your commitment to success must be so strong that quitting would never even occur to you.

When you have accomplished your goals, you need to begin the process again. Successful people never get to a target and sit down; they are always *becoming*. They reach one goal and begin dreaming, planning, preparing for the next accomplishment.

A Goal Is Anything You Can Have, Be, or Do

Before you work on your goals, think about goals in these terms: you can *have* a boat; you can *be* a member of the student government, or you can *play* a musical instrument. Use the following questions to help you decide what goals to set.

■ DO, BE, OR HAVE EXERCISE

What do I want to do? _____

_____

_____

> To thine own self
> be true.
>   **Shakespeare**

What do I want to be? _____

_____

_____

What do I want to have? _____

_____

_____

CHARACTERISTICS OF ATTAINABLE GOALS

It is usually easier to set goals than to achieve them. To be able to set attainable goals, you need to know their characteristics. Attainable goals must be

- **Reasonable.** Your goals need to be based on your abilities, desires, and talents. If you got terrible grades in English composition and hate to sit at a computer, it may be unrealistic to set a goal to become a writer. On the other hand, if you are a star athlete and love to work with young people, your goal might be to become a coach.

- **Believable.** To achieve a goal, you must really believe it is within your capacity to do so. You may want a sailboat very badly, but the cost may be prohibitive. If you want it, but don't believe you can get it, you are probably fooling yourself—at least at this stage of the game.

- **Measurable.** A goal needs to be concrete and measurable in some way. If you set a vague goal, such as "I want to be happy," you cannot know if you've attained your goal, because you have no way of measuring it.

- **Adaptable.** Your goals may need to be adapted to changing circumstances in your life. You may begin with a goal and find that you have to change direction for one reason or another. Maybe you don't like this goal once you learn more about it or perhaps some insurmountable obstacle arises. You might have to adjust your expectations and the goal itself in order to achieve it.

- **Controllable.** Your goals should be within your own control; they should not depend on the whims and opinions of anyone else. For example, if your goal is to learn to play golf well enough to score 90, you need to control your practice and the times you play; you do not want to practise based on the needs of your golf partner, who may have strengths and weaknesses different from yours.

- **Desirable.** To attain a difficult goal, *you* must want it very badly. You cannot make yourself work for something just because someone else wants it. If you have always dreamed about becoming a teacher of young children set this as your goal; it will be extremely difficult for you to stay on course to become a medical researcher because your parents want you to follow in their footsteps.

Look at your responses in the Do, Be, or Have Exercise. Measure them against the characteristics of attainable goals. Do you think the goals you discussed are within your reach? Can you control events that could prevent you from attaining them? Do you really believe you can do what you want to do? Can you measure your success? Can these goals be adjusted if necessary? Do you really want to do, be, or have the things you listed?

HOW TO WRITE GOALS

Webster's New Collegiate Dictionary defines a goal as "the end toward which effort is directed." The process of goal setting involves deciding what you want and working to get it. Goals can be short term or long term. Short-term goals can usually be accomplished within six months or a year, although they could be accomplished in a much shorter time. "Within six months I will save enough money to spend a week skiing in Banff" is a short-term goal; "Within six years, I will become a chartered accountant (CA)" is a long-term goal.

When you write goals you need to include a goal statement, action steps, and target dates. The goal statement should be specific and measurable, that is, it should entail some tangible evidence of its achievement. An example of a goal statement is "I will lose ten pounds in six weeks." You can make goal statements from intangibles if you can devise a way to measure the desired outcome. For example, "I will develop a more positive attitude by the end of six weeks as evidenced by at least three people's commenting on my improved attitude and by my dealing positively with at least three negative situations weekly."

After you write the goal statement, you'll need to create specific action steps that explain exactly what you are going to do to reach your goal. Then decide on a target date for reaching your goal.

The final step in writing goals is to write a narrative about what your goal accomplishments will mean to you. If your goals don't offer you significant rewards, you are not likely to stick to your plan. An example format for a goal statement, with action steps, target date, and narrative follows.

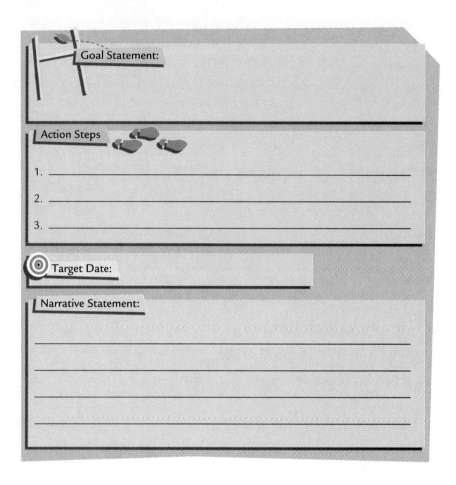

Goal Statement: _____

Action Steps

1. _____
2. _____
3. _____

Target Date: _____

Narrative Statement:

_____
_____
_____
_____

Now you are ready to begin the exciting adventure known only to goal setters. To help you get started, we'll discuss some common areas for which you might want to set goals. After reading this section, however, you might want to venture off in a different direction. That's perfectly all right, since these are *your* goals.

■ CATEGORIES FOR GOALS

Personal or Self-Improvement. Set a goal that relates to your personal life. For example, you might want to work on punctuality.

Goal: I will be on time and prepared for all my classes this semester.

Academic. You might set a goal of reaching a certain grade point average. A word of caution: don't set an average of 4.0 as your goal if you have always been a B student; strive first for a B+. Remember the "a little better every day" philosophy.

Goal: I will earn at least a B+ on my first English exam.

Family. You might want to do something nice for your parents or for a younger sibling.

Goal: I will go home for my brother's birthday and will spend the weekend doing whatever he wants to do.

Career. You could decide to take a weekend seminar or workshop that will allow you to explore new areas of interest.

Goal: I will take a computer programming seminar next month to determine if this field appeals to me.

Financial. Now is a good time to focus on managing your money, even if you don't have a great deal of it. Set a goal that will help you to establish good financial management practices.

Goal: I will save $400 by Christmas so I can buy my family gifts.

Community Service. Set a goal to become involved in community service. Serving other people can be as rewarding for you as it is for those you help.

Goal: I will volunteer ten hours of my time each week to the children's hospital in the area of physical therapy.

Social. You might want to work on certain social skills, such as restaurant etiquette or dancing, or you might want to limit your social life to certain activities.

Goal: I will take a gourmet cooking course to improve my social skills.

Health. Set goals that will help you to relieve stress and stay in top condition. You might set goals that involve exercise, proper diet, or enough rest.

Goal: I will limit my fat gram intake to 36 grams per day.

Spiritual. Set goals to keep you spiritually fit. Anything that makes you feel alive and well can be part of your spiritual goal, such as walking on the beach or watching a touching movie.

Goal: I will participate in at least three activities each week that are spiritually rewarding and renewing for me.

GOALS DON'T HAVE TO BE SET IN CONCRETE

Sometimes a few weeks or months after setting a goal, it becomes apparent that you are not moving in the right direction to achieve that goal. For example, suppose you were recruited by a university to play varsity volleyball, but after practising for a while you realize that you don't have the time both to play volleyball and to pursue the rigorous curriculum that will enable you to become a computer systems specialist. You can always change your goal. If you change just because accomplishing the goal is difficult, you are defeating yourself. But if something happens to prevent you from ever achieving your goal, or you realize it isn't right for you, or you decide to move in a new direction that is more appealing or important to you, it is appropriate to change your goals.

You are ready to build someone unique and special! As a first-year student, you have a great opportunity to become someone very special, the best you can be. Setting goals and motivating yourself to achieve those goals is one of the most important steps you can take as you begin your college career.

On the following pages, you will be given the opportunity to set three goals to begin working on right away. These goals should be short-term goals. By working on short-term goals first, you will be able to feel the excitement of accomplishing a goal rather quickly. Think carefully about the three most important things you could do to improve yourself and to make you feel better about yourself. Review the list in your double-entry journal of things you want now to see if they can help you determine what to work on. Remember that success depends on your selecting goals that mean a great deal to you.

Use the Personal Strategic Success Plan form to write a goal statement with action steps, target date, and narrative statement for a goal that can be accomplished in a month. Then begin working on a plan to accomplish the three most important goals you need to reach this semester. At the same time you are working on your three most important semester goals, focus on completing the short-term, one-month goal. Reward yourself when you complete this goal. You may reproduce this sheet as often as you like.

■ PERSONAL STRATEGIC SUCCESS PLAN This is going to be the best year I have ever experienced. I am going to college, where I will succeed because I am prepared to succeed. I have a head start on most people because I have an excellent attitude, I am willing to work hard, and I have a plan for what I want to accomplish. Every day I will get a little better. I will think positive thoughts, act decisively, push myself out of my comfort zone, and take care of my body and my mind. *Nothing will stop me from accomplishing my goals!*

Once you have mastered the steps in goal setting and motivation outlined in this chapter, you are on the way to building the best person you are capable of becoming. Use these ideas as you move through college and later in your career. Remember that goal setters usually accomplish the most.

After you have finished writing your goals, use the following evaluation plan to determine if your goals are appropriate.

EVALUATION PLAN FOR YOUR GOALS

Do I really want to achieve this goal enough to pay the price and to stick with it?

What is the personal payoff to me if I achieve this goal?

Who will notice if I achieve this goal? Does that matter to me?

How realistic is this goal? Am I way over my head for this stage of my development?

Do I need to reduce my expectations so I won't be disillusioned in the beginning and increase the difficulty of my goal only after I have reached the first steps?

Can I control all the factors necessary to achieve this goal?

Is this goal specific and measurable?

Does this goal contribute to my overall development? Is this goal allowing me to spend my time in the way that is best for me right now?

How will I feel when I reach this goal?

Will my parents and friends be proud that I accomplished this goal?

Will the achievement of this goal increase my self-esteem?

Goal Statement:

Action Steps

1. _____

2. _____

3. _____

4. _____

Target Date:

Narrative Statement:

_____
_____
_____
_____
_____
_____
_____
_____
_____
_____
_____
_____
_____
_____
_____
_____
_____
_____
_____
_____
_____
_____
_____
_____
_____

I hereby make this promise to myself.

Date _____ Signature _____

Goal Statement:

Action Steps

1. _____
2. _____
3. _____
4. _____

Target Date:

Narrative Statement:

_____
_____
_____
_____
_____
_____
_____
_____
_____
_____
_____
_____
_____
_____
_____
_____
_____
_____
_____
_____
_____
_____
_____

I hereby make this promise to myself.

Date _____ Signature _____

Goal Statement:

Action Steps

1. _____
2. _____
3. _____
4. _____

Target Date:

Narrative Statement:

_____
_____
_____
_____
_____
_____
_____
_____
_____
_____
_____
_____
_____
_____
_____
_____
_____
_____
_____
_____
_____
_____
_____

I hereby make this promise to myself.

Date _____ Signature _____

The one minute journal

Write about one specific piece of information that you read in this chapter that you think will motivate you.

Outside Looking In: Developing Positive Self-Esteem

Chad was one of the brightest, most creative, and most inquisitive students I had ever taught, so I had a difficult time understanding why he always wrote about his very low self-esteem. One day after reading a paper in which he had written many cynical, self-defeating remarks about himself, I asked him to come to my office to talk. Three hours later, I felt that I understood

Chad much better.

Chad attended kindergarten when he was four. Because he had a speech impairment, he left the classroom several times a week for speech therapy. An insensitive teacher made some negative remarks about Chad's problems, and his young classmates soon began to follow suit. Chad was taunted and teased; he began to feel bad about himself and began to develop poor self-esteem.

As he sat in my office, this bright young man, who appeared fine on the outside, talked about how he had turned to alcohol and drugs to escape the pain that he had felt for so many years. He said, "No one ever calls me on Friday night. I hate the way I look; I feel like a freak." He had a lot going for him, but none of it mattered because he didn't like himself.

I referred Chad to a counsellor, and he agreed to seek help. As the semester progressed, Chad often stopped by after class to let me know how things were going. He seemed to be making a great deal of progress. One day I asked for a volunteer to lead a computer project, and Chad volunteered. He had never done so before. I could tell that he was somewhat uncomfortable when he spoke up, but he knew that he had to take this step if he was ever to rebuild his self-esteem.

Chad has worked to overcome feelings of loneliness, isolation, frustration, and unwor-

Asking for help, taking chances, and believing in your talents can save your college career, and maybe your life.

thiness. With the help of extensive therapy, he has conquered his addictions and learned how to interact with people on a more personal level. He's pushed himself to participate in extra-curricular activities so that he is around people more often. Now he takes responsibility for inviting someone to do something on Friday nights. He does not wait around for other people to make him happy. None of this has been easy for Chad, but if you ask him, he will tell you that asking for help, taking chances, and believing in your talents can save your college career, and maybe your life.

his chapter will help you develop more positive feelings about yourself. After completing this chapter, you will be able to

■ Define self-esteem

■ Discuss the importance of self-esteem

■ Evaluate your own self-esteem

■ Discuss the concept of the inner child

■ List strategies for improving self-esteem

■ Demonstrate "feel good about me" behaviours

■ Display a winning attitude and image

■ Incorporate the cornerstones for positive self-esteem into your life

You and Your Personal

Self-Esteem Level

efore discussing reasons and strategies for changing, complete the questionnaire to see where you stand right now.

5 = Strongly Agree

4 = Agree

3 = Don't Know

2 = Disagree

1 = Strongly Disagree

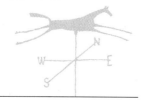

1. I like who I am.
   1 2 3 4 5

2. I feel confident in my ability to do well in college.
   1 2 3 4 5

3. I have friends on whom I can rely. *1 2 3 4 5*

4. I feel comfortable interacting with classmates.
   1 2 3 4 5

5. I am able to speak up in class.
   1 2 3 4 5

6. I can laugh at myself.
   1 2 3 4 5

7. I can make mistakes and accept them. *1 2 3 4 5*

8. I am able to talk to professors comfortably. *1 2 3 4 5*

9. I can plan for my future with confidence. *1 2 3 4 5*

10. I think positive thoughts about myself and have a positive mental image of myself.
    1 2 3 4 5

A SELF-ASSESSMENT Total your points from these ten questions. Refer to the following rating scale to evaluate your level of self-esteem.

0–10 *You have problems feeling good about yourself and often suffer from anxiety and feelings of insecurity.*

11–20 *You seem to have more anxiety than most people.*

21–30 *You experience low self-esteem in some areas, but you are confident in many aspects of your life.*

31–40 *You feel reasonably secure and confident; only a few areas cause you stress and insecurity.*

41–50 *On almost all occasions, you feel confident and competent and can laugh at your mistakes and learn from them.*

Now, turn to your journal and respond to the following questions.

1. What is my major cause of insecurity and low self-esteem?

2. Who makes me insecure and unsure?

3. On what occasions do I feel most secure and capable?

4. Who makes me feel good about myself?

What Is Self-Esteem and
Why Is It so Important?

Self-esteem is how you feel about yourself; it is the value you place on who you are as a person. You might think of self-esteem as a photograph of yourself that you keep locked in your mind. It is a cumulative product developed through many experiences and through relationships with many people.

People who demonstrate a high degree of self-esteem and confidence usually have five characteristics.

CONDITIONS OF SELF-ESTEEM

1. A sense of security   4. A sense of purpose

2. A sense of identity   5. A sense of personal competence

3. A sense of belonging

These characteristics are considered key to a person's ability to approach life with confidence, maintain self-direction, and achieve outstanding accomplishments. In high school or on the job, you might have felt pretty good about yourself, but since you have entered a new environment, have you become somewhat shaky where self-esteem is concerned? It is natural to be nervous or to feel threatened as you move into a new environment. If your self-esteem is healthy, you will soon feel comfortable again.

Although most of us don't carry as much baggage from bad experiences as Chad did, all of us have in our past some experiences that have negatively affected our self-esteem and kept us from being as successful and happy as we could be. Can you think of experiences in your past that have had a negative impact on your self-esteem? In your double-entry journal discuss one experience that caused you to feel less than good about yourself. Can you see how this experience and the people involved in it have helped control your feelings about yourself?

Before reading any further, familiarize yourself with these important things to remember about self.

SELF
What Makes Me Who I Am

- Your self is made up of all experiences, beliefs, opinions, and attitudes that relate to you.

- Taking care of, protecting, and improving the self is the foundation of everyone's behaviour.

- The protection of self causes people to position themselves in the best light.

- Your self needs your acceptance as much as it needs the acceptance of others.

- Most of your behaviours are consistent with how you feel about your self.

- Your self is constantly changing as you accept new ideas and discard old ones. (This idea is encouraging, because it means that you can change your self-esteem and make it better. It also suggests the necessity of constantly working on your self-esteem because as you change, your self-esteem will change, too.)

- If you change your feelings about your self, your behaviour will change. Learning to love your self will most likely result in better marks, improved relationships, and more direction and focus in your life.

■ Your self needs routine, consistency, and patterns; therefore, introducing change to your self may bring some resistance. (Change is the hardest thing for human beings to face, even when they want it and when they know that in the long run, it will be best.)

Influences on Poor Self-Esteem

All self-esteem, positive or negative, is learned. All young children, indeed all people, need unconditional love—love that is given with no strings attached. We all need to feel loved just as we are, with all our faults and shortcomings. Parents often do a very good job of loving unconditionally. However, because they want their children to do well, parents sometimes use conditional love as a way to motivate their children. An example of conditional love is for a mother to pout if her daughter went out with her friends but to reward her with a new outfit if she stayed home. Although most parents do not intend to harm their children, conditional love can be damaging to a child's self-esteem.

When you were a young child, you probably received messages that made you think you were good. Your self-esteem might have been bolstered by praise or encouragement. You were probably praised for taking your first step and for saying your first word. When you were older, your parents, teachers, or peers may have praised you for good grades, for scoring a goal, or for being elected class president. Perhaps you won approval from classmates because you were witty, athletic, or musical. Any accomplishments that made you feel good and successful helped build positive self-esteem.

As a child you probably also received messages that registered disapproval. Your self-esteem might have been damaged by well-meaning parents, teachers, and others who criticized you in an effort to motivate you. Sometimes parents have unrealistic expectations of their children's behaviour, and when those expectations aren't met they make their children feel inadequate without realizing it.

_____ *Feel that I must always be dressed perfectly*

_____ *Place too much importance on brand-name clothing*

_____ *Always arrive late*

_____ *Always arrive early*

_____ *Have difficulty establishing intimacy*

_____ *Am preoccupied with what others may think of me*

_____ *Cannot adequately face the demands of life*

Now look over your responses and list the three items that you think have the most negative impact on your self-esteem.

1. _____

2. _____

3. _____

Later you will refer to this list and work on improving these areas.

More about You and Your

Personal Self-Esteem

"Two perspectives create your self-esteem: your history and your view of this history. Your history is how you grew up, where and with whom. This history colors your thought patterns, feelings, attitudes, and belief systems" (Berenblatt and Berenblatt, 1994). As children we rated ourselves and compared ourselves to others. According to Berenblatt and Berenblatt, "If you held onto that childhood bad rating, it still affects everything you do and every relationship you have, even today."

■ HOW I FEEL ABOUT ME EXERCISE Complete this exercise to learn more about your current self-esteem level.

1. John never performed well in school, so he learned to be the class clown to gain recognition and to direct negative attention away from himself. Did you work to excel in areas outside academics? Did these efforts help shape your self-esteem?

_____

_____

_____

2. We don't all learn the same way. Some people can learn well by reading, others need to see what is being taught, and still others need to do something to learn. How do you learn best? Do you think your self-esteem was affected by someone who tried to teach you in a way that was not best for you? _____

_____

_____

_____

_____

3. Kelly can make anything with the right tools and materials. Juan writes very creatively. Soo Lin can make everybody laugh with her creative characters. What can you do that is creative? _____

_____

_____

4. Most people have a self that is their real self and a self that they present to others. How do your real self and your other self differ? What do you think you would have to do to be able to be your real self most of the time? _____

_____

_____

_____

5. Sometimes a person's image influences how he or she feels about herself or himself. Do you have any image concerns that might influence your personal self-esteem? Do you have any self-damaging habits that relate to your personal image? Is there anything you can do to improve your image and your self-esteem?

_____

_____

_____

6. Do you have a friend who puts you down, makes you feel dumb or insignificant, or hurts your feelings with snide remarks? What could you do to improve your own self-esteem and let your friend know that you don't like such remarks?

_____

_____

_____

No one expects you to be perfect or to know everything.

WHY SHOULD YOU DO IT?

You may be wondering why you should worry about self-esteem when you already have concerns about grades, work, laundry, relationships, and a million other things. Maybe you think you can wait to worry about your self-esteem after you graduate. The reason you need to be concerned *now* is that your marks, work, social life—everything—are tied up with your self-esteem.

Several outstanding psychiatrists and professors stress the importance of addressing self-esteem in the educational process, believing that self-esteem goes hand-in-hand with academics. Carl Rogers (1972), a noted psychiatrist who has developed many psychological theories and ideas about self-esteem, wrote, "Sometimes I feel our education has as one of its major goals the bringing up of individuals to live in isolation cages." Leo Buscaglia (1982), a well-known professor who has taught for years on the subjects of love and relationships, asks, "How many classes did you ever have in your entire educational career that taught you about you?"

Your relationships with others—friends, parents, children, professors, bosses, spouses—depend on how well you have developed your own self-esteem. You are not an isolated human being. Every day you must relate to others, and your self-esteem will influence the kinds of relationships you build. You will continue to meet new people and face new challenges with the people you know as you grow and mature, and these challenges are likely to increase in complexity. Unless you are planning to live a life alone in the woods, you will rely on your ability to relate positively to all kinds of people. The basis for those relationships lies within you, in your self-esteem.

HOW DO YOU DO IT?

If you are like most people, you will admit that your self-esteem could use a little improvement. You might even admit that a great deal of the time you are faking it and that everything isn't nearly as wonderful as you pretend. So that makes you normal. The good news is that you can change things if you really want to.

You can't all of a sudden become a new person, and there is no reason to throw away everything from your past. But you can mend or heal feelings that make you feel inadequate and unsure of yourself. Even if you have a great self-esteem, you can still find ways to get better.

Improving your self-esteem is a life-long undertaking. Self-fulfilled people are always becoming, constantly striving to improve in all areas of their lives. Many highly educated and successful people seek continually to improve. No one achieves greatness overnight, although it may appear so at times. World-class athletes have spent a lifetime perfecting their skills; presidents of major corporations have struggled for years to reach the top; career politicians usually start at the bottom of the ladder.

As a new college student, you have a wonderful opportunity to grow. You can observe others, ask questions, and try new ideas. Extraordinary people are just ordinary people who believe in themselves and get a little better every day.

Some people think that they can't change. Their attitude is: "This is who I am—take it or leave it." Buscaglia (1982) says, "I believe that wherever you are in life, and however you learned it, . . . if you want to learn it differently, anything that can be learned can be unlearned and relearned. So there's always hope and there's always wonder." Do you feel that you can't change, that you can't do anything about what has already happened? As you look within, do you see ways in which you might improve how you feel about yourself? Have you been using excuses to justify why you won't change? Are these excuses causing you to be unhappy with who you are? Answer the following questions to help assess your own attitudes about change.

1. Do I really understand myself and why I do what I do? Discuss one of your present behaviours that is tied to a past experience. _____

_____

_____

2. How good are my personal relationships with my family, friends, colleagues, classmates? Discuss a technique for improving one of your relationships.

_____

_____

3. Am I reasonably happy with the way I feel about myself and what is happening in my life right now? _____

_____

_____

4. Do I need to quit making excuses and get on with becoming who I can be? If so, how can I do it? _____

_____

_____

■ UNCOVER YOUR GOLDEN INNER SELF There is a story called *"Temple of the Golden Buddha."* The golden Buddha of the title is a beautiful solid gold sculpture standing 3 metres tall and weighing 5 1/2 tonnes. The value of the gold alone is approximately $100 million.

More than 200 years ago, when the Burmese army invaded Thailand, the people in the village where the Buddha was located covered the Buddha with clay to hide its worth from the invaders. The Burmese army killed everyone in the village, so there was no one to tell the story of the clay-covered golden Buddha. In 1957 the Buddha was being moved. When it began to rain, the monks who were moving the statue, unaware that its clay was cracked, covered it with a tarpaulin. During the night, one of the monks examined the Buddha to see if it had dried. He noticed a gleam reflecting from the beam of his flashlight and risked further damage to the Buddha by using a sharp tool to chip away the clay. The monk discovered the solid gold art that had been hidden for over 200 years.

Self-esteem is very much like the golden Buddha. We all have wonderful talents and capabilities waiting to be developed, but all too often we hide those talents under poor self-esteem. By taking the proper steps and focusing on the positive things about yourself, you can begin to chip away the clay that may have covered the golden Buddha inside you.

■ ATTITUDE! You may feel that you have had enough of attitude. Your parents talked to you about it, your teachers hounded you about it. But it is important! The impact of a bad attitude on your self is overpowering, and the importance of a good attitude to your self-esteem should not be underestimated. Focusing on the positive can bring dramatic changes in your life.

We all know that life sometimes deals bad blows, but your goal should be to be positive much more often than you are negative. Positive attitudes go hand in hand with energy, motivation, and friendliness. People with positive attitudes are more appealing to others; negative people drive others away.

Listen to yourself for a few days. Are you whining, complaining, griping, and finding fault with everything and everybody around you? Do you blame your roommate for your problems? Is your bad grade the professor's fault? Are your parents responsible for everything bad that ever happened to you? If these kinds of thoughts are coming out of your mouth or are in your head, your first step toward improved self-esteem is to clean up your act.

■ LOSE THE VICTIM MENTALITY Many people grow up with a "victim mentality." They expect bad things to happen to them and they may feel they deserve to have bad things happen to them. The victim mentality means letting things happen to you instead of deciding what you want your life to become.

If you have a victim mentality, you work to get rid of it! See where you fit in the following chart.

VICTIM MENTALITY VERSUS PERSONAL RESPONSIBILITY

Victim Mentality	Personal Responsibility
are not your genuine self	are who you are
change your personality to accommodate whomever you are with	exhibit same personality most of the time
are overly critical	are nonjudgmental
hold back for fear of earning someone's disapproval	can function without others' approval
are a perfectionist	can accept work that is less than perfect
envy the success of others	are happy for others' accomplishments
love with conditions	are able to provide unconditional love
hide real feelings, including anger	express true feelings and demonstrate anger in a healthy manner
are unable to play, tease, laugh, and have fun	can laugh at yourself and tease others appropriately
distrust others	are able to trust people who have earned your trust
seek to control others; withdraw when unable to do so	control yourself; do not need to control others

Source: Adapted from Charles Whitfield, *Healing the Child Within,* Deerfield Beach, Fla.: Health Communications (1987).

Do some of the victim behaviours describe you? You can develop a strategy for changing these behaviours. Select an item from the victim side of the chart. In your double-entry journal discuss why you think you have these feelings. Next, select an item from the personal responsibility side of the chart and describe how you managed to develop this positive emotion. Can you see how attitude plays a great role in whether you accept being a victim or insist on having a great life?

Positive self-esteem enables you to plan your life, chart a course, and step boldly forward, making things happen as you envision them rather than accepting what life gives you. Since self-esteem affects how you think, feel about yourself, relate to others, love and establish relationships, study, react to stress, parent your children, and experience intimacy, you can see what an important topic it is for you to study. Even more important is the need for you to examine your own self-esteem, to learn to recognize signs and examples of low self-esteem, and to determine how to correct problems. Studies show a high correlation between self-esteem and school performance and the ability to learn. As you begin your college career, one of your highest priorities should be to raise your level of self-esteem, regardless of what it is now.

> In my own work with thousands of students of all ages, I have observed that the vital ingredient of a satisfying life, in and out of the classroom, is a positive reflection of self.
>
> Sharon L. Hanna, author

■ MAKE A CONSCIOUS CHOICE TO FEEL GOOD ABOUT YOURSELF

How you feel about yourself ultimately is up to you. You can keep negative remarks, planted by you or others, in your mind, or you can push them out and replace them with feel-good messages. It may sound a little hokey, but it works. Begin by writing down three feel-good messages about yourself.

1. _____

_____

2. _____

_____

3. _____

_____

Begin each day thinking of these messages. When you get into bed at night, close your eyes and silently repeat to yourself the same three messages, or three other feel-good messages. Many successful people talk to themselves frequently to keep their self-esteem at a high level. Do whatever it takes.

■ SHOW OFF YOUR TALENTS AND STRENGTHS Make a list of five of your most important strengths.

Great Things About Me!

1. _____

2. _____

3. _____

4. _____

5. _____

What can you do to showcase your strengths? If you play the guitar, perhaps you could join a band. If you are a great floor hockey player, perhaps you could join an intramural team. Think about how you could use your experiences to create positive opportunities on campus now. What talents do you have that can help you improve your self-esteem?

■ DECIDE TO DO SOMETHING DIFFERENT So you don't like that you are always late? Decide to stop it, right now. Set your alarm clock 30 minutes early. Get up and take your time instead of rushing and feeling stressed out.

Do you feel bad because your father always seems to be on your case about something? Discuss it with him. Try to help him understand how it makes you feel and how important it is to you to please him.

Has a friend hurt your feelings and made you feel inadequate by teasing you? Discuss your feelings with your friend and take responsibility for overcoming those feelings.

Do you give up too easily when things get tough? Decide to stick with one really important task until you get it done well. Then select another, and another, until sticking to something becomes a habit. Remember: 21 straight days, an action becomes a habit. Start now!

■ BUILD POSITIVE RELATIONSHIPS A large portion of your self-esteem, positive or negative, derives from your peers. Is your self-esteem enhanced by your friends, or do they drag you down and make you feel insignificant? Picture your friends in your mind and recall the last time you were with each one of them. Was the experience encouraging or demeaning? Did you hear remarks that made you feel good? Did you make any comments that made your friends feel good? Sometimes one of the best ways to build your self-esteem is to help others who are struggling with theirs.

Describe the most positive experience you have had recently with a friend who made you feel good. _____

_____

_____

_____

Describe the most negative experience you have had recently with a friend or acquaintance who made you feel lousy and worthless. _____

_____

_____

_____

Does writing about these experiences help you to see qualities that you admire in certain people? Does it help you identify certain things about some of your acquaintances that are bad for you?

■ PREPARE FOR THE FUTURE When you were little, did you want to be a ballet dancer or a firefighter or a garbage collector or a veterinarian? You are probably still struggling with who you want to become. Many people in their fifties and sixties are still becoming.

En route to becoming whomever it is you want to become, you can develop characteristics that will help you to feel good about yourself and at the same time earn the respect and confidence of other people.

What five qualities do you admire most in other people?

1. _____

2. _____

3. _____

4. _____

5. _____

Design a plan for developing one of these qualities in your own life.

_____

_____

_____

_____

_____

Start now.

■ WHEN PARENTS WANT TO RUN YOUR LIFE Parents or guardians sometimes have plans and dreams for their children that are very different from what the children want for themselves. For example, a parent who owns a small manufacturing firm may have aspirations for a child to take over the family business, whereas that child may dream of becoming a forest ranger because he or she loves the outdoors. If you are a young adult beginning to identify your direction in life, you will want to listen to the advice of your parents or guardians, your professors and advisors, and others who can provide information for you, but you will ultimately have to make your own decisions. More about career development can be found in Chapter 15 of this book.

Some cultures value independence from family more than others. You will have to decide whether to make your own decisions or honour those of others who have made plans for you. You may have to endure the stress of living between two cultures whose values sometimes conflict. Always be true to yourself, and remember, the stronger and more positive your self-esteem, the easier it will be for you to make decisions for yourself, whatever your culture.

When you make your own decisions, you must take responsibility for your choices. Before you make a decision that directly conflicts with parental advice, ask questions, research it carefully to be sure to make a wise choice. For example, some questions you might ask about a career choice are: "What is the job market like?" "Does this kind of job pay well enough to support the lifestyle to which I aspire?" "Will this career provide the kind of challenge that will make me look forward to going to work?"

Parents will always give you advice, and that advice will be based on their experiences and what they think is best. Listen respectfully, use what you can, and explain why you are doing what you are doing. In the long run, you'll need to decide for yourself.

■ PRAISE AND REWARD YOURSELF We have discussed many ways to improve self-esteem and you will uncover others that work for you on your own. Positive self-esteem arises from experiences that generate

> My mother has always been unhappy with what I do. She would much rather I do something nicer, like be a bricklayer.
> **Mick Jagger, lead singer for The Rolling Stones**

feelings of value and worth. Recognition for accomplishments also promotes a feeling of positive self-esteem. Sometimes your accomplishments may not be recognized by anyone else. For example, since coming to college, you may have stopped procrastinating about doing your homework, but it may be that no one at college knows that you used to procrastinate. In these cases you need to celebrate your success by congratulating yourself. Each time you reach a goal or do something that improves your self-esteem, you should praise and reward yourself.

If there are things about you that you would like to change, you need to make up your mind to change them. It will take work, motivation, and desire. In the process of changing bad habits, you will begin to turn loose negative feelings about yourself. The following chart identifies strategies for letting go of bad feelings.

GETTING ON WITH MY LIFE—LEARNING TO LET GO

When I feel nervous or stressed because of memories from the past I will breathe deeply, focus on doing well, and tell myself that all those negative things are behind me now.

When I feel pain from the past restricting my intellectual growth, I will visualize a quiet path in the woods, where I am walking with a large suitcase. In that suitcase are all the painful incidents that used to cause me problems. I will visualize myself leaving that suitcase on the ground deep in the woods. When I come out of the woods, I will see bright sunshine.

I will surround myself with positive people who praise easily and laugh often. And I will remember how important it is that I give them praise and encouragement in return.

I will remember to praise myself for small and large accomplishments, to put positive words of congratulations in my mind, and to push aside negative remembrances.

I will concentrate on the fact that no one can control me unless I allow it. I will control myself and my thoughts!

IF IT IS TO BE, IT IS UP TO ME

You *can* reshape your self-esteem and you *can* determine many things and feelings about your future.

Earlier in this chapter, in the section about behaviours associated with poor self-esteem, you identified the three top problems you have with self-esteem. Now write a goal for overcoming each one of them, using what you learned in Chapter 2 about writing goals: define the goal in measurable terms, determine the steps you need to take to accomplish the goal, and set a deadline for reaching the desired behaviour.

Goal #1

_____
_____
_____

Steps to Achieve Goal #1:

1. _____
2. _____
3. _____
4. _____

Deadline: _____
Reward for Accomplishing This Goal: _____

Goal #2

_____
_____
_____

Steps to Achieve Goal #2:

1. _____
2. _____
3. _____
4. _____

Deadline: _____
Reward for Accomplishing This Goal: _____

Goal #3

_____
_____
_____

Steps to Achieve Goal #3:

1. _____
2. _____
3. _____
4. _____

Deadline: _____
Reward for Accomplishing This Goal: _____

BECOMING YOUR BEST IN SELF-ESTEEM

How can you become your best in self-esteem and stay there? Well, you probably can't. Self-esteem fluctuates according to many factors. You might arrive at class on top of the world only to have your ego deflated by a sharp-tongued professor who did not like your essay and decided to make you the example of the day. You could be anticipating a great evening on a first date and then be stood up—suddenly your ego hits rock bottom. Perhaps you went into a baseball game feeling great because you were three for four in your last game; then you bat zero, and your self-esteem plummets. Self-esteem is not stable and unchanging; if your self-esteem acts like a yo-yo at times, you are normal.

Most of the time, though, your self-esteem should be fairly stable—maybe not a 10, but not a zero either. If you have positive self-esteem and good mental and emotional health, you should be able to check off most of the items on the positive self-esteem checklist.

POSITIVE SELF-ESTEEM CHECKLIST

- Physically fit and active

- Creative

- Joyful and energetic

- Involved in extracurricular activities

- Free from constant worries and anxiety

- Feel confident and competent

- Have positive relationships with people of both sexes

- Act assertively; do not let anyone run over you

- Feel good about where you are headed with your life

- Free of people who make you feel bad, put you down, or abuse you mentally, emotionally, or physically

- Free of self-destructive habits, such as addictions to drugs, cigarettes, and alcohol

- Free of physically destructive habits, such as overeating, starving, binging; free from anorexia and bulimia

So you are probably saying, "Well, nobody can do all that stuff all the time." And you are right. But you can do most of it most of the time. Your positive self-esteem is like the golden Buddha, waiting to be discovered, admired, and praised. The more you love you, the happier and more successful you will become and the more you will be able to love and help others. Developing positive self-esteem is hard work, but it's worth all the effort it requires.

Developing positive self-esteem is hard work, but it's worth all the effort it requires.

CORNERSTONES for developing positive self-esteem

- Love yourself.

- Reparent yourself if necessary.

- Celebrate your own successes.

- Learn to celebrate others' successes.

- Turn loose old pains and negative thoughts.

- Face fears and overcome them.

- Solicit advice and opinions but make your own decisions.

- Display your genuine self and like who you are.

- Take responsibility for yourself and look forward to the freedom it brings.

- Study new ideas and concepts and embrace those that are right for you.

- Be open to having relationships with all kinds of people, secure in the knowledge that all people don't have to be just like you.

- Emulate the characteristics and traits you admire in others.

- Picture yourself happy, winning, and successful.

- Focus on the positive things about you.

- Use positive "I" statements.

The one minute journal

n a minute or less, jot down one lesson you learned from this chapter.

Understanding Differences: A Celebration of Diversity

The professor called him Jimmie, but the class would later learn that his name was Jhi' Ming. He was a small, quiet man who sat in the front row of the communication class. During the fifth week of class, four team leaders were asked to choose members to form a group that would work together to solve a problem. The first leader chose Parvinder, the second leader chose Phillip, the

third leader chose Clifford, and the fourth leader chose Carolyn. The selection process continued until everyone had been chosen except Jimmie. The first leader, Stephanie, was forced to include Jimmie in her group by the process of elimination. There were no audible sounds of dismay, but everyone in the class knew that Jimmie had not been chosen because he was different. Jimmie was considered different because he was older than the others, because he was married, because he had children, and because he was Vietnamese.

The groups began working right away. Stephanie asked for advice on solving her group's problem. Several times, Jimmie suggested solutions, but his opinions were ignored and others were sought. Jimmie finally stopped contributing to the conversation and sat quietly with his group until time was called.

After class, Stephanie told another group leader that she was disappointed that she had to "get stuck with that oddball!" They laughed and continued down the hall to another class. Fortunately, Jimmie did not hear the conversation as he had already left.

Little did Stephanie, the other members of her group, or their classmates know what they were to learn from Jimmie during the remaining weeks of the semester. This shy, quiet man had a remarkable history which would change the lives of every student who had the

Stephanie began to realize what a wealth of information, history, and honour each of us carries in our souls.

privilege of being in his class. This man called Jimmie, whose opinions were shut out by his group, would send shock waves through the hearts of 24 students during his presentation the next week. Those students would never again call him an "oddball."

"My name is Jhi' Ming Yen," he began. "Today, I will share with you the history of my life and the triumph of my family." The class was somewhat uninterested at first, but within a minute, Jhi' Ming's story had begun to affect every person in the class. "Fifteen years ago, my family left Vietnam in a small boat in the middle of the night. We had been planning our escape for some time, ever since the communist government had taken over. Life had become unbearable for us. Fear dominated our lives, and nobody knew when a soldier would come visit with demands from the government. I was a successful businessman in Vietnam, and I owned a company that employed several hundred people. Little by little I sold my family's possessions so that I could save enough money to buy a boat and to pay my way out of the country. Anyone caught leaving Vietnam would be killed, so the night we left was terrifying. We walked away from everything — our house, family, friends and our country — all for a chance at freedom." The class was completely silent.

"Our boat was small, and it was a long, dangerous journey to safety. The waves were huge, and many of us were seasick. We made it Cambodia where we lived in a refugee camp for more than a year. The conditions were terrible, and many people were sick much of the time. We were so grateful when we were told that a church in Canada was going to sponsor us and bring us to this wonderful country. My wife and I have worked at menial jobs for the past 15 years to support our children, to give them opportunities for a good life in a free society."

His story unfolded like a book of horrors and triumphs as the class listened, for the first time, to the quiet man who sat in the front row. He continued, describing what had happened in the 15 years since he left his country, and the only life and world he knew. Jhi' Ming was no longer a stranger. When the class was over, Stephanie and her classmates finally understood how important it is to give people who are different a chance. They began to realize what a wealth of information, history, and honour each of us carries in our souls. As others shared their lives and histories, the class began to see that people of a different culture, age, marital status, sexual orientation, ethnicity, race, religion, and educational level can add monumental dimensions to another's life. They began to learn how to celebrate diversity, because they allowed Jhi' Ming to share the priceless gift of his life's story. Equally important, perhaps, they learned how Jhi' Ming had adjusted to Canadian culture; he and his family worked hard, earned respect, and made it in a new world.

You Are a Culture of One

During our formative years, each of us develops a unique set of values, beliefs, and customs. We are virtually programmed, based on who raises us, as to our race, our nationality, where we live, where we go to school, our religion or lack of religion, our friends, our relatives, and our experiences and opportunities. Like fingerprints, no two people with their beliefs, customs, and experiences are exactly alike. This amazing phenomenon is what makes human beings interesting and makes the differences we see in people from cultures other than our own especially interesting as well as personally educational.

Culture is learned. People are born into a culture, but their culture is not a physical trait, such as eye colour or hair texture. You probably developed, or absorbed, most of your personal culture from your family. The process is almost like osmosis in plants; it is as though culture seeps gradually through your skin. Many of the beliefs and values you embrace have been passed from one generation to another.

In college, you are likely to find your values, beliefs, and actions changing as you meet new people and become involved in new situations and as your horizons broaden. Quite simply, your college experience enhances your understanding, and your cultural beliefs change as a result. This change is known as **cultural adjustment**. You can, and should, expect to have your beliefs greatly tested—and perhaps adjusted—before you graduate.

Cultural adjustment doesn't mean that you must abandon your family, church, basic values, and friends. It may mean, however, that you need to reevaluate why you feel the way you do about certain situations and certain groups. You may have been taught that people belonging to a certain group are bad. As you learn and grow, you may find that they are not bad at all, just different from you, and, like Stephanie and her classmates, you will probably discover that this different culture is one to be celebrated.

In this chapter you will be given an opportunity, through a series of scenarios, to put yourself in other people's shoes and thereby gain a better understanding of how someone different from you may feel. After studying this chapter you will be able to

- Discuss different types of prejudices, including racial, religious, sexual, gender, regional, and international

- Develop communication skills for relating to people from different cultures and backgrounds

- Identify your own biases, attitudes, and expectations

- Learn to examine critically your own thinking and actions relative to people from different cultures

- Plan ways in which you can eliminate your personal prejudices and biases

- Discuss strategies for interacting more effectively with people from a variety of cultures

Take a moment now to assess your current feelings relative to people who are different from you.

5 = Strongly Agree

4 = Agree

3 = Don't Know

2 = Disagree

1 = Strongly Disagree

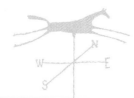

1. Many of my friends have backgrounds different from mine. *1 2 3 4 5*

2. I readily accept people from different regions. *1 2 3 4 5*

3. I am interested in knowing people whose ethnic background is different from mine. *1 2 3 4 5*

4. I am open to relationships with people who are of a different race from me. *1 2 3 4 5*

5. I can accept people who are homosexual or bisexual. *1 2 3 4 5*

6. I have been taught things by my parents or others that may contribute to my personal biases. *1 2 3 4 5*

7. I am accepting of people who belong to religions that promote beliefs very different from my own. *1 2 3 4 5*

8. I would be comfortable dating someone from another nationality, race, or religion. *1 2 3 4 5*

9. I am accepting of the attitudes, values, and beliefs of people of generations other than mine. *1 2 3 4 5*

10. I am comfortable around people who are physically, emotionally, or mentally challenged. *1 2 3 4 5*

A SELF-ASSESSMENT Total your points from these ten questions. Refer to the following rating scale to determine where you stand in relation to dealing with cultural diversity.

0–10 You have a great deal of difficulty relating to and accepting people from different cultures, nationalities, races, religions, sexual orientations, and age groups.

11–20 You have some difficulty relating to and accepting people who have different beliefs and backgrounds from yours.

21–30 You have learned to accept some cultural differences, but you still have some difficulty fully accepting all people.

31–40 You are more accepting of cultural differences than the average person.

41–50 You have very few biases or problems relating to people of different cultures and beliefs.

Now, refer to your journal and respond in writing to your findings. Consider the following questions when writing in your journal.

1. Why is it important to understand someone from another culture?

2. Discuss one prejudice you have toward a particular group of people. Why do you have these beliefs?

3. What steps do you think you can take to reduce your biases?

The Components of Culture

Sometimes we can tell that people are from a different culture or ethnic group because of the way they look and dress or by the way they speak—dress and speech are two visible signs of culture. Other components of culture are not so visible. Sociologist David Popenoe (1993) identifies five components of culture.

- Symbols
- Language
- Values
- Norms
- Sanctions

Symbols are items that stand for something, such as the Canadian flag. Most Canadians respect the flag and know that it stands for honour, duty, patriotism, service, and freedom. People of other nationalities might not understand that the maple leaf on the Canadian flag is a significant symbol in Canadian culture. The key to relating to people from any culture is understanding. Some common symbols and what they stand for are as follows:

purple signifies royalty in some cultures

a *dove* is a sign of peace in countries around the world

red is associated with anger in some cultures

a *hexagonal sign* indicates Stop! in several countries

Name a symbol from your culture: _____

What does this symbol mean? _____

Language is another important component of culture; the meaning of a word can vary across cultures. For example, if you were to ask for a biscuit in England, you would get a cookie. How many different words can you think of for that nonalcoholic, carbonated beverage many of us like to drink? Pop? Soda? Soft drink? Coke?

Canadian culture has given some words meanings that are specific to our culture. For example, a "boom box" is typical of language used by young Canadians. Other cultures have developed their own sets of words and meanings.

What is a phrase specific to your culture? _____

_____

What does it mean? _____

_____

Values are typically based on family traditions and religious beliefs. What is wrong in one society may be acceptable in another. Most young people in Canada would be unwilling to allow their parents to choose their future spouse, yet in many countries this practice is quite common. Some religious services are joyous celebrations; others are formal and solemn. Some churches are usually filled with soulful, joyous singing, while others may include songs not accompanied by musical instruments and may be more solemn—there is no one proper way to conduct a religious ceremony. Like so much else, what is correct depends on the culture.

Name a value of the culture in which you were raised. _____

_____

Why is this value important to you? _____

_____

Norms relate directly to the values of a culture or society—they are how we expect people to act based on those values. In an elegant restaurant, for example, you expect people to conduct themselves with more dignity than you might expect in a fast-food restaurant.

What is a norm in your culture? _____

_____

Why do you think it is a norm? Why is it important? _____

_____

Sanctions are the ways in which a society enforces its norms. When a society adopts a set of norms that are upheld as valuable, it typically seeks a way to enforce these norms through formal laws. In every society there are people who do not abide by the rules, people who break the law. A person in Canada who breaks the law may be sent to jail or may be required to perform community service. In other cultures the penalty for minor offences might involve corporal punishment. In Canada this punishment would not be acceptable, but elsewhere it is.

What is a sanction in your culture? _____

_____

Why do you think it is a sanction? _____

_____

_____

If you have a desire to understand and appreciate others, you can learn to celebrate diversity and gain valuable lessons from almost everyone you meet.

The Power of an Open Mind

To experience other people and to receive the benefits of knowing someone, you need to enter all relationships with an open mind. If you have a derogatory mindset toward a race, an ethnic group, a sexual orientation, or a religion, for example, you have internal barriers that can keep you from getting to know who a person really is.

Everyone you meet is a game player to a certain extent. Most people do not allow you to see who they are until they know they can trust you. We protect ourselves and our egos by holding back, covering up, and otherwise shielding ourselves from possible hurt and pain until we know a person will accept us for who we are. Regardless of background, all people want to be accepted for themselves; they want to be able to act naturally and to be comfortable just being themselves.

Learning to interact with people from different cultures is a matter of keeping an open mind and looking at each person as an individual, not as a race, a class, or a religion. We cannot help but be influenced by what we have been taught and what we have experienced, but we can overcome prejudices and biases if we view people as individuals. If you intend to grow as an educated person and as a human being, you will need to expand your capacity to accept and understand people from different cultures within and outside your country.

MY CULTURE OF ONE

Take some time now to identify exactly who you are as a culture of one.

Describe the place(s) where you grew up—the people, the size of the city or

town, the schools you attended. _____

_____

> **You are not educated as long as you have prejudices against anyone for any reason other than his or her character.**
> **Martin Luther King, Jr., civil rights leader**

____

____

____

____

Discuss some of the basic beliefs you learned from your family. _______________

____

____

____

____

____

____

Do you think some of the beliefs you learned from your family might not be right for you today? Why or why not?

____

____

____

____

____

____

Discuss some of the basic beliefs you learned from your teachers.

____

____

____

____

____

Name some ways in which your background is reflected in your culture of one, for example, what you wear, your hairstyle, some of the slang phrases you use.

____

____

____

____

____

_____

_____

_____

_____

_____

_____

Discuss how you may have been influenced by extracurricular activities, sports,
friends, or travel. _____

_____

_____

_____

_____

_____

Discuss how religious teachings or the absence of religious training has influ-
enced your beliefs. _____

_____

_____

_____

_____

If you are in a relationship, describe how your partner has influenced your
beliefs, actions, or values. _____

_____

_____

_____

_____

If you have children, discuss how your values, ideas, and associations have
changed since you became a parent. _____

_____

_____

_____

_____

_____

You Are the Centre
of Your Own Universe

Make use of your responses to the "Culture" exercise together with other pieces of information from your personal background to complete the next exercise. The figure inside the box represents you as you are today. The boxes the figure is juggling represent all aspects of your cultural background that have shaped your beliefs, customs, and habits. In each box, list one source of your personal cultural development. On the lines below, write the basic beliefs, rules, or values you learned from that source. For example, your religious background (source) may have prohibited attending movies (rule). Looking very carefully at your personal background, try now to identify those unique beliefs and experiences that make you who you are. (See the examples provided.)

The Colours of My Life

#1
Parents
*Hard workers
* Work ethic
*Strict

#2
Family
*8 brothers
*1 sister
*Loving

#3
Environment
*Small town
*Few neighbours
*Country living

#4
Education
*Rural
*Small
*Homogeneity

The Colours of My Life

Changing Demographics of Canada

The demographics of Canada are radically different from what they were 50 years ago. Projections point to an increasingly diverse mixture of people with whom you will work and interact; therefore, it is increasingly important for you to learn to understand, work effectively with, and accept that you live in a global community with people from a variety of cultures.

According to the Canadian Human Rights Commission Annual Report 1995, the number of women in the workforce increased by 9 percent between the years 1987-94; the number of males decreased by 5 percent, and the number of visible minorities increased by 66 percent in the same time period.

Perhaps the best opportunity for you to experience multiculturalism will be at college, particularly if you are attending a large or metropolitan college or university. When you graduate you will have a great advantage if you have become cross-culturally oriented and learned to communicate effectively with people who embrace values, beliefs, and customs that are different from yours.

Researchers Gardenswartz and Rowe (1993) suggest that one cultural mindset determines our behaviour and attitudes, from when to smile and with whom to make eye contact, to how to deal with conflict and talk to a supervisor. For example, a teenager's not looking an adult in the eye during a conversation may be considered disrespectful in one culture, but is a sign of respect in another. One of the great problems we all face in dealing with diversity is that we typically interpret other people's behaviour through our own cultural mindset. Canadians may find it strange that in some cultures parents arrange their children's marriages. People from other cultures may have difficulty understanding the relative lack of respect many Canadians show toward elders compared with their culture, in which older people are revered. You can greatly enhance your education this term if you make up your mind to look beyond your own cultural mindset.

Maxwell Yalden, Commissioner of the Canadian Human Rights Commission, suggests that we should try to "accept that one is not the only one with one's eyes on the truth; and remember, in the end, that 'all human beings are born equal in their dignity and their rights.'"

Who Are You?

in *Managing Diversity,* Gardenswartz and Rowe (1993) refer to "individuals as being like the proverbial onion with layer upon layer of cultural teaching." They suggest that cultural identity is shaped by the following factors:

- **Ethnicity**—the ethnic group with which a person identifies and the person's native language

- **Race**—the racial group or groups with which a person identifies

- **Religion**—the organized denomination or sect to which a person subscribes or rejects

- **Education**—the level and type of learning a person receives

- **Profession/Field of Work**—the type of work a person is trained to do

- **Organizations**—groups or associations to which a person belongs or has belonged, such as the military, a scouting group, a labour union, or a fraternal organization

- **Parents**—the messages, verbal and nonverbal, given by a person's parents about ethnicity, religion, values, cultural identity, etc.

In addition to these powerful cultural influences, gender, family, peers, and place of birth also significantly determine a person's cultural identity.

The Golden Rule
for Celebrating Diversity

At one time or another, most of us have been exposed to the Golden Rule: Do unto others as you would have them do unto you. As you work to improve and expand your knowledge of cultural diversity, it may help you to look at this rule from a different angle. In considering the following scenarios, first by yourself and then with a group, see if you can apply a new version of the Golden Rule: **Do unto others as they would have you do unto them.**

Respond to each scenario in the space provided. Discuss how the situation makes you feel, how you would feel if you were the person in the cultural minority depicted, and what you might do or say to improve this situation for everyone involved.

After you have responded to all the scenarios, your instructor may divide the class into groups so that you can discuss your beliefs with others and gain an understanding of how other people feel about the same situation.

You may find that some of your beliefs change slightly—or maybe even dramatically—as you work on these exercises. Growth that allows you to open up your mind, to move beyond biases and prejudices, and to seek to understand people who are different from you is positive growth.

■ SCENARIO #1 You and Jack, a friend from high school, are attending the same university. Jack has a physical disability that requires him to use a wheelchair. He was an outstanding basketball player and swimmer prior to a diving accident, which left him a paraplegic. Jack is an honour roll student. He is an avid basketball fan, attends all the games, and plays on a wheelchair team. He has a great sense of humour. He long ago dealt with his personal situation and now he even jokes about it. Jack is one of your favorite people.

Since you and Jack have been in class together, you have been noticing that people tend to treat him differently from others. Sometimes people talk loudly when talking to Jack, as if he couldn't hear. Because getting to and from classes is difficult, Jack has someone to help him maneuver around campus. One day you overhear a student talking to the person who is helping Jack as if Jack weren't there. "What happened to him?" "Can he use his arms?" Although Jack is handsome, friendly, and personable, he is usually left out of the many social activities in which other classmates participate. You know that your classmates would like and admire Jack if they got to know him.

How do you think Jack feels when people treat him as though he doesn't exist?

_____

_____

_____

_____

Why do you think some people have difficulty relating to people who have physical disabilities? _____

_____

_____

_____

What could you do to help Jack become accepted just like any other student?

_____

_____

_____

What could you say to classmates that might help them understand how to relate to Jack better and might make them and him feel more comfortable?

_____

_____

_____

After your group discusses this scenario, make an entry in your journal. Discuss any changes in feelings and beliefs brought about by this discussion.

■ SCENARIO #2 Douglas met Andy on the first day of class. Douglas struck up a conversation with Andy because he saw a tennis racket in Andy's gym bag—a welcome sight. Douglas had not found anyone to play tennis with since his arrival on campus. The two decided to get together later in the afternoon to play a game. When the game was over, each knew that he had found a friend. They discovered that they lived in the same neighbourhood, had the same professor for marketing, only at different times, and both loved to play tennis. As the semester progressed, Douglas and Andy became very close friends; they studied history together, went to parties together, ate together when their schedules permitted, and double-dated once or twice.

Douglas and Andy enjoyed many of the same sports and movies and had tastes similar in music. Douglas felt that he had met a true soul mate, and Andy could not have been happier to have Douglas to talk to and hang around with. Andy knew, however, that things could soon change. He had made a serious decision; before the Christmas break he would tell Douglas that he was gay.

Exams ended on Wednesday. Andy decided to break the news to Douglas on Tuesday night. They talked and laughed sitting on a bench outside the athletic centre; then the conversation grew still, and Andy chose his words carefully. He told Douglas that he was gay and that he had been involved with someone at home for almost a year.

If you were Douglas, what would your reaction have been? _____

_____

_____

Was Andy right to risk their friendship by telling Douglas about his sexual orientation? _____

_____

_____

Should Andy have told Douglas sooner? _____

_____

_____

If Douglas were to walk away from the friendship, how do you think Andy would feel? _____

_____

_____

Imagine that Douglas, a heterosexual, accepted Andy's orientation, but that Andy went on to say that he was interested in having a relationship with Douglas. How do you think Douglas would have reacted? _____

_____

_____

Does being gay carry a cultural or social stigma? Why or why not? _____

_____

_____

After your group discusses this scenario, make an entry in your journal. If your feelings have changed based on this discussion, explain how they have changed.

■ SCENARIO #3 You are from a small town in Northern Alberta where you attended a local college to take some university courses offered on campus. Your siblings attended the local high school. One has graduated, and the other dropped out and got married when she was 16. Your father is a farmer and your mother is a homemaker; neither parent graduated from high school. You excel as a student, but because your educational background is so superior to that of the rest of your family, you begin to feel like an outsider at home.

You are awarded an academic scholarship to a prestigious eastern university; a great majority of the university's student body are from wealthy families. Your mother doesn't understand why you want to go east just to go to school. Your father thinks you should stay at home, take a few secretarial courses, and get a job. As he says, "After all, you are just going to get married and stay at home; an education is wasted on you." One of your sisters, the dropout, begins to call you uppity. When you arrive at university, you realize that you are definitely out of place, but you are determined to stay and to excel. You experienced the feeling that you can't go home again long before you graduated from high school. Yet university doesn't seem like home either. You are suffering from culture shock.

One night you are taking part in a discussion with a group of students in your dorm. One of them asks what your father does. Other students have already revealed that their parents are prominent doctors, lawyers, and corporate executives. After you answer, you notice that some students are keeping you much more at a distance than they did before.

How do you feel? _____

_____

_____

How will you behave after this experience? _____

_____

_____

How could one of the other students present have helped you feel more comfortable? How could this student help the others to accept this person from another culture? _____

_____

_____

What part does money play in developing a person's culture? _____

_____

_____

After you have had a discussion with your group, make an entry in your journal. If your feelings have changed as a result of your discussion, note these changes in your journal.

■ SCENARIO #4 Tonya was a first-year student at a major research university. She had an excellent academic background. She had always loved science and math and was seriously considering a major that would allow her to incorporate her love of these subjects into a career. In her second semester at the university she enrolled in a calculus class taught by Dr. Ralph Bartlett. This class was especially important to Tonya for two reasons. First, Dr. Bartlett was the department chair for the program she was considering pursuing, and second, the course was her first post-secondary math course, so she wanted to start off strong.

On the first day of class Dr. Bartlett made some disparaging jokes about women in the field of science. Although these comments made Tonya uncomfortable, she thought perhaps she was being oversensitive. As the semester progressed, so did Dr. Bartlett's derogatory asides about women. Nonetheless, Tonya loved the course; she was earning A's and she felt that she had found her niche. She decided to major in this area. Tonya made an appointment to discuss possible career opportunities with Dr. Bartlett. Shortly into the appointment, Dr. Bartlett made it clear to Tonya that he didn't think she could cut it and suggested that she look for another program.

How would you feel if you were in Tonya's shoes? _____

_____

_____

What action should Tonya take in regard to Dr. Bartlett? _____

_____

_____

How would you feel if you were a male in Tonya's class? _____

_____

_____

Do you think women face discrimination in higher education? In the workforce?

_____

_____

After you have held your group discussion, make an entry in your journal relating to this scenario. If any of your feelings have changed based on this discussion, write about those changes.

■ SCENARIO #5 Gregg is in an orientation class for new students. He loves the class and most of the students in it. He is particularly close to Jesse. Gregg and Jesse were both raised in small towns, were active in their high school student councils, and love sports. They also have strong religious convictions, although they act on them differently. Gregg holds firmly to his own beliefs, but he also believes in free choice and people's right to choose their own religion. Jesse is extremely conservative as well as vocal in his approach to religion, and he readily condemns views that differ from his. Although Gregg believes that Jesse has a right to express his feelings and share his views with others, he also believes that Jesse should be more tolerant of others' beliefs.

Gregg has noticed that students avoid talking with Jesse in class and that they share less and less during class discussion. This concerns Gregg because he really likes Jesse, but he doesn't want the class to lose its openness. One day during a discussion on abortion, Jesse openly condemned a student when she shared that she had had an abortion. After class Gregg heard several students say how much they disliked Jesse's attitude.

Would you be willing to share your views in class if Jesse were one of your class-mates? _____

_____

_____

_____

If you were Gregg, how would you deal with Jesse? _____

_____

_____

_____

How tolerant are you of people's differing religious views? _____

_____

_____

_____

Can people be too religious? _____

_____

_____

_____

Do some religions carry a social stigma? _____

_____

_____

_____

CORNERSTONES for celebrating diversity

■ Accept the fact that each person is a culture unto himself or herself.

■ Be willing to change some of your attitudes, beliefs, and values in order to grow.

■ Recognize that some of your personal values and beliefs may need cultural adjustments.

■ Spend more time on inclusivity than on exclusivity.

■ Learn to appreciate that different is not necessarily bad or wrong.

■ Develop relationships with people from a variety of backgrounds, religions, races, and nationalities.

■ Make an effort to relate to people with disabilities as just people.

■ Listen to people whose sexual orientation differs from yours and try to understand them.

■ Be open to relationships with people from different socioeconomic backgrounds and understand that their value systems may be very different from yours.

■ Strive to rid yourself of filters that may skew your thinking against a person or a group of people.

■ Read about various cultures and explore ways to understand more.

■ Try to accept people for who they are.

The one minute journal

in a minute or less, jot down one major lesson you learned
from this chapter.

UNIT

INTERNET

ACTIVITY

How Well Do You Understand Yourself?

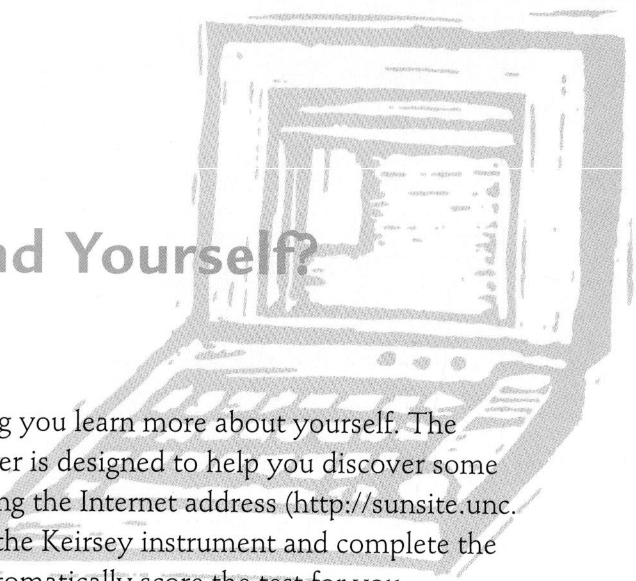

Unit 1 is devoted to helping you learn more about yourself. The Keirsey Temperament Sorter is designed to help you discover some new things about you. Using the Internet address (http://sunsite.unc.edu/jembin/mb.pl), locate the Keirsey instrument and complete the test. The computer will automatically score the test for you.

By examining your score, what did you learn about yourself? __________

What are your dominant factors? __________

What are your secondary factors? _____

_____

_____

_____

_____

_____

_____

_____

_____

How do you think your self-esteem correlates with your dominant factors? _____

_____

_____

_____

_____

_____

_____

_____

_____

UNIT

Sharpening the Tools of Life

■ **AN INSIDER'S VIEW**
Raymond Barnes
Age 38
Seneca College
Career-related Education
Toronto, Ontario

As I see it, learning is a lifelong habit. I am a network analyst for ISM (a division of IBM), where I provide technical support for corporate clients. I've worked with computers since I took data processing in high school. And since technology is a fast-changing industry, I'm continually taking industry-related computer courses to upgrade what I learned about computers at Seneca College 17 years ago. Over the years, I've also developed academic learning skills in the classroom that are directly applicable to my workplace.

One of the most important of these skills is note taking. When I'm in class, I concentrate on listening effectively, which to me means being keen about the subject content, and trying to absorb as much as I can. I take notes in point form, and I make sure that I get down the key words and ideas on paper. It's impossible to remember everything that's said in class unless you've got a good set of notes to refer to. Later that day, I look over my notes. The key words jog my memory so that I can elaborate on any areas that need clarification and detail. At work, I use the same skills when I'm solving my clients' computer problems. I listen carefully to what they're saying, and I have to document lots of detailed, specific information. My job depends on accurate data records. In fact, most jobs require this type of skill, whether you're taking minutes in a meeting or you're tracking customer information for marketing purposes

— to be successful, companies depend on accurate information.

I have worked hard to get to where I am today. It's doing the little things right that make a person successful. Work ethic, pride in a job well done, positive attitude, discipline and belief in yourself are the things that matter. If you've got the right attitude and if you take responsibility for your life, you'll be successful. Too many people have a chip on their shoulder and blame other people or their background, race, or family circumstances if things don't go their way. I've got a lot of pride in my family background, and I've never used my colour or anything else as an excuse. I expect people to see me as an individual, not a colour, and to evaluate me based upon my strengths as a person. I believe that this perspective has been instrumental in my personal success. I rely on myself to make positive things happen, and I know that if I work hard enough, I'll be successful in anything I undertake.

I make sure that I get down the key words and ideas on paper.

■ AN INSIDER'S VIEW

Peter Keech
Age 45
Nova Scotia Community College
Burridge Campus
Yarmouth, Nova Scotia

A year ago I started on one of the most rewarding journeys of my life. I'd been working for 14 years at a job I hated, and I was so burned out that I took time off to explore other career options. During my free time I did some volunteer work at the local hospital. It wasn't long before I realized that I came alive when I was working there, and I knew I had found my new career.

I enrolled in the Certified Nursing Assistant (CNA) program at NSCC, and while I knew that I was heading in the right direction, I was a wreck during the weeks leading up to the program. I had a tremendous fear of failing, and I was putting far too much pressure on myself to succeed. I guess I was afraid of letting everybody down.

The first 5 or 6 weeks were pretty tough. I considered quitting on more than one occasion, and particularly when I received the results of my first test. I had studied like a madman, but nothing had really sunk in — when I got to the test, I couldn't remember much of anything. I recall thinking that I just didn't have what it takes to get through college. What saved me were three conversations: two with a couple of my instructors, and one with the college counsellor. They encouraged me to stick it out, and they helped me see that there are many different ways of studying. I just had to find out what would work for me. Just as importantly, they suggested that I learn to relax and ease up on the pressure I was creating for myself. I found that when I did, I

absorbed the material much more easily and I started to really enjoy being at college.

I also have ADD (attention deficit disorder), so college was a lot of work for me. I studied for 2 1/2 hours every night. I couldn't afford to miss even one evening of studying, and many times I was absolutely exhausted. However, I knew that the hard work I was putting in would pay off, and the new study techniques I was using were proving to be successful. I did a terrific amount of writing because my courses required a lot of memory work. I'd write out the medical terminology and their definitions 10 times each (just like the old lines kids had to write when they were kept after school), as I found that the repetition reinforced the material. I also did a lot of word associations to help me remember the information.

Writing a test was easier once I knew how. Before each test I would practice relaxation techniques so that my whole mind would be available to work on the testing material. I also found it helpful to speed read the entire test first, because some of the questions would help me remember the answers to other questions on the test. I felt like I was on top of the world when I got my first 100% result!

If I have one thought to leave with you, it would be to perservere no matter what. If you're finding it all too difficult, ask for help. Nobody will know you're having trouble if you don't say anything. Just don't give up. With the love and support of my wife and children, I am now a graduate of the CNA program. I am working at the local hospital and now I look forward to going to work. I care deeply about my patients, and there's nothing like knowing that I really make a difference in their lives.

Life is a grindstone. Whether it

grinds a man down or polishes him

up depends on what he is made of.

Proverb

So Much to Do, So Little Time to Do It: Priority Management

Ying was in my class several years ago. She impressed me as the most organized person I had ever known. She always had her calendar with her, she took meticulous notes and transcribed them every day, and she never missed a deadline. In her notebook, she had carefully written goals and objectives for every class. She had a regular schedule, which she

followed exactly, that detailed on which day she would do laundry, on which day she would shop for groceries, and at what time she would exercise. Ying adhered to a carefully organized schedule so she would have plenty of time for studying, reviewing her notes, and meeting with professors. Although she was not naturally outstanding academically, through these efforts Ying was able to keep her grades among the highest in the class.

Her organization and adherence to her priorities also enabled Ying to serve on the student council, to be a peer tutor, and to work 15 hours a week. I have never known a student to be more disciplined about her work. One of the best things about her self-management style was that she always took time to have fun and to be with her friends. Ying noted in her calendar "Sacred Day." These were days that were reserved for her to have fun, to renew her spirit, to do nothing—days on which work would not be allowed to interfere with life. Ying had learned some of the most important time-management and organizational strategies at a very young age: make a plan, stick to the plan, work hard, play hard, and reward yourself when you have performed well.

One of the best things about her self-management style was that she always took time to have fun and to be with her friends.

THE CROSS-CAMPUS "I'VE-GOT-TO-MAKE-MY-8 A.M.-CLASS-FOR-ONCE" DASH.

You may think, "That's great for Ying, but it wouldn't work for me." And you may be right. The important thing to consider as you read this chapter *is* how to design a plan that is right for you, a plan based on your schedule, your interests, and your most productive times of day. You'll want to consider how to manage your time and set priorities based on you and your individual needs. This chapter offers some pointers for getting things accomplished; some of them will work for you and some of them won't, but when you have finished the chapter, you should have a better handle on how to get the job done and still have time for yourself.

If you can't follow a schedule as rigid as Ying's, that's fine. Design a schedule you can follow. You might have heard the old saying, "All work and no play makes Jack a dull boy." This statement is true, but so is "All play and no work will make Jack flunk out of school." The trick is to find a happy medium.

What Is Time ?

Have you ever tried to define time? It's almost like trying to catch a sunbeam or stretching to put your arms around a rainbow. Time is elusive and flexible and also restrictive and binding. Most of us have the idea that time is external to our bodies. We make plans to manage time as though it were a concrete object that could be placed in a box and manipulated at will.

After completing this chapter, you will be able to

- Assess your current status of organization

- Differentiate between "doing" time and "being" time

- Design a plan for accomplishing your daily, weekly, and monthly goals

- Organize your schedule to include all components of a balanced life

- Understand the importance of scheduling the most taxing items on your list for your personal peak performance time

- Say "no" if saying "yes" would cause you to be stressed, unhappy, and unable to focus on your own goals and interests

- Include in your plan some time for rest, relaxation, and doing nothing

- Learn to take fun breaks

- Put into practice the cornerstones for using effective organization and time management

Managing Time So You'll Have More Fun

As you focus on managing and organizing your time and using it wisely, remember that you are not learning to manage your time just so you can accomplish more work. The real reward of time and priority management is that it allows you to have more *fun*. Most of us prefer play to work. So if you approach the concept of time management with the idea that you will be gaining play time—time to relax, go to the movies, play with your children, be with a special person, laugh with friends, exercise, or just do nothing—you are much more likely to stick to your plan. Before studying organization and priority management practices, take a minute to assess the techniques you are using now.

1. I lead a balanced life with a reasonable amount of time devoted to play.
   1 2 3 4 5

2. I usually plan my days and weeks carefully.
   1 2 3 4 5

3. My daily plans are related to my short-term and long-term goals.   *1 2 3 4 5*

4. I know how to prioritize tasks for best results.
   1 2 3 4 5

5. I plan projects carefully before plunging in.
   1 2 3 4 5

6. I have a specific place for supplies and items I use frequently. *1 2 3 4 5*

7. I feel that I have control over events in my life.
   1 2 3 4 5

8. I have a clear understanding of my value system.
   1 2 3 4 5

9. I am able to say no when a request does not fit with my personal objectives.
   1 2 3 4 5

10. I use a personal calendar that allows me to manage all my school, personal, and work time. *1 2 3 4 5*

5=Strongly Agree

4=Agree

3=Don't Know

2=Disagree

1=Strongly Disagree

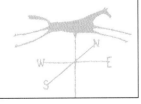

Total your points from these ten questions. Now, refer to the following rating scale to see where you stand in relation to priority management.

0–10   *Your priority-management skills are very weak. You use little planning and feel little control over the events in your life. You are usually late with assignments, and time rules your life.*

11–20   *Your priority-management skills are weak. You try to get things accomplished on time, but you usually do not plan in advance, and you spend a great deal of time catching up.*

21–30   *Your priority-management skills are average. You have some success getting things done. You plan some of your day, but you may not stick to your schedule.*

31–40   *Your priority-management skills are very good. You develop a daily and weekly plan and follow it closely. Your assignments are usually turned in on time, and you have some free time for fun activities.*

41–50   *Your priority-management skills are excellent. You are a planner, and you get things done that need to be done. You set goals and work in a timely fashion to accomplish them. You use a calendar and update it daily.*

Ann McGee-Cooper, author and consultant, refers to the top line as the quality and joy in your life and to the bottom line as productivity. While in college, be sure to devote time to both the top and bottom lines of your life. In the past, do you think you have had balance between the top and bottom lines?

> Ordinary people think merely how they will *spend* their time; people of intellect try to *use* it.
> Arthur Schopenhauer,
> Aphorisms on
> the Wisdom of Life

Working Hard and Playing Hard

Developing and perfecting priority-management skills are critical to your success as a college or university student. You have probably wondered how some people get so much done, how some people always seem to have it together, stay calm and collected, and are able to set goals and accomplish them. At the same time, you are aware of others who are always late with assignments and are unable to complete projects and live up to commitments.

Although college students' abilities may vary greatly, most have the intellectual ability to succeed; the difference between success and failure is often a person's ability to organize and manage time and to set priorities. Have you ever thought about the statement "Life is a series of choices"? You can't do everything, so you have to make choices! Making choices is what priority and time management are all about.

This chapter presents guidelines to help you focus on managing your time so that you can devote a sufficient part of your day to your work and studies but still be able to have fun and develop the top line.

THE DIFFERENCE BETWEEN BEING AND DOING

Do you know the importance of being as well as doing? If you are a doing person, you focus on what you accomplish, how many awards you win, how much money you make, how many offices you hold. In other words, you are focused on a destination. If you allow some time for being, you will experience the journey that life is meant to be. You will take time to walk on the beach, to work out in the gym, to enjoy a play or a football game. The measure of your life should be much more than facts and figures. Can you think of people who spend all their time doing and very little time being? Chapter 15 provides more information about being and doing.

Discuss ways in which you have spent your time doing since you arrived

on campus. _____

_____

_____

_____

Discuss ways in which you have spent your time being since you began your post secondary education. _____

_____

_____

_____

_____

At this point of your development, are you spending too much time either doing or being?

You know that you will experience many hectic days when you won't have balance, quiet, and being time, but the goal is to have it as often as you can. Balance doesn't mean that you should play as much as you work; the demands of today's schedules usually don't allow for that. Balance does mean that a reasonable portion of every day should be devoted to that elusive top line—quality and joy. Some days you may feel like a juggler as you look for ways to live as well as to work.

■ FOCUSING ON QUALITY AND JOY Focus on this idea: you are building you. So don't take a haphazard approach. Consider your choices carefully, but leave time for spontaneity.

If part of your overall organizational plan is to include joy and quality of life, you need to identify what these two concepts mean to you in concrete terms. Later you will use your responses here to help you design your own unique priority-management plan.

WHAT BRINGS ME JOY?	*WHY?*
_____	_____
_____	_____
_____	_____
_____	_____
_____	_____

WHO BRINGS ME JOY?	*WHY?*
_____	_____
_____	_____
_____	_____
_____	_____
_____	_____

Select your favorite item from those you listed as bringing you joy, and in your double-entry journal discuss how you might find time to enjoy this activity more.

As you think about quality of life, relate to it as *enjoying this day.* Some college students, especially nontraditional students, can be so focused on getting that piece of paper that they don't take time to taste what college is and should be about. Savour the college experience, squeeze every drop from it, start a foundation on which you will continue to build all your life—a foundation that includes joy and quality of life, as well as work and accomplishments.

Now look over the checklist of activities or experiences that might have a part in a plan that includes quality of life. Since quality of life is a personal matter, some of the things on this list may not appeal to you. Place a check by each item you might like to do or experience. Then add others to your personal list of things that are important to your quality of life now or that you think you might like to experience.

◼ QUALITY OF LIFE EXPERIENCES CHECKLIST

____ Watching a sunset   ____ Talking to a friend

____ Walking on the beach   ____ Writing a letter

____ Reading a book   ____ Chatting on the Internet

____ Listening to music   ____ Working out in the gym

____ Skiing in the mountains   ____ Playing basketball or other sport

____ Dancing

____ Doing volunteer work in the community   ____ Learning a computer game

____ Preparing a gourmet meal

____ Hiking   ____ Taking a spontaneous trip

____ Going to the zoo   Others: _____

____ Attending football games   _____

____ Ice-skating   _____

____ Painting   _____

____ Doing aerobics   _____

____ In-line skating   _____

Later, you will use this list to help you design your own personal priority-management plan.

Sometimes you need to be in several places at once, but of course you can't be. These situations can be extremely frustrating unless you learn to set priorities. Practice dealing with such a situation by working on the following problems.

■ DECISIONS, DECISIONS You are walking out of your room and the telephone rings. A friend with a problem is calling, and you can tell that this conversation needs to be a long one—your friend has boyfriend problems. You have only 12 minutes until your student council meeting starts, and it is important that you arrive on time.

Explain how you would handle this situation in such a way that you could make your meeting and still be helpful to your friend.

_____

_____

_____

_____

_____

_____

You have been assigned a group project with a deadline of October 15. At every meeting, the group seems to spend all its time on "What if we did this?" and never reaches a decision. The deadline is approaching rapidly, and no one is completing the assignment.

How could you demonstrate your leadership abilities and priority-management skills? _____

_____

_____

_____

_____

_____

You have been in your room working on your computer for four hours without a break. You have been using the Internet to research information for a paper. Your eyes are tired, you are hungry, and your back is beginning to ache. You had hoped to finish this paper by noon, but because some of the references were difficult to locate, you now realize that you will have to work at least two more hours. You obviously need a break.

Explain what you would do on a break to energize you, relieve your stress, and help you come back to this task refreshed. _____

_____

_____

_____

_____

After working for six hours on a beautiful Saturday, you finish your paper at 3 PM. You feel wonderful because the paper is finished and the deadline is still a week away. You have been working on this paper gradually, instead of throwing it together at the last minute. You feel that you have done your very best work, and you will be proud to turn the paper in to your professor.

How would you reward yourself for the discipline you have used to finish this project? _____

_____

_____

_____

_____

YOUR BODY'S CYCLES

Priority management and the ability to concentrate are closely linked. Since many people are able to concentrate on visual or auditory stimuli for only about 20 to 30 minutes before they begin to make errors, cramming for tests rarely works. Some people are able to concentrate effectively for longer periods of time, and some people for shorter periods; you'll need to determine your own ability to concentrate and then to plan for short breaks to avoid making errors.

Other factors affect concentration in different ways.

- **Complexity of material.** May lead to frustration.

- **Time of day.** Effect depends on type of task.

- **Noise.** Improves concentration for some people if it is not too loud.

- **Hunger.** Makes it difficult to concentrate.

- **Environment.** Positive or negative feedback and support or lack of support affect concentration.

- **Pace.** If too fast may result in errors; if too slow may result in boredom.

You have a prime time when you are most capable of performing at your peak.

If you are interested in sports or exercise, you know that your body responds to exercise and physical activity differently at different times of the day. Time of day affects your mind similarly. For instance, you may find that you complete work involving comparison and memory best in the morning; or, if you have gathered all the statistics and information needed to make a decision, you may handle this type of task best in the afternoon. You have a prime time when you are most capable of performing at your peak. For many people, even if they don't like to get up early, the peak performance time is in the morning if they have had enough rest. Other people function best late at night. Of course, you want to work on the most important and demanding jobs at your peak working time. To determine your best working time answer the following questions:

1. Are you lethargic in the morning until you have been up for an hour or so?

2. Did you try to schedule your classes this semester after 10 AM so you could sleep later?

3. Do you feel a little down around 5 PM but feel ready to go again around 8 PM?

4. Have you tended to pull all-nighters in the past?

5. Do you wake up early and spring right out of bed?

6. Do you have a hard time being productive during the late afternoon hours?

7. Is it impossible for you to concentrate after 10 PM?

8. Are you one of those rare college students who loves 8 AM classes?

If you answered yes to questions 1 through 4, or to most of them, you are a night person; if you answered yes to questions 5 through 8, or to most of them, you are a morning person. Being a morning person does not mean that you can never get anything done at night, but it does mean that your most productive time is morning. If you are a morning person, you should tackle difficult, complex problems early in the morning when you are at your peak. If you are a night person you should wait a few hours after getting up in the morning before you tackle difficult tasks.

MAXIMIZING YOUR TALENTS

The first step toward productivity is to organize so that your talents, skills, and work habits are used to their fullest potential. You know the saying "A place for everything and everything in its place." A certain amount of "everything in its place" is critical to productivity, but execution of this concept may be different for the highly organized person from what it is for the person who works among stacks of projects. Some suggestions for organizing according to your best working style follow. These suggestions are guidelines, which you can adjust to fit your personal needs.

TIPS FOR HIGHLY ORGANIZED PEOPLE

- Select a place on your desk or a desk drawer to keep your stapler, scissors, tape, pens, pencils, paper clips, and so on. Always return these items to their proper place.

- Purchase a book bag, and organize your materials by class. Take with you only those materials that you will need until you can return to your room or home to pick up different materials.

- Use a separate notebook for each class.

- Purchase a small filing cabinet (or a cardboard file box) and some file folders, and file your materials by class. *Save all old tests.*

Planning—The Secret to Priority Management

> The more time we spend . . . on planning . . . a project, the less total time is required for it. Don't let today's busy work crowd planning time out of your schedule.
> —Edwin C. Bliss, *Getting Things Done*

"I don't have time to plan." "I don't like to be fenced in and tied to a rigid schedule." "I have so many duties that planning never works." *No more excuses!* To manage your time successfully, you need to spend some time planning. Follow the steps for effective planning for one week. Then see how your productivity at the end of the week compares to your productivity before you used these ideas. Some of these ideas will work for you, and others won't.

STEPS FOR EFFECTIVE PLANNING

■ PLANNING AND ORGANIZING FOR SCHOOL Use the priorities chart to make a list of your highest priorities for this semester.

- Focus on a few key things that you value the most

- Include both long-range and short-range tasks

- Focus on some items that are fun, relaxing, and growth oriented

Priorities
for This Semester

1.
2.
3.
4.
5.
6.
7.
8.
9.
10.

Next, use the chart called "Everything I Know I Need To Do Now." Check your list of priorities to be sure not to overlook any.

- Include long-range projects, such as term papers

- Include any special events that you really want to attend and that may be rewarding to you

- Exclude anything that other people want you to do, but that you don't really have time for and that are not important to you and your goals and objectives

No more excuses! To manage your time successfully, you need to spend some time planning.

Learning to say no is important. Before you say yes to another committee or social activity, ask yourself, "Is this something I really want to do? Will it help me achieve my goals, or will it stress me out and divert my time and thinking away from what I really want to accomplish this semester?" If you are unsure, say, "Let me think about this overnight, and I will give you an answer tomorrow." Don't let other people make their priorities yours. You have your own set of priorities.

If you are a visual thinker who needs to see things to remember to do them, try one of the following approaches. Put your list on colourful Post-it notes so that you can move items around on a poster board or stick them on a typing stand and place it on your desk among the clutter. You might consider three columns of notes—school, work, fun. Alternatively, you might transfer your list to a poster and use coloured markers to highlight priorities. Or, you might function best with a neat list in a notebook or on a section of your daily calendar. Visualizing your work may help you to stay focused.

1. _____
_____
_____

2. _____
_____
_____

3. _____
_____
_____

4. _____
_____
_____

5. _____
_____

6. _____
_____
_____

7. _____
_____
_____

8. _____
_____

9. _____
_____
_____

10. _____
_____
_____

Things I Need

to Purchase to Put My Priority-Management Plan in Place

1. _____
   _____
   _____

2. _____
   _____
   _____

3. _____
   _____
   _____

4. _____
   _____
   _____

5. _____
   _____

6. _____
   _____

7. _____
   _____
   _____

8. _____
   _____
   _____

9. _____
   _____

10. _____
    _____
    _____

Now, carefully look over the examples of "Today" lists for traditional and nontraditional students. Then use the blank form to make a list of everything you can reasonably do tomorrow and still take some fun breaks and spend some time being instead of just doing. Schedule no more than 60 to 75 percent of your time; leave time for thinking, planning, and interacting.

- Include segments of long-range projects (e.g., going to the library to begin research for a paper or project that isn't due for six weeks)

- Build in flexibility, in case a project takes longer than foreseen

When you have completed your Today list, place a 1, 2, or 3 by each item in the priority code column. Place a 1 by those items that absolutely must be done on this day if you are to avoid a major crisis. For example, you absolutely must finish a paper that is due the following day because the professor will not accept late papers. Place a 2 by those items that should be done today if possible because they are important, and further delay of these items could create a stressful situation and become a major problem. For example, you should read the three chapters in your psychology textbook that will be discussed in class the following day. The professor has indicated that it is important to read these chapters prior to the discussion. *Preparation relieves*

TODAY

Date _____ Jan. 25 _____

List of Priorities		Appointments and Classes		
Priority Code		End-of-Day Checklist		
3	Buy Mom's Gift		8:00	Math Class
3	Wash Car		9:00	History Class
1	Study - French Test	✓	10:15	Student Gv. Mtg.
1	Exchange Work Hours	✓	11:30	Canteen w/ John
2	Run 3 km		12:30	Lunch w/ Chantal
1	Read Ch.14	✓	2:00	Study
2	Write 2/15 Paper		5 - 6	Run w/ Chantal

Expenses for Today	Phone Numbers Needed Today
lunch - 2.50 gas - 5.00 notebook - 3.79	Mary - 555 -1234

Fun Breaks

Canteen @ 11:30 w/ John   Run w/ Chantal

Sacred Day to Look Forward to: Ski Trip !! Feb. 18

TODAY

Date _____ Jan. 25 _____

List of Priorities		Appointments and Classes		
Priority Code		End-of-Day Checklist		
1	Crystal's Play	✓	8:00	History Class
1	Meet w/ Boss	✓	9:30	Meet w/ Boss
1	Study for 1/26 Psy Test	✓	10:00	Write Report
2	Grocery Store		11:30	Walk w/ Ann
3	Call Smith @ Party		12:15	Call Kyle's Teacher
1	Pick up Children	✓	3:30	Pick up Children

Expenses for Today	Phone Numbers Needed Today
gas - 20.00 chicken - 12.70 groceries - 75.99	Mrs. Choi - 555-1212 Smiths - 555-0013

Fun Breaks

Walk w/ Ann   Crystal's Play

Sacred Day to Look Forward to: Feb.15 - Weekend in Mtns.

TODAY

Date _____

List of Priorities		Appointments and Classes	
Priority Code		End-of-Day Checklist	

Expenses for Today	Phone Numbers Needed Today

Fun Breaks

Sacred Day to Look Forward to:

stress and improves your confidence. Place a 3 by those items that could be done today if time permits, but that have no major bearing on your overall goals and objectives. For example, shopping for a new pair of shoes would rate a 3. If it is not done today, you will not have a major crisis.

Now, put your plan to work. As soon as you have any time that is free from class, work, meals, committees, athletic practice, and so on, focus on accomplishing the first priority item on your list. Work hard to discipline yourself to finish this item in a certain amount of time. When you have finished the first task, move to the next one. As you work, occasionally focus on the fact that you will get a reward when you finish this task.

Reward yourself with short, fun breaks—watch a brief TV program, call a friend to talk for a few minutes (but limit your time), drink some juice, or eat an apple. Then go back to work! Work as long as you continue to be productive and don't feel that you are getting stale and performing inadequately. If you are a nontraditional student with a family, a fun break might be to talk with your children or partner about their day, to play a game, to take a walk together, or to ride bikes. Nontraditional students and their family members feel time pressures keenly. Don't expect to put your life and theirs on hold while you go to school. If you do, you all will begin to build resentments, which can damage your family life.

Write appointments and meetings in a calendar that you keep with you at all times. Own only one calendar. It is a mistake to try to keep a big calendar at home and carry a small one with you. *Always* take your calendar to meetings and classes. You might try placing stickers in strategic spots on your calendar to help you focus on important tasks that you might otherwise overlook, such as fun breaks and sacred days. Fun breaks, sacred days, and rewards give you something to look forward to. They are diversions from work that you enjoy *after* you have earned them!

Determine what style of calendar works best for you. Since you have to carry it everywhere, you'll probably want to select one that is not too heavy or bulky. Until you find a calendar you like, feel free to duplicate the Today sheet or any other forms in this book as often as you like.

After you have used your plan for four days, make an entry in your journal describing the progress you think you are making toward managing your time more effectively.

		1	②	3	4	⑤	6
			Pick up Children			7 pm Crystal's Play	
7	8	9	10	⑪	12	13	
	7–9 pm Study		7–9 pm Study	Meet w/ Boss		Football game w/Kyle	
14	15	16	17	18	19	20	
	7–9 pm Study		7–9 pm Study	*Psy test			
21	22	㉓	24	25	26	27	
	7–9 pm Study	Pick up Children	7–9 pm Study		Ski trip! →		
28	29	㉚	31				
Ski trip! →	7–9 pm Study	Pick up Children	7–9 pm Study				

■ PLANNING AND ORGANIZING FOR WORK Some supermen and superwomen work full-time and go to school full-time while they juggle families and other responsibilities. *We don't recommend this schedule unless it is for one semester only, when you are pushing to graduate.* If kept up for a long period, you will burn out from the stress such a pace imposes on your mind and body, and if you have children, they may be adversely affected by your overfull schedule. If you work less and, if necessary, take longer to graduate, you will have more opportunity to savour your college or university experience.

Of course, regardless of our best advice, we know that most of you will do what you feel like you need to do to survive. What we can do here is to offer encouragement—perhaps you'll find it helpful when you feel overwhelmed with work and school and have no time for yourself. Use the following questions to help you get organized.

What are your most important responsibilities at work? _____

_____

_____

_____

_____

Be sure to plan carefully to accomplish these tasks. Your job and your reputation at work depend on their accomplishment, and this job may be the one that gets you your dream job later on.

What measures do your employers use to evaluate your work? _____

_____

_____

_____

_____

All bosses have pet things they want done—always get these done on time! If you are given a formal evaluation, read it carefully to be sure that you are performing well in all categories.

Must you keep strict hours or can you use flexible scheduling? _____

_____

_____

_____

_____

If your talents are in great demand, such as graphic arts skills or computer skills, if you can teach a sport or activity, such as swimming, or if you have an academic strength and can tutor, you may be able to set your own hours to a greater extent than if you have to meet an employer's schedule.

 **CORNERSTONES**

for priority management at work

- Organize your materials at work as they are organized at home. If you have a desk in both places, keep your supplies in the same place in both desks. Simplify your life by following similar patterns at work and at home.

- If you are a visual thinker and need to see different assignments, be considerate of others who may work close to you. Keep your work area as orderly as you can and still have it work for you. Clear plastic boxes, coloured file folders, and coloured file boxes will work as well for you on the job as they do at home.

- Write directions down. Nothing is so irritating to busy bosses as having to give directions multiple times. Keep a notebook for repetitive tasks, use a software program, or do whatever helps you to remember.

- Some jobs, for example, working the night desk at a hotel, are ideal for students because they allow time for study. If you have such a job, use the time after you have finished your work responsibilities to read chapters or study for exams. Never let your work responsibilities slide because you are studying on the job. Employers always notice.

- Build relationships with fellow employees. Go out of your way to be polite, personable, and thoughtful. Remember people's birthdays with cards; compliment people; congratulate employees who are promoted or recognized in other ways. Don't engage in too much idle chatter. You are being paid to work. Other employees may resent you if you create disturbances with behaviour that is out of place at the office. Don't waste time on gossip. Avoid negative people—they drain your energy.

- When you are given projects that require working with others, plan carefully to do your work well and on time. Never hold up other employees' work because you have failed to get your job done. If necessary, come in early or stay late to get your job done. It will make a positive impression on your employer.

- Keep a Rolodex file of important phone numbers and addresses that you use frequently. Cut off nonproductive telephone calls. Never use the telephone at work for social chats. Employers hate this habit!

- Perform difficult, unpleasant tasks as soon as you can so you don't have them hanging over your head.

- When you plan your work schedule, allow for unexpected problems that might interfere with the schedule. Plan what you can realistically accomplish so that you won't get frustrated.

Use these tips to help generate ideas for managing your time better, performing more effectively, and reducing stress at work. List your ideas in the space provided.

_____

_____

_____

_____

_____

■ PLANNING AND ORGANIZING AT HOME Some people organize effectively at work and school and allow things to fall apart at home. Whether you are a traditional student living in residence or a nontraditional student living in a house with your family, your home should be pleasant and safe. It should be a place where you can study, relax, laugh, invite your friends, and find solitude. The following ideas about home organization will help you maximize your time.

 **for priority management at home**

For Traditional Students:

■ Organize as effectively at home as you do at work.

■ If you have roommates, divide the chores. Insist on everyone doing his or her share. If your roommate is a slob and is driving you crazy, get a new roommate at the first opportunity.

■ Break bad habits, such as leaving dishes in the sink or letting laundry pile up. Plan a rotation schedule for major household chores and stick to it—do laundry on Mondays and Thursdays, clean bathrooms on Saturdays, iron on Wednesdays, and so on. Your parents will be much happier to see you if you don't expect them to do five weeks' worth of mildewed laundry when you are home for the weekend.

- Organize your closet and your dresser drawers. Get rid of clothes you don't wear.

- Put a sign by your telephone that reads "TIME" to remind yourself not to waste it on the phone.

- If you can't study in your room because of drop-in visitors, loud roommates, and the like, go to the library.

- Pay bills twice monthly. Pay them on time so you don't ruin your credit rating.

- If you drive to class, work, or appointments, fill up your tank ahead of time so you won't be late.

For Nontraditional Students:

If you are a nontraditional student and have children, teach them to be organized so they don't waste your time searching for their shoes, books, and assignments. Teach family members responsibility! You can't work, go to school, and hold everybody's hand all the time. Give each of your children a drawer in a filing cabinet. Show them how to organize their work. You will be preparing them to be successful.

- If you are a perfectionist and want everything in your home to be perfect, get over it! You have many more important things to do than to spend your valuable time cleaning floors until you could have dinner on them.

- Get rid of the clutter in your garage, basement, or closets. Perhaps you can persuade your children to sell some of their old toys and other items that are cluttering up their rooms if you tell them they can keep the money. The idea is to reduce most of the clutter in your home.

- Establish a time for studying in your home. Children do their homework, and you do yours. Any other adults in the house could read or work on their own during this time so that the house is quiet.

- If you have a family, insist that all of you organize clothes for school or work for several days.

- Put a message board in a convenient place for everyone to use.

- If your children are old enough to drive, have them run errands at the cleaner's, post office, and grocery store.

- Carpool with other parents in your neighbourhood.

SO MUCH TO DO, SO LITTLE TIME TO DO IT

- Delegate, delegate, delegate! You are not superwoman or superman. Tell your family you need help. Children can feed pets, make their beds, fold clothes, vacuum, sweep, iron, and cut the grass if they are old enough.

- Schedule at least one hour alone with each of your children each week. Make this a happy, special time—a fun break!

- Plan special times with your spouse or partner if you have one so that he or she does not get fed up with your going to school. Nontraditional students must have support from their families in order to perform well at school.

- Tell your family and friends when you have to study; ask them to respect you by not calling or dropping by at this time.

- Post a family calendar where everyone can see it. Put all special events on it—for example, Kirsten's Recital, Mike's Baseball Game, Yasmina's Company Party. Plan to be able to attend special functions as much as possible. Be sure to put these dates on your personal calendar.

- Put sacred days on this calendar so that your entire family has something to look forward to.

- Take time to smell the roses.

Building a Priority-
Management Plan

IF YOU NEED TO BE HIGHLY ORGANIZED

(If structure is not your strong suit, go to the next section.) Traditional time-management principles will probably work best for you because you are more likely to be organized, time conscious, and disciplined. For you, time management will consist largely of controlling the events in your life—getting to them on time, being prepared, being in control, working within a carefully designed system, starting and ending on time, and filing things in the right place.

You can never gain total control of all the events in your life—and perhaps it is good that you can't. One main goal for you is to control selectively as much as you can and to learn to relax and enjoy being during a segment of free time. Another goal is to learn to deal with frustration when you can't control events, other people, or circumstances so that you can avoid over stress.

Look through the chapter and make a list of major points that relate to you and your work style. _____

_____

_____

_____

_____

Use these key points and the forms provided in this chapter to design a time-management plan that suits your needs. Be sure to build in fun and relaxation time and strive for balance!

Refer to the exercise you completed earlier in this chapter on who and what brings you joy. Include in your management plan a few of the things that you enjoy most.

Now review the Quality of Life Experiences checklist that you completed. If you plan carefully and discipline yourself, how many of these items can you work into your plan as fun breaks, rewards, or sacred days?

IF YOU LIKE LESS STRUCTURE

You know by now that there is really nothing wrong with the way you do things. You may need to tighten up your time-management style, but you can still manage your time and avoid having your life geared to a rigid format that is uncomfortable and unnatural for you.

Make a list of the key points you learned in this chapter that will help you design a time-management plan. Look back through the chapter and find major ideas you want to remember. _____

_____

_____

_____

_____

_____

_____

Now use the ideas in this chapter to design a plan for one week. Be sure to build in some techniques that require you to meet deadlines and to bring some degree of organization to your supplies and belongings.

Refer to the list you made earlier in this chapter of people and things that bring you joy. How many of these favorite people and experiences can you work into your schedule as fun breaks, rewards, or sacred days?

Remember to work first—and then reward yourself!

Your priority-management and organizational system should be individualized and tailored to your own unique work style. The main consideration in creating a plan should be: "Does it work for me?" If your grades are good, you feel good, your work performance is above average, your social life is active, your home is reasonably clean and orderly, your personal appearance is as good as you can make it, and you have some time to have fun and relax, you have a good system. Stick to it, and work to improve it!

 **of priority management and organization**

- Understand the importance of "balance" in your life.

- Realize that you are preparing to work in a new and different work environment.

- Know the difference between "being" and "doing."

- Focus on quality and joy.

- Be able to list *who* and *what* bring you joy.

- Include fun breaks, rewards, and sacred days.

- Learn to organize in a manner that maximizes your abilities.

- Devise strategies for managing your time effectively at school, work, and home.

- Keep a calendar and use other planning guides to keep you on track.

The one minute journal

i n a minute or less, jot down what you learned in this chapter.

I Heard You! I Heard You! What Did You Say?: The Art of Active Listening

Carole had been through a rough evening. She had received a phone call from home to say that her grandmother was very ill and had been taken to the hospital. As she sat in math class the next morning, her mind was flooded with images of home. She had lived with her grandmother most of her life. In her mind's eye, she saw a house filled with people and

she could smell the bread baking in the oven. She saw her grandmother calling her down to eat before the arrival of the school bus. Her daydream was so vivid that for a moment, Carole could feel the gentle kiss of her grandmother on her forehead.

Carole was filled with anxiety wondering whether her grandmother would be all right. Her mind was a million miles away when a deep voice rang through her daydream. "Do you agree with the solution to this problem, Ms. Chen?"

Carole knew the voice was speaking to her, but it took her a few seconds to focus on it. Again the instructor asked, "Do you agree with the solution to this problem, Ms. Chen?" Carole had no idea whether she agreed or not. She had not heard the problem or the solution. She looked at the instructor and out of embarrassment and intimidation, she answered, "Yes, I do."

The situation took a turn for the worse. "Why do you think this is the proper way to solve this problem, Ms. Chen?" Carole sat, bewildered, at her desk. She looked down at her notes for help, but she had written only the date and the topic for the day on her

A deep voice rang through her daydream.

notepad. The tension grew as the entire class waited for her answer. "I don't know, Sir, I don't know."

How many times has this happened to you? We have all probably been in a similar situation recently. It isn't uncommon. Sometimes a person's mind wanders because of anxiety, dullness, or lack of interest; sometimes, because of simple mathematics. What does that mean? Well, most people speak at a rate of 125 words per minute, and most listeners can listen at almost 700 words per minute (Beebe and Beebe, 1994). This simple mathematical fact means that it is easy for people to lose concentration and fail to listen actively. If we toss in

personal anxiety or problems such as what Carole faced, or a boring speaker who causes you to lose interest, the problem of actively listening is compounded.

One of the practical traits most common to successful students is the ability to listen actively. Listening actively means knowing how to listen, what to listen for, how to evaluate the information you hear, and where to store the information you gain. This chapter is intended to help you to become an active listener. After completing this chapter, you will be able to

- Differentiate between listening and hearing
- Define active listening
- List the benefits of active listening
- Identify active and passive listening characteristics
- Identify key phrases and words for effective note taking
- Identify obstacles to active listening
- Listen visually
- Describe and use the cornerstones for effective listening

Take some time now to assess what types of listening skills you possess.

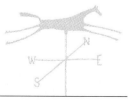

A SELF-ASSESSMENT Total your points from these ten questions. Refer to the following rating scale to determine where you stand in relation to your active listening skills.

0–10   You have a great deal of difficulty focusing on the message and listening actively.

11–20   Your ability to focus and your listening skills are below average.

21–30   Your ability to focus and listen actively is average.

31–40   Your ability to focus and listen actively is above average.

41–50   You have excellent listening skills. You are able to focus on the message and weed out distractions.

Now, refer to your journal and respond in writing to your findings. Consider the following questions when writing in your journal.

1. Do you agree or disagree with the results of the assessment? Why?

2. Do you know an excellent active listener? What qualities does that person have?

3. What do you feel you need to do to become a more active listener?

The Importance of Listening

Listening is one of the most important and useful skills human beings possess. For all animals, listening is a survival skill needed for hunting and obtaining food; for humans, listening is necessary for establishing relationships, growth, survival, knowledge, entertainment, and even health. It is one of our most widely used tools. How much time do you think you spend listening every day? Research suggests that we spend almost 70 percent of our waking time communicating, and 53 percent of that time is spent in listening situations (Adler, Rosenfeld, and Towne, 1989). Effective listening skills can mean the difference between success or failure, A's or F's, relationships or loneliness.

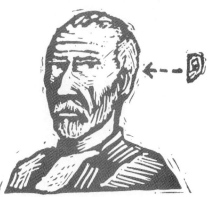

For students, good listening skills are critical. Over the next two to four years you will be given a lot of information in lectures. Cultivating and improving your active listening skills will help you to understand the lecture material, take accurate notes, participate in class discussions, and communicate with your peers.

The Difference Between Listening and Hearing

We usually do not think much about listening until a misunderstanding occurs. You've no doubt been misunderstood or misunderstood someone yourself. Misunderstandings arise because we tend to view listening as an automatic response when it is instead a *learned, voluntary* activity, like driving a car, painting a picture, or playing the piano. Having ears does not make you a good *listener*. After all, having hands does not mean you are capable of painting the Mona Lisa. You *may* be able to paint the Mona Lisa, but only with practice and guidance. Listening, too, takes practice and guidance. Becoming an active listener requires practice, time, mistakes, guidance, and active participation.

Hearing, however, is not learned; it is *automatic* and *involuntary*. If you are within range of a sound you will probably hear it although you may not be listening to it. Hearing a sound does not guarantee that you know what it is, or what made it. Listening actively, though, means making a conscious effort to focus in on the sound and to determine what it is.

Listening is a four-step cycle, represented by the mnemonic ROAR.

R—Receiving the information

O—Organizing the sounds heard and focusing on them

A—Assigning meaning

R—Reacting

Receiving means that you were within the range of the sound when it was made. Receiving a sound is not the same as listening. To become an active listener, when receiving information make an effort to

1. Tune out distractions other than the conversation at hand.

2. Avoid interrupting the speaker.

3. Pay close attention to nonverbal communication, such as gestures, facial expressions, and movements.

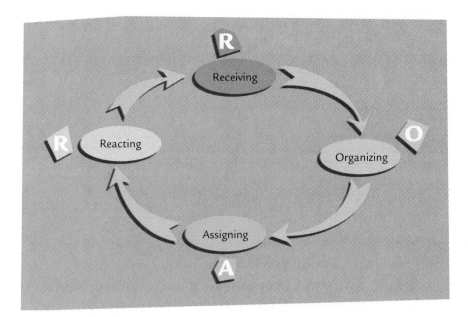

4. Concentrate on what is being said at the moment, not on what will be said next.

5. Listen for what is not said. Were important facts omitted?

Take a moment to determine what sounds you are receiving right now. List them.

_____

_____

_____

_____

_____

Organizing and Focusing means choosing to listen actively to the sound, to pay attention to its origin, direction, and intention. When you completed the preceding exercise you were organizing and focusing.

Spend the next few moments talking with a partner in your class. Put your pen down and listen carefully and actively; do not take notes. Spend at least four to five minutes asking about your partner's goals, dreams, plans, academic program, and life's work.

To become an active listener, when organizing and focusing on information make an effort to

1. Sit up straight or stand near the person speaking, so that you involve your entire body.

2. Make eye contact with the speaker; listen with your eyes and ears.

3. Try to create a visual picture of what is being said.

Paraphrase what your partner said to you. _____

_____

_____

_____

_____

_____

_____

_____

If you listened actively, you would have been able to write about your partner's goals, major, dreams, and career plans. How did you do? Were you actively listening?

Assigning refers to mentally assigning a name or meaning to what you have been listening to. Sometimes you may have to pay special attention to sounds in order to assign the correct name or meaning to them. Have you ever been sitting inside and heard a crash? You might have had to hear it again before you could identify the sound as dishes falling, books dropping, or static on the radio. Your brain tries to create a relationship between what you hear and what you have heard before; it tries to associate one piece of information with another. Once the association is made, you will be able to identify the new sound by remembering the old sound.

To become an active listener, when assigning meaning to information make an effort to

1. Relate the information to something that you already know.

2. Ask questions to ensure that there are no misunderstandings.

3. Identify the main ideas of what is being said.

4. Try to summarize the information into small "files" in your memory.

5. Repeat the information to yourself (or out loud if appropriate).

When you are actively listening in class, you will be able to relate new information to information you have heard previously. For instance, if you hear about Maslow's Hierarchy of Needs in psychology class, you might immediately relate it to workplace motivation you learned about in management class. If you hear about spreadsheets in computer class, you will probably make the connection from accounting. Active listening allows you to make associations that help create learning patterns for your long-term memory. Simply hearing information does not allow you to make these associations.

Reacting is nothing more than making a response to the sound you hear. If you hear a crash, you might jump; if you hear a baby cry, you might pick the baby up; if you hear a voice, you might turn to see who is speaking. Reacting can be a barrier to active listening. Tuning out because you are bored or do not agree with the speaker's point of view is a way of reacting to information.

To become an active listener, when reacting to information make an effort to

1. Leave your emotions behind; do not prejudge.

2. Avoid overreacting.

3. Avoid jumping to conclusions.

4. Ask yourself, "How can this information help me?"

Practical Definitions of Listening

According to Ronald Adler (Adler, Rosenfeld, and Towne, 1989), the drawing of the Chinese verb meaning "to listen" provides the most comprehensive and practical definition of listening. To the Chinese, listening involves the ears, the eyes, the mind, and the heart. Do you make it a habit to listen with more than your ears? The Chinese view listening as a whole-body experience. People from Western cultures seem to have lost the ability to involve their whole body in the listening process. We tend to use only our ears and sometimes, we don't even use them—remember Carole at the beginning of the chapter.

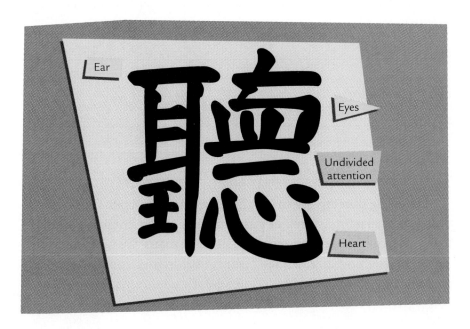

The Oxford Dictionary defines listening as follows: "To make an effort to hear something; to pay attention." This standard definition is not very concrete nor does it offer much direction. Listening needs to be personalized and internalized. To understand listening as a whole-body experience, we can define it on three levels:

1. Listening with a purpose

2. Listening objectively

3. Listening constructively

Listening with a purpose suggests a need to recognize different types of listening situations— for example, class, worship, entertainment, and relationships. People do not listen the same way in every situation. When you go to a concert, you turn on your concert ears; you listen for enjoyment and excitement. Unless you are a musician, you are unlikely to take notes on the music. When you go to class, you listen to gain a deeper understanding of the material presented. Have you ever listened to a friend who needed advice? You were listening with different ears from those you use in a classroom or an entertainment setting. Unless you understand that the listening situations that involve you differ, you will find listening a difficult adventure. As you enter a situation you need to know what type of listening will be required. This is called listening with a purpose.

List different listening situations in which you will be involved this semester.

1. _____

2. _____

3. _____

How do they differ?

1. _____

2. _____

3. _____

Listening objectively means listening with an open mind. You will give yourself few greater gifts than the gift of knowing how to listen without bias and prejudice. This is perhaps the most difficult aspect of listening. If you have been cut off in mid-conversation or -sentence by someone who disagreed with you or if someone has left the room while you were giving your opinion of a situation, you have had the experience of talking to people who do not know how to listen objectively.

We all tend to shut out or ignore information with which we do not agree or that is obscure and removed from our lives. To listen objectively, we need to listen with an open mind and then draw our conclusions rather than make a judgment and then try to listen, as we often do. Have you ever done the latter?

List three situations in which you might be involved this semester that would require you to listen with an open mind.

1. _____

2. _____

3. _____

Why would you need to listen objectively in each of these situations?

1. _____

2. _____

3. _____

Listening constructively means listening with the attitude of, "How can this be helpful to my life or my education?" This type of listening involves evaluating the information you are hearing and determining whether it has meaning to your life. Sound easy? It is more difficult than it sounds because, again, we all tend to shut out information that we do not see as immediately helpful or useful. To listen constructively, you need to know how to listen and store information for later dates.

Dario was a student who disliked math very much. He could never understand why, as a history major, he had to learn algebra. So, he automatically tuned out when the math professor presented information that he did not consider important. From time to time, we've all probably felt this way about some piece of information. However, when we tune out because we cannot see, or because we refuse to see, the relationship of certain information to our lives, we are not listening constructively.

When was the last time you tuned out of a listening situation for any reason? What was your reason? _____

_____

_____

_____

_____

_____

Looking back, could you have benefited from the information or the source of the information if you had not tuned out of the listening situation? Why or why not?

_____

_____

_____

Obstacles to Listening

Several major obstacles stand in the way of your becoming an effective listener. To begin building active listening skills, you first have to remove some barriers.

OBSTACLE ONE: PREJUDGING

Prejudging means that you automatically shut out what is being said; it is one of the biggest obstacles to active listening. You may prejudge because of the content, because of the person communicating, or because of your environment, culture, social status, or attitude.

Rebecca enrolled in a religion class called "Faith, Doubt, and Reason" at her college. Right from the start, the instructor asked questions and made statements that challenged beliefs that Rebecca had held all her life. The instructor was trying to get the class to explore new ideas. After two weeks in the class, Rebecca decided to drop the course because she did not want to hear the instructor's comments. Rebecca was prejudging. She shut out what the instructor was saying because it went against what she believed. It is almost impossible to prejudge and actively listen. It is best first to listen with an open mind, and then to make judgments.

■ DO YOU PREJUDGE INFORMATION OR ITS SOURCE? Answer yes or no to the following questions.

1. I tune out when something is boring.   Yes   No

2. I tune out when I do not agree with the information.   Yes   No

3. I argue mentally with the speaker about information.   Yes   No

4. I do not listen to people I do not like.   Yes   No

5. I make decisions about information before I
understand all of its implications or consequences.   Yes   No

If you answered yes to two or more of these questions, you tend to prejudge in a listening situation.

TIPS FOR OVERCOMING PREJUDGING

1. Listen for information that may be valuable to you as a student. Some material may not be pleasant to hear but may be useful to you later on.

2. Listen to the message, not the messenger. If you do not like the speaker, try to go beyond personality and listen to what is being said, without regard to the person saying it. Conversely, you may like the speaker so much that you automatically accept the material or answers without listening objectively to what is being said.

3. Try to remove cultural, racial, gender, social, and environmental barriers. Just because a person is different from you or holds a different point of view does not make that person wrong; and just because a person is like you and holds a similar point of view does not make that person right. Sometimes you have to cross cultural and environmental barriers to learn new material and see with brighter eyes.

OBSTACLE TWO: TALKING

Not even the best listener in the world can listen while he or she is talking. The next time you are in conversation with a friend, try speaking while your friend is speaking—then see if you know what your friend said. To become an effective listener, you need to learn the power of silence. Silence gives you the opportunity to think about what is being said before you have to respond. This short amount of time can be invaluable to effective listeners. Silence also allows you to listen. The physical effort of trying to listen and talk at the same time is taxing and always unsuccessful. Finally, silence provides the opportunity to consider what others are saying; it allows time for reflection.

1. I often interrupt the speaker so that I can say what I want.   Yes   No

2. I am thinking of my next statement while others are talking.   Yes   No

3. My mind wanders when others talk.   Yes   No

4. I answer my own questions.   Yes   No

5. I answer questions that are asked of other people.   Yes   No

If you answered yes to two or more questions, you tend to talk too much in a listening situation.

TIPS FOR OVERCOMING THE URGE TO TALK TOO MUCH

1. Force yourself to be silent at parties, family gatherings, and friendly get-togethers. We're not saying you should be unsociable, but force yourself to be silent for ten minutes. You'll be surprised at what you hear. You may also be surprised how hard it is to do this. Test yourself.

2. Ask someone a question and then allow that person to answer the question. Too often we ask questions and answer them ourselves. Force yourself to wait until the person has formulated a response. If you ask questions and wait for answers, you will force yourself to listen.

OBSTACLE THREE: BRINGING YOUR EMOTIONS TO THE TABLE

Emotions can form a strong barrier to active listening. Worries, problems, fears, and anger can keep you from listening to the greatest advantage. Have you ever sat in a lecture, and before you knew what was happening your mind was a million miles away because you were angry or worried about something, like Carole in the opening story? If you have, you know what it's like to bring your emotions to the table.

■ DO YOU BRING YOUR EMOTIONS TO THE LISTENING SITUATION? Answer yes or no to the following questions.

1. I get angry before I hear the whole story. Yes No

2. I look for underlying or hidden messages
   in information. Yes No

3. Sometimes I begin listening on a negative note. Yes No

4. I base my opinions of information on what others
   are saying or doing. Yes No

5. I readily accept information as correct from people
   whom I like or respect. Yes No

thoughts

If you answered yes to two or more of these questions, you tend to bring your emotions to a listening situation.

TIPS FOR OVERCOMING EMOTIONS

1. Know how you feel before you begin the listening experience. Take stock of your emotions and feelings ahead of time.

2. Focus on the message and determine how you can use the information.

3. Try to create a positive image about the message you are about to hear.

ACTIVE AND PASSIVE LISTENING CHARACTERISTICS

ACTIVE LISTENERS	PASSIVE LISTENERS
Lean forward and sit up straight	Slouch and lean back in their chairs
Make eye contact with the speaker	Look around the room
Listen for what is not said	Hear scattered information
Are patient	Are easily frustrated
Leave emotions outside the discussion	Get angry at the speaker
Avoid jumping to conclusions	Make immediate assumptions
Ask questions	Speed the speaker along
Focus on the topic	Daydream
Have an open mind	Prejudge the speaker
React to ideas	React to the person speaking

ACTIVE LISTENERS	PASSIVE LISTENERS
Do not argue mentally	Create mental arguments
Empathize	Criticize
Tune out distractions	Are distracted easily

Listening for Key Words, Phrases, and Hints

Learning how to listen for key words, phrases, and hints can help you to become an active listener and a more effective note taker. For example, if your English professor begins a lecture saying, "There are ten basic elements to writing poetry," jot down the number 10 under the heading "Poetry" or number your notebook page 1 through 10, leaving space for your notes. If at the end of class you have only listed six elements to writing poetry, you know that you missed a part of the lecture. At this point, you need to ask the professor some questions.

Some key phrases and words that may help you to become an active listener are

in addition	another way	above all
most important	such as	specifically
you'll see this again	therefore	finally
for example	to illustrate	as stated earlier
in contrast	in comparison	nevertheless
characteristics	the main issue is	moreover
on the other hand	as a result of	because

Picking up on transition words will help you filter out less important information, and thus listen more carefully to what is most important. There are other indicators of important information, too. You will want to listen carefully when the professor

Writes something on the board

Uses an overhead

Draws on a flip chart

Uses computer-aided graphics

Speaks in a louder tone or changes vocal patterns

Uses gestures more than usual

Once you have learned how to listen actively, you will reap several key benefits as a student, as an employee, and as a citizen.

TOP 10 REASONS FOR ACTIVELY LISTENING

1. You will be exposed to more information and knowledge about the world, your peers, and yourself.

2. You will be able to help others if you listen to their problems and fears, and you will gain a greater sense of empathy.

3. You will avoid problems at school or work that result from not listening.

4. You will be able to participate in life more fully, because you will have a keener sense of what is going on in the world around you.

5. You will gain friends and healthy relationships, because people are drawn to those to whom they can talk and who they feel listen sincerely.

6. You will be able to ask more questions and to gain a deeper understanding about subjects that interest you or ideas you wish to explore.

7. You will be a more effective leader. People follow people who they feel listen to their ideas and give their views a chance.

8. You will be able to understand more about different cultures from around the world.

9. You will be able to make more logical decisions regarding pressing and difficult issues in your life and studies.

10. You will feel better about yourself because you will know in your heart and mind that you gave the situation your best.

Test Your Listening Skills

Your professor will assist you with the following activities to test your active listening skills in a variety of listening situations. You will need to use several types of listening skills to participate.

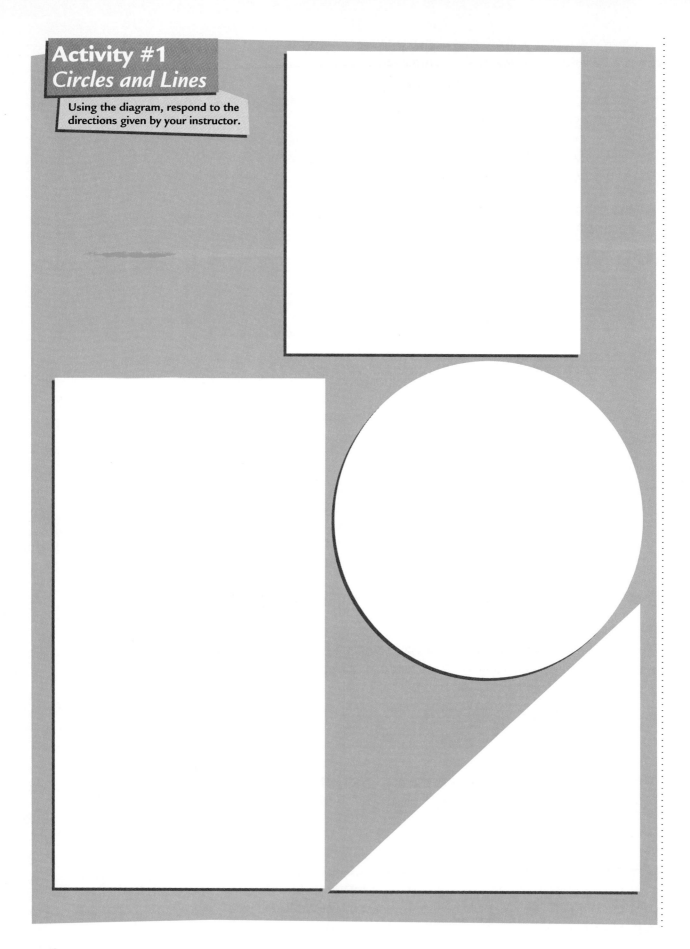

Activity #1
Circles and Lines

Using the diagram, respond to the directions given by your instructor.

Close your book, listen to the instructor's story, and then follow the instructor's directions.

_____ 1. A thief approached the cabdriver at a traffic light.

_____ 2. The thief demanded money.

_____ 3. The thief was a man.

_____ 4. The cabdriver's window was down all the way when the thief approached the cab.

_____ 5. The cabdriver gave the thief the money.

_____ 6. Someone sped away with the money.

_____ 7. The money was on the dash of the cab.

_____ 8. The amount of money was never mentioned.

_____ 9. The story mentions only two people, the cabdriver and the thief.

_____ 10. The following statements are true:

Someone demanded money; the money was snatched up; a person sped away.

Activity #3
The Accident

Listen as your instructor reads the scenario, then follow your instructor's directions

	Listener	Additions	Deletions
1.			
2.			
3.			
4.			
5.			

Activity #4
Visual Listening

Listen to your peers and draw the design that they verbally create.

Having ears does not make you a good *listener.*

Activity #5
Whispers

Write down what the person next to you whispers in your ear.

After listening, answer the questions your instructor asks.

1. _____

2. _____

3. _____

4. _____

5. _____

Becoming an active listener requires practice, time, mistakes, guidance, and active participation.

 **CORNERSTONES** for active listening

- Make the decision to listen. Listening is voluntary.

- Approach listening with an open mind.

- Leave your emotions at the door.

- Stop talking.

- Eliminate as many distractions as possible.

- Focus on the material at hand. How can it help you?

- Listen for key words and phrases.

- Listen for *how* something is said.

- Listen for what is *not* said.

- Listen for major ideas and details.

- Take notes; this makes you actively involved in listening.

- Paraphrase the speaker's words.

- Relate the information to something you already know.

- Encourage the speaker with your body language and facial expressions.

- Don't give up too soon; listen to the whole story.

- Avoid jumping to conclusions.

The one minute journal

in a minute or less, jot down one major idea you learned from this chapter.

Will This Be on the Test?: The Essentials of Note Taking

Sanjay loved to play pool. Pool was his passion, his hobby, his job, and his first love. Few things ever got in the way of Sanjay's pool game. On more than one occasion, Sanjay skipped class to go to the pool hall with his buddies. "I'll just get the notes from Wanda," he would say. "She's always in class."

When class met on Monday morning, Sanjay asked Wanda for her notes.

She told him that her handwriting was not very good and that she took notes in her own shorthand. "Oh, that's all right," Sanjay said. "I'll be able to get what I need from them." Wanda agreed to make a copy of her notes and to bring them to Sanjay on Wednesday.

Wanda kept her promise and brought a copy of her notes. Sanjay put them into his backpack just before class began. The notes stayed in his backpack until the night before the midterm exam. He had not taken them out to look at them or to ask Wanda any questions about them. When he unfolded the notes, he was shocked at what he found. The notes read:

Psy started as a sci. disc. from Phi and Physio. Wihelm Wundt/GERM and Will James/US= fndrs. in lt. 19th cent. APA est. by Stanely Hall in US.
5 mjr Pers in PSY=
> *Biopsy. Per*
> *Psychodym. Per*
> *Humanistic. Per*
> *Cog. Per.*
> *Beh. Per.*
Psy wk in 2 mjr. areas 1. Acad.
2. Practising

Sanjay was in trouble. He could not understand Wanda's shorthand, and it was too late to ask her to translate her notes. To add insult to injury, he had lost his textbook a few weeks earlier. After

Psy started as a sci. disc. from Phi and Physio.

trying unsuccessfully to make sense of the notes, he gave up and went to the pool hall to relax and have fun before the test. Sanjay failed his midterm.

We've all missed a few classes from time to time. Very few students have not missed a class for one reason or another. Still, there are two important reasons for attending every class meeting: first, if you are not there, you will not get the information presented; second, although you may borrow notes from a classmate, there is no substitute for your own notes. Sanjay had several problems, including setting priorities, but one of his biggest problems was that he was not in class to take his own notes. To compound this problem, he did not bother to review the notes with Wanda and thus gain some insight into understanding them.

This chapter will address note taking and developing a system of note taking that works for you. At the end of this chapter, you will be able to

■ Identify key phrases and words for effective note taking

■ Understand why note taking is essential to successful students

■ Use the L-STAR system

■ Develop and use a personalized, shorthand note-taking system

■ Use the outline technique for taking notes

■ Use the mapping (or webbing) technique for taking notes

■ Use the Cornell (T or modified) technique for taking notes

■ Put into practice the cornerstones of effective note taking

Take a moment now to assess your current skills in taking notes.

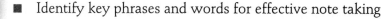

AT THIS MOMENT...

5 = Strongly Agree

4 = Agree

3 = Don't Know

2 = Disagree

1 = Strongly Disagree

1. I am an excellent note taker.
   1 2 3 4 5

2. I am a good listener.
   1 2 3 4 5

3. I have a personal note-taking system.   *1 2 3 4 5*

4. I use abbreviations when taking notes.
   1 2 3 4 5

5. I use symbols when taking notes.   *1 2 3 4 5*

6. I preread each chapter before class.   *1 2 3 4 5*

7. I ask questions in class.
   1 2 3 4 5

8. I know how to listen for clues.
   1 2 3 4 5

9. I rewrite my notes after each class.   *1 2 3 4 5*

10. I reread my notes before each class.   *1 2 3 4 5*

A SELF-ASSESSMENT Total your points from these ten questions. Refer to the following rating scale to determine where you stand in relation to note taking.

0–10   *You do not have a personalized system for note taking and you probably do not take accurate notes.*

11–20   *You have some note-taking skills, but you need to refine your skills by listening and using symbols and abbreviations.*

21–30   *You are an average note taker. You pay some attention to style and content and you probably read over your notes occasionally.*

31–40   *Your note-taking skills are above average. You probably read your notes weekly, correct any mistakes, and make additional notes in the margins.*

41–50   *Your note-taking skills are excellent. You rewrite your notes, know how to use symbols and abbreviations, listen well, and probably have a personalized system of note taking.*

Now, refer to your journal and respond in writing to your findings. Consider the following questions when writing in your journal.

1. Do you have a personalized note-taking system? What is it?

2. Do you have trouble reading your notes after class? Why?

3. Do you feel you need to upgrade your note-taking skills? Why?

Why Take Notes?

Sometimes it all seems like a big, dull chore. Go to class, listen, and write it down. Is note taking really important? Actually, knowing how to take useful, accurate notes can dramatically improve your life as a student. If you are an effective listener and note taker, you have two of the most valuable skills any student could ever use. It is important to take notes for several reasons.

- You become an active part of the listening process.

- You create a history of your course content when you take notes.

- You have written criteria to follow when studying.

- You create a visual aid for your material.

- Studying becomes much easier.

Just as listening is a learned skill, so is note taking. Simply writing information down does not constitute note taking. Note-taking systems and helpful clues can enable students to become more effective note takers.

In this chapter we will discuss, review, and analyze note-taking systems and methods to help you determine which works best for you. Just because your friend uses the outlining method does not make it right for you. If you are a visual learner, you may need to consider the mapping system. A note-taking system is personal and individualized. You will discover the best style for you as you read through this chapter.

Simply writing information down does not constitute note taking.

Do I Need to Write That Down?

Every day professors hear, "Do we need to write this down?" Although most professors would love students to write down the majority of what is said in class, doing so is impossible. Therefore, you need to figure out how to listen actively and distinguish the most important material covered to be an effective listener and note taker. Remember from Chapter 6 that to be an effective listener, you need to know how to listen for key words and phrases.

When you hear these phrases, as outlined in Chapter 6, you can be assured that the instructor is making a major point and that you need to listen carefully and write it down. If material is presented on an overhead, chalkboard, whiteboard, or similar medium, you will also need to take notes. And when your professor uses a handout, it is usually a good idea to take notes on it as the professor reviews.

Preparing to Take Notes

Just as an artist must have materials, such as a brush, palette, canvas, paints, and oils in order to create a painting, you must have certain materials and prepare to become an effective note taker.

- **Attend class.** This may sound like stating the obvious, but it is surprising how many students feel they do not need to go to class. "Oh, I'll just get the notes from Wanda," said Sanjay in the opening story. The only trouble with getting the notes from Wanda is that they are Wanda's notes. You may be able to copy her words, but you may very well miss the meaning behind them. If she has developed her own note-taking style, you may not be able to read many of her notes. She may have written something like this:

> *T/Tmsn dnt lv to see fml crtn of G/7.*

Can you decode this? How would you ever know that these notes mean "Tom Thomson didn't live to see the formal creation of the Group of Seven?" To be an effective note taker, class attendance is crucial; there is no substitute for it.

- **Come to class prepared.** Do you read your assignments nightly? Professors are constantly amazed at the number of students who come to class and *then* decide they should have read their homework. Doing your homework—reading your text, handouts, or workbooks or listening to tapes—is one of the most effective ways to become a better note taker. It is always easier to take notes when you have a preliminary understanding of what is being said. As a student, you will find fewer tasks more difficult than trying to take notes on material that you have never seen or heard before. Coming to class prepared means doing your homework and coming to class ready to listen.

Coming to class prepared also means bringing the proper materials for taking notes: your textbook or lab manual, at least two pens, enough sharpened pencils to make it through the lecture, a notebook, and a highlighter. Some students also use a tape recorder. If you choose to use a tape recorder, be sure to get permission from the instructor before recording.

■ **Bring your textbook to class.** Although many students think they do not need to bring their textbook to class if they have read the homework, you will find that many professors repeatedly refer to the text while lecturing. Always bring your textbook to class with you. The instructor may ask you to highlight, underline, or refer to the text in class, and following along in the text as the professor lectures may also help you organize your notes.

■ **Ask questions and participate in class.** Two of the most critical actions you can perform in class are to ask questions and to participate in the class discussion. If you do not understand a concept or theory, ask questions. Don't leave class without understanding what has happened and assume you'll pick it up on your own. Many professors use students' questions as a way of teaching and reviewing materials. Your questioning and participation will definitely help you, but they could also help others who did not understand something!

Beginning the Building Process

Y ou have been exposed to several thoughts about note taking: first, you need to cultivate and build your active listening skills; second, you need to overcome obstacles to effective listening, such as prejudging, talking when others are talking, and bringing emotions to the table; third, you should be familiar with key phrases used by professors; fourth, you need to understand the importance of note taking; fifth, you need to prepare yourself to take effective notes; and finally, you must scan, read, and use your textbook to understand the materials presented.

THE L–STAR SYSTEM

One of the most effective ways to take notes begins with the L-STAR system.

L Listening

S Setting It Down

T Translating

A Analyzing

R Remembering

This five-step program will enable you to compile complete, accurate, and visual notes for future reference. Along with improving your note-taking skills, using this system will enhance your ability to participate in class, help other students, study more effectively, and perform well on exams and quizzes.

L—Listening. One of the best ways to become an effective note taker is to become an active listener. A concrete step you can take toward becoming an active listener in class is to sit near the front of the room where you can hear the professor and see the board and overheads. Choose a spot that allows you to see the professor's mouth and facial expressions. If you see that the professor's face has become animated or expressive, you can bet that you are hearing important information. Write it down. If you sit in the back of the room, you may miss out on these important clues.

S—Setting it down. The actual writing of notes can be a difficult task. Some professors are organized in their delivery of information, others are not. Your listening skills, once again, are going to play an important role in determining what needs to be written down. In most cases, you will not have time to take notes verbatim. You will have to be selective about the information you choose to set down. One of the best ways to keep up with the information being presented is to develop a shorthand system of your own. Many of the symbols you use will be universal, but you may use some symbols, pictures, and markings that are uniquely your own. Some of the more common symbols are

w/	with	w/o	without
=	equals	≠	does not equal
<	less than	>	greater than
%	percentage	#	number
@	at or about	$	money
&	and	^	increase
+	plus or addition	–	minus or subtraction
*	important	etc	and so on
eg	for example	vs	against
esp	especially	"	quote
¿	question	...	and so on

These symbols can save you valuable time when taking notes. Because you will use them frequently, it might be a good idea to memorize them. As you become more adept at note taking, you will quickly learn how to abbreviate words, phrases, and names.

Using the symbols listed and your own shorthand system, practice reducing the following statements. Be sure that you do not reduce them so much that you will be unable to understand them later.

1. *It is important to remember that a greater percentage of money invested does not necessarily equal greater profits.*

Reduce. _____

_____

2. *She was quoted as saying, "Money equals success." Without exception, the audience disagreed with her logic.*

Reduce. _____

_____

3. *He found many more books at the new store than he expected. For example, there were more than 100 dictionaries available; a far greater number than at any other store.*

Reduce. _____

_____

4. *The increase in financial aid has allowed a greater number of students to attend college and university.*

Reduce. _____

_____

T—Translating. One of the most valuable activities you can undertake as a student is to translate your notes immediately after each class. Doing so can save you hours of work when you begin to prepare for exams. Many students feel that this step is not important, or too time-consuming, and leave it out. Don't. Often, students take notes so quickly that they make mistakes or use abbreviations that they may not be able to decipher later.

After each class, go to the library or some other quiet place and review your notes. You don't have to do this immediately after class, but before the end of the day, you will need to edit and translate your classroom notes. This process gives you the opportunity to put the notes in your own words and to incorporate your text notes into your classroom notes. You can correct spelling, reword key phrases, write out abbreviations, and prepare questions for the next class. Sounds like a lot of work, doesn't it? It *is* a great deal of work, but if you try this technique for one week, you should see a vast improvement in your comprehension of material. Eventually, you should see an improvement in your grades.

Translating your notes helps you to make connections between previous material discussed, your own personal experiences, and readings and new material presented. Translating aids in recalling and applying new information. Few things are more difficult than trying to reconstruct your notes the night before a test, especially when they were made several weeks earlier. Translating your notes daily will prove a valuable gift to yourself when exam time comes.

A—Analyzing. This step takes place while you translate your notes from class. When you analyze your notes, you are asking two basic questions: (1) What does this mean? and (2) Why is it important? If you can answer these two questions about your material, you have almost mastered the information. Though some instructors will want you to spit back the exact information you were given, others will ask you for a more detailed understanding and a synthesis of the material. When you are translating your notes, begin to answer these two questions using your notes, textbook, supplemental materials, and information gathered from outside research. Once again, this process is not simple or quick, but testing your understanding of the material is important. Remember that many lectures are built on past lectures. If you do not understand what happened in class on September 17, you may not be able to understand what happens on September 19. Analyzing your notes while translating them will give you a more complete understanding of the material.

R—Remembering. Once you have listened to the lecture, set your notes on paper, and translated and analyzed the material, it is time to study, or remember, the information. Some effective ways to remember information include creating a visual picture, speaking the notes out loud, using mnemonic devices, and finding a study partner. Chapter 8 will help you with these techniques and other study aids.

Putting It all Together:
Note-Taking Techniques

There are as many systems and methods of note taking as there are people who take notes. Some people write too small, others too large. Some write too much, others not enough. Some write what is really important, others miss key points. The aim of this section is to help you use the L-STAR system with a formalized note-taking technique. The L-STAR system can be used with any of the techniques presented.

Before examining the three most commonly used note-taking systems, let's review a few principles about basic note taking.

- Always date your notes and use a heading

- Keep notes from each class separate by using dividers or separate notebooks

- Use loose-leaf paper with a three-hole punch

- Copy any information that is written on the board, used on an overhead, or presented in charts and graphs

- Organize and review your notes the same day you take them

- Use your own shorthand system

- Incorporate related handouts with appropriate notes

The three most common types of note-taking systems are: (1) The outline technique; (2) The Cornell, or split-page technique (also called the T system); (3) The mapping technique.

THE OUTLINE TECHNIQUE

The outline system uses a series of major headings and multiple sub-headings formatted in hierarchical order. The outline technique is one of the most commonly used note-taking systems, yet it is also one of the most misused systems. It can be difficult to outline notes in class, especially if your professor does not follow an outline while lecturing.

When using the outline system, it is best to get all the information from the lecture and afterward to combine your lecture notes and text notes to create an outline. Most professors would advise against using the outline system of note taking in class, although you may be able to use a modified version in class. The most important thing to remember is not to get bogged down in a system during class; what is critical is getting the ideas down on paper. You can always go back after class and rearrange your notes as needed.

If you are going to use a modified or informal outline while taking notes in class, you may want to consider grouping information together under a heading as a means of outlining. It is easier to remember information that is logically grouped than to remember information that is scattered across several pages. If your economics lecture is on taxes, you might outline your notes using the headings "Municipal Taxes," "Provincial Taxes," and "Federal Taxes."

After you have rewritten your notes using class lecture information and material from the textbook, your pages may look something like this.

Study Skills 101   Oct.17
                                    Wednesday
Topic: Listening
I. The Process of Listening (ROAR)
    A. R= Receiving
        1. W/in range of sound
        2. Hearing the information
    B. O = Organizing & focusing
        1. Choose to listen actively
        2. Observe the origin, direction & intent
    C. A = Assignment
        1. You assign a meaning
        2. May have to hear it more than once
    D. R = Reacting
        I. Our response to what we heard
        2. Reaction can be anything
II. Definitions of Listening (POC)
    A. P = Listening w/ a purpose
    B. O = Listening w/ objectivity
    C. C = Listening constructively

THE CORNELL (MODIFIED CORNELL, SPLIT PAGE, OR T) SYSTEM

The basic principle of the Cornell system, developed by Dr. Walter Pauk of Cornell University, is to split the page into three sections, each section to be used for different information. Section A is used for questions that summarize information found in section B; section B is used for the actual notes from class; and section C will be used for a summary. The blank note-taking page should be divided as shown.

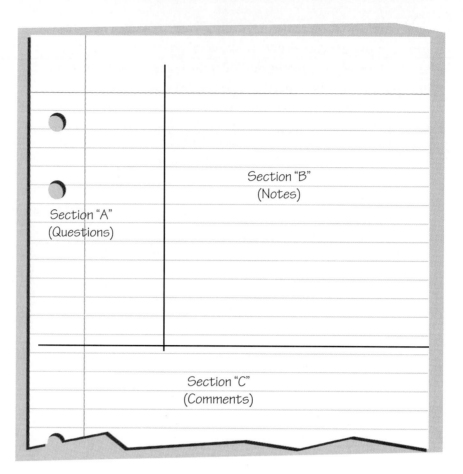

Section "A"
(Questions)

Section "B"
(Notes)

Section "C"
(Comments)

To implement the Cornell system, you will want to choose the technique that is most comfortable and beneficial for you; you might use mapping (discussed later) or outlining on a Cornell page. An example of notes outlined using the Cornell system follows.

Study Skills 101   Oct. 19
Topic: Listening   Friday

What is the listening Process? (ROAR)	*The Listening Process or (ROAR)
	A= Receiving
	1. Within range of sound
	2. Hearing the information
	B = Organizing
	1. Choose to listen actively
	2. Observe origin
Definition of Listening (POC)	*Listening Defined
	A. Listening w/ a purpose
	B. Listening objectively
	C. Listening constructively
Obstacles (PTE)	*What interferes w/ listening
	A. Prejudging
	B. Talking
	C. Emotions

The listening process involves Receiving, Organizing, Assigning &
Reacting - Talking, Prejudging & Emotions are obstacles.

THE MAPPING SYSTEM

If you are a visual learner, this system
may be especially useful to you. The
mapping system of note taking generates a picture of the information. The
mapping system creates a map, or web,
of information that allows you to see
the relationships among facts, names,
dates, and places. A mapping system
might look something like
what follows.

Oct. 22
Monday

Topic: Listening

① Receiving
get info w/in range
Hear information

② Organizing
Choose to listen
observe origin

The Process of Listening (ROAR)

③ Assignment
assign a meaning
May have to hear it more than once

④ Reacting
our response
Response can be anything

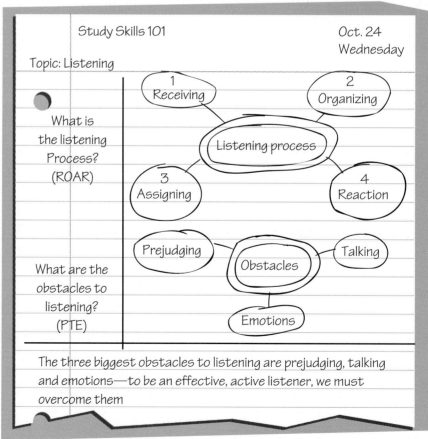

Study Skills 101

Oct. 24
Wednesday

Topic: Listening

What is the listening Process? (ROAR)

1 Receiving
2 Organizing
Listening process
3 Assigning
4 Reaction

What are the obstacles to listening? (PTE)

Prejudging
Obstacles
Talking
Emotions

The three biggest obstacles to listening are prejudging, talking and emotions—to be an effective, active listener, we must overcome them

The most important thing to remember about each note-taking system is that it *must* work for you. Do not use a system because your friends use it or because you feel that you should use it. Experiment with each system or combination to determine which is best for you.

Always remember to keep your notes organized, dated, and neat. Notes that cannot be read are no good to you or to anyone else. The note-taking system illustrated here would probably be inappropriate for anyone.

Use the spaces provided here to practise your note-taking skills.

■ THE OUTLINE METHOD

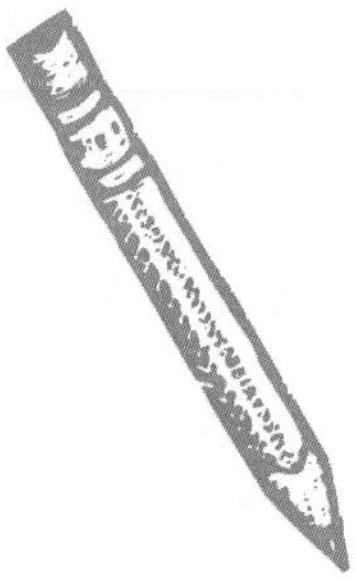

_____

_____

_____

_____

_____

_____

_____

_____

_____

_____

_____

_____

_____

_____

_____

_____

_____

■ THE CORNELL METHOD

_____

_____

_____

_____

_____

_____

_____

_____

_____

_____

_____

_____

_____

_____

_____

_____

_____

_____

_____

_____

_____

_____

■ THE MAPPING METHOD

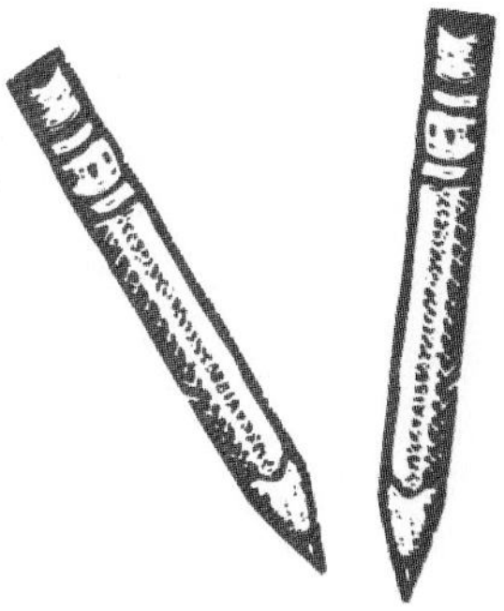

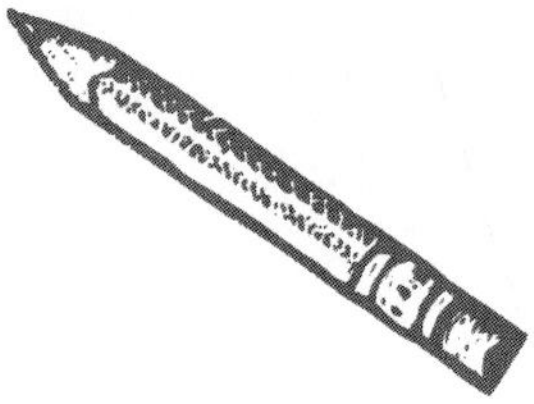

_____

_____

_____

_____

_____

_____

_____

_____

_____

_____

_____

_____

_____

_____

_____

_____

_____

_____

_____

_____

 **CORNERSTONES** of effective note taking

- ■ Attend class.

- ■ Be prepared for every class by doing homework assignments.

- ■ Sit where you can see and hear the professor.

- ■ Edit your notes after each class.

- ■ If it's on the board or overhead, write it down.

- ■ Use loose-leaf paper.

- ■ Keep the notes for each course separate from one another.

- ■ Develop your listening abilities and tune out chatter.

- ■ Ask questions.

- ■ Use abbreviations and special notes to yourself.

- ■ Keep your notes neat and clear.

- ■ Participate in class.

If you remember the concepts of the L-STAR system (listening, setting it down, translating, analyzing, and remembering) and use this system as a study pattern, and if you find a note-taking system that is comfortable and useful to you, then you will begin to see significant improvement in your ability as a note taker and in your performance as a student.

The one minute journal

in one minute or less, jot down one major idea you learned from this chapter.

Avoiding the "All-Nighter": Studying for Success

Tyrone walked into class beaming. He was happy, joking, and smiling, and he spoke to everyone on the way to his seat. He was always a delightful student, but today he seemed even happier than usual. Several classmates asked how he could possibly be so up. They could not understand his jovial attitude because today was test day. How could he be happy today of all days? How could anyone be happy on test day?

Tyrone told his classmates that he was happy because he was prepared. "I'm ready for the world," he said. "I studied all week and I know this stuff." Most of his classmates ribbed him and laughed. In the final moments before the test began, all the other students were deeply involved in questioning each other and looking over their notes. Tyrone stood by the window finishing his coffee until the test was to begin.

After all was said and done, Tyrone got the highest mark on the exam of all his peers—a 98. Several students asked him how he did so well. Intrigued by their curiosity, I asked Tyrone to share his secret to successful test taking.

I found his answer extremely useful, especially in light of his active life; Tyrone was on the basketball team, held a part-time job, cared for his elderly grandmother, dated, and worked on the college newspaper.

"You have to do it in steps," Tyrone said. "You can't wait until the night before, even if you have all evening and night." He explained that he incorporated study time into his schedule several weeks before the test. If the test was to cover four chapters, he would review two chapters the first week and two chapters the second week. "I use a study room at the library because my house is so full of people. I make an outline of my notes, review my text, answer sample questions in the book, and many times I find someone to quiz me on the material."

"You have to do it in steps," Tyrone said. "You can't wait until the night before, even if you have all evening and night."

s this how you approach studying? Do you have a positive attitude about taking tests? Many of us fear the whole process, and not everyone goes to the trouble that Tyrone did to prepare so well. Unfortunately, lack of study and poor test-taking skills are reflected in marks. Studying is one of the most essential skills a student can master. This chapter will introduce you to a variety of study and memory techniques. At the end of this chapter, you should be able to

- Identify studying strategies

- Create a notebook system that works for you

- Determine the proper environment for successful studying

- Identify new methods of reading, highlighting, and taking notes from texts

- Use the SQ3R method

- Use the READ method

- Create and use mnemonic devices and jingles

- Identify and use the Cornerstones of Effective Studying

- Use strategies for studying with small children in the house

Why Study? I Can Fake it

didn't have to study very hard in high school, why should I do it now?" This thought may have crossed your mind by this point in the semester. Many students feel that there is no real reason to study. They believe that they can glance at their notes a few moments before a test and fake it. Quite truthfully, some students are able to do this. Some tests and instructors lend themselves to this type of studying technique. More than you imagine, however, this is *not* the case. Some college professors are notorious for thorough exams, lengthy essay questions, tricky true–false statements, and multiple choices that would confuse Einstein. If you want to succeed in your classes in college, you will need to make studying a way of life.

Effective studying requires a great deal of commitment, but learning how to get organized, take effective notes (see Chapter 7), read a textbook, listen in class, develop personalized study skills, and build memory techniques will serve you well in becoming a successful graduate. Faking it is now a thing of the past. Take a moment to assess your study skills now.

1. I have a workable study plan.
   1 2 3 4 5

2. I am a very organized person.
   1 2 3 4 5

3. I use a different notebook for each subject.
   1 2 3 4 5

4. I know how to use a variety of study techniques.
   1 2 3 4 5

5. I understand how memory works.   *1 2 3 4 5*

6. I understand the SQ3R study method.   *1 2 3 4 5*

7. I know how to transfer information into long-term memory.   *1 2 3 4 5*

8. I know how to use mnemonics and jingles.
   1 2 3 4 5

9. I read my notes daily.
   1 2 3 4 5

10. I know how to survey a chapter.   *1 2 3 4 5*

5 = Strongly Agree

4 = Agree

3 = Don't Know

2 = Disagree

1 = Strongly Disagree

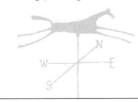

A SELF-ASSESSMENT Total your points from these ten questions. Refer to the following rating scale to determine where you stand in relation to your study habits and skills.

0–10   *You probably do not have a study plan, spend a great deal of time looking for materials, and have difficulty remembering information.*

11–20   *Your study skills are below average. You probably do not maintain a study plan, you have some trouble remembering information, and you are somewhat unorganized.*

21–30   *Your study skills are average for a new college student. You know the importance of using a study plan, but you probably don't follow it often. You can use memory techniques, and you are somewhat organized.*

31–40   *Your study skills and habits are above average. You probably know exactly where your supplies are, have developed a study plan, and use memory techniques wisely.*

41–50   *Your study skills and habits are excellent. You are probably a very organized person. You keep your supplies together and you know to use memory techniques, read and survey chapters, and take notes from the text.*

Now, refer to your journal and respond in writing to your findings. Consider the following questions when writing in your journal.

1. Is studying easy and part of a routine for me? Why or why not?

2. Is remembering information difficult for me? Why or why not?

3. I do or do not spend a great deal of time studying. Why?

The Importance of Your

Study Environment

> Order and simplification are the first steps toward mastery of a subject.
> Thomas Mann, author

You may wonder why your study place is important. The study environment can determine how well your study time passes. If the room is too hot, too noisy, too dark, or too crowded, your study time may not be productive. In a room that is too hot and dimly lit, you may have a tendency to fall asleep. In a room that is too cold, you may spend time trying to warm yourself. Choose a location that is comfortable for *you*.

Different students need different study environments. You may need to have a degree of noise in the background, or, you may need complete quiet. You have to make this decision. If you always have music in the background while you are studying, try studying in a quiet place one time to see if there is a difference. If you always try to study when it is quiet, try putting soft music in the background to see if it helps you. You may have to try several environments before you find the one that is right for you.

Describe your current study environment. _____

_____

_____

_____

_____

_____

_____

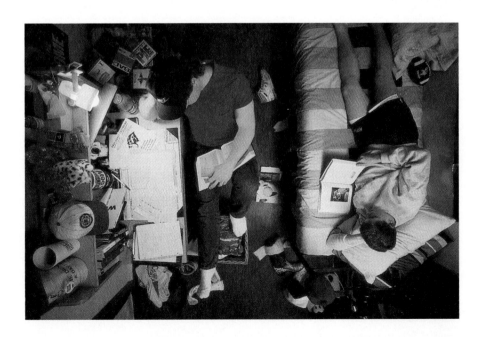

Has this environment served you well? Why or why not? _____

_____

_____

_____

_____

_____

_____

How could this environment be improved? _____

_____

_____

_____

_____

_____

_____

_____

_____

Ready, Set, Go!!

In Chapter 5 you got organized, collected all your materials together, and developed a notebook system. In Chapters 6 and 7 you actively listened and developed a note-taking system. So far in this chapter you've found the appropriate study environment. Now it's time to study. And studying doesn't have to be a horrendous chore. All it takes is a positive attitude and an open mind. Next you'll learn about several methods of studying that you can use to put yourself in charge of the material. After you've reviewed these methods, you may want to use some combination of them or you may prefer to use one method exclusively. The only set standard in choosing a study plan is that the plan must work for you. You may have to spend a few weeks experimenting with several plans and methods to determine the one with which you are most comfortable. Don't get discouraged if it takes you a while to find what is right for you.

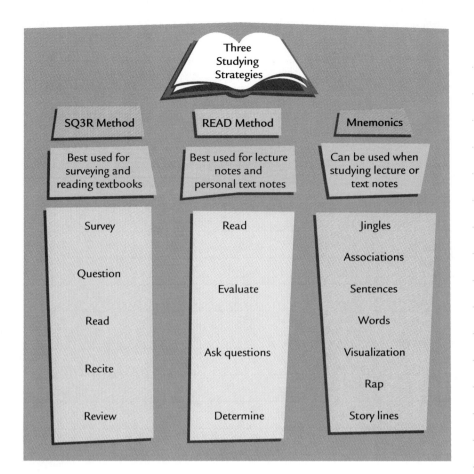

SQ3R

The most basic and often-used studying system is the SQ3R method, developed by Francis P. Robinson in 1941. This simple, yet effective, system has proved to be a successful study tool for millions of students. SQ3R involves five steps: Survey, Question, Read, Recite, and Review. The most important thing to remember about SQ3R is that it should be used on a daily basis, not as a method of cramming.

1. **Survey.** The first step of SQ3R is to survey, or preread, an assigned chapter. You begin by reading the title of the chapter, the headings, and each subheading. Look carefully at the vocabulary, time lines, graphs, charts, pictures, and drawings included in each chapter. If there is a chapter summary, read it. Surveying also includes reading the first and last sentence in each paragraph. Surveying is not a substitute for reading a chapter. Reading is discussed later. Before going any further, select a chapter from any book, or one assigned by your professor, and survey that chapter.

■ CHAPTER SURVEY

1. What is the title of the chapter? _____

2. What is the subheading of the chapter? _____

_____

_____

_____

3. How many sections does the chapter have? _____

List them. _____

_____

_____

_____

_____

4. What are the chapter objectives? _____

_____

_____

_____

_____

5. Does the chapter include vocabulary words? _____

List the words you will need to look up. _____

_____

_____

_____

_____

6. If the chapter contains quotations, which one means the most to you? Why? __

_____

_____

_____

_____

7. What is the most important graph or chart in the chapter? Why? _____

_____

_____

_____

2. **Question.** The second step is to question. The five most common questions you should ask yourself when you are reading a chapter are: Who? When? What? Where? and Why? As you survey and read your chapter, try turning the information into questions and seeing if you can answer them. If you do not know the answers to the questions, you should find them as you read along.

3. **Read.** After you survey the chapter and develop some questions to be answered from the chapter, the next step is to read the chapter. Remember, surveying is not reading. There is no substitute for this step in your success plan. Read slowly and carefully. The SQ3R method requires a substantial amount of time, but if you take each step slowly and completely, you will be amazed at how much you can learn and how much your grades will improve.

   Read through each section. It is best not to jump around or move ahead if you do not understand the previous section. Paragraphs are usually built on each other, and so you need to understand the first before you can move on to the next. You may have to read a chapter or section more than once, especially if the information is new, technical, or difficult.

   Another important aspect of reading is taking notes, highlighting, and making marginal notes in your textbook. You own your textbook and should personalize it as you would your lecture notes. Highlight areas that you feel are important, underline words and phrases that you did not understand or that you feel are important, and jot down notes in the margins.

   "If I mark in my text, I may not get much for it when I sell it back to the bookstore," you might say. Right now you need to be concerned with learning the information in the most beneficial and efficient way possible. Don't worry about selling your textbook after the class is over. You might even want to consider keeping your book especially if it relates to your major field of study or chosen career.

   As you begin to read your chapter, mark the text, and take notes, keep the following in mind.

- Read the entire paragraph before you mark anything

- Identify the topic or thesis statement of each paragraph and highlight it

- Highlight key phrases

- Don't highlight too much; the text will lose its significance

- Stop and look up words that you do not know or understand

When you have finished marking in your text, it may look something like this example.

Interacting=
Dynamic
Process

It is not easy to initiate, develop, and maintain positive relationships. It takes work and considerable skill. (Interacting) with others, for example, is a dynamic process. The interaction is constantly shifting and changing as you and the other person respond and react to each other. Sometimes communication will be clear; other times you may misunderstand each other. Sometimes you will have common goals and needs; other times your goals and needs will conflict. Everything you do will affect the relationship to some degree. Everything the other person does will affect your perceptions and feelings about the other person and the relationship.

Neg feelings
= hard to
lose

There is a general rule that positive perceptions of and feelings toward another person are hard to acquire but easy to lose; however, negative perceptions of and feelings toward another person are easy to acquire and hard to lose. A perception of another person (A) as kind, for example, may develop as you see the person act in sympathetic and generous ways towards others. But one instance of deliberate cruelty can change your perception of the person dramatically. On the other hand, the sight of a person kicking a dog on a single occasion would probably stick in your memory, and repeated evidence of kindness would not wipe out the impression that the person can be cruel. (2) The complex and constantly (changing nature of relationships) the (slowness) with which positive feelings and impressions are built, and the (fragileness of relationships) all point to the difficulty in developing friendships. Loneliness, however, pushes most people into the effort to do so. The experience of feeling lonely is a central fact of human existence.

From David W. Johnson, *Reaching Out: Interpersonal Effectiveness and Self-Actualization*, 5/e. © 1993, Allyn and Bacon.

While reading, you will want to take notes that are more elaborate than your highlighting or marginal notes. Taking notes while reading the text will assist you in studying the material and committing it to memory. Among the several effective methods of taking notes while reading are

- Charts
- Outlines
- Key words
- Mind maps
- Flash cards
- Summaries
- Time lines

■ CHARTS Charts assist visual learners in seeing relationships and differences.

Aeschylus	Tragedy	* 7 Against Thebes * Agamemnon * The Persians
Sophocles	Tragedy	* Oedipus The King * Antigone * Electra
Euripides	Tragedy	* Medea * Hippolytus * The Cyclops
Aristophanes	Comedy	* The Clouds * The Birds
Menander	New Comedy	* The Grouch * The Arbitration * The Shorn Girl

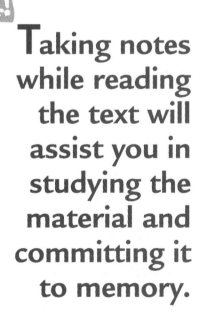

Taking notes while reading the text will assist you in studying the material and committing it to memory.

■ OUTLINES Outlines organize information into clusters or under separate headings.

```
              Internal Sexual Organs          p. 73
                     (Female)
   I. The Vagina
       A. - Extends back & upward from opening
       B. - @ 7 - 13 cm. long at rest
   II. The Cervix
       A. - Lower end of the uterus
       B. - Produces secretions (chemical)
   III. The Uterus
       A. Pear shaped (called the womb)
       B. Slants forward
   IV. The Fallopian Tubes
       A. Extend from upper uterus to ovaries
       B. @ 10 cm. in length
   V. The Ovaries
       A. Almond-shaped
       B. @ 8 cm. long
```

■ KEY WORDS Key words help define terminology, phrases, names, and people.

```
   Fat Soluble Vitamins: A, D, E & K (p. 237)

   Vitamin A          1st to have been recognized; there
                      are 3 forms: retinol, retinal &
                      retinoic acid


   Vitamin D          Different from all other nutrients
                      Body can't synthesize it w/out
                      help of sunlight
```

■ MIND MAPS Mind maps help show relationships among people, places, and things; they can also help show progression and time.

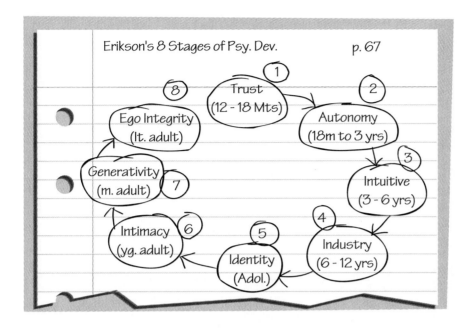

■ FLASH CARDS Flash cards are portable and easily accessible. They are useful for remembering key words, phrases, definitions, and procedures. It is best to write the word or phrase on the front and define it on the reverse side.

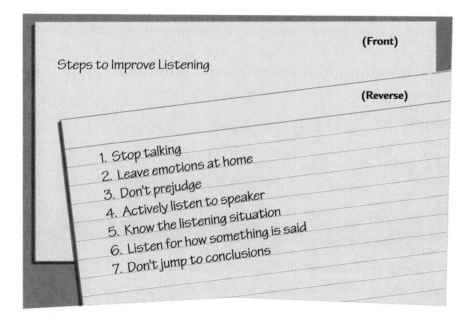

■ SUMMARIES Summaries are used for very detailed information that cannot be reduced to note cards, outlines, or time lines.

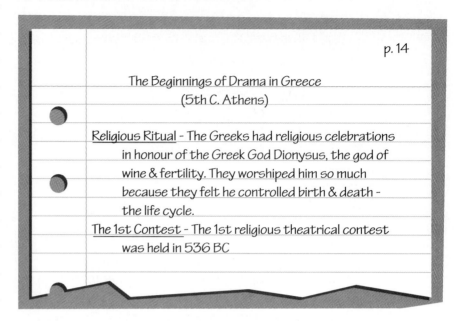

p. 14

The Beginnings of Drama in Greece
(5th C. Athens)

Religious Ritual - The Greeks had religious celebrations
in honour of the Greek God Dionysus, the god of
wine & fertility. They worshiped him so much
because they felt he controlled birth & death -
the life cycle.
The 1st Contest - The 1st religious theatrical contest
was held in 536 BC

■ TIME LINES Time lines are an excellent way to show chronological relationships among events.

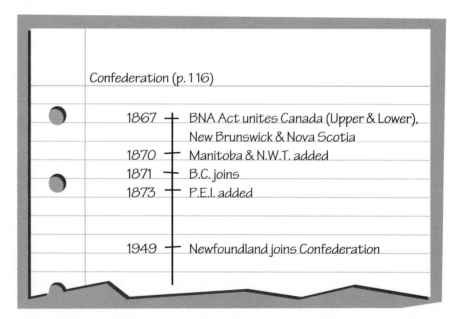

Confederation (p. 116)

1867 — BNA Act unites Canada (Upper & Lower),
New Brunswick & Nova Scotia
1870 — Manitoba & N.W.T. added
1871 — B.C. joins
1873 — P.E.I. added

1949 — Newfoundland joins Confederation

As you read through a chapter in your textbook, you may find that you have to use a variety of these techniques to capture information. Try them for one week. Although taking notes while reading a chapter thoroughly is time-consuming, you will be amazed at how much you remember and how much you are able to contribute in class after using these techniques.

4. **Recite.** Recitation is simple, but crucial. Skipping this step may result in less than full mastery of the chapter. Once you have read a section, ask yourself this simple question, "What was that all about?" Find a classmate, sit down together, and ask questions of each other. Discuss with each other the main points of the chapter. Try to explain the information to each other without looking at your notes. If you are at home, sit back in your chair, recite the information, and determine what it means. If you have trouble explaining the information to your friend or reciting it to yourself, you probably did not understand the section and you should go back and reread it. If you can tell your classmate and yourself exactly what you just read and what it means, you are ready to move on to the next section of the chapter.

5. **Review.** After you have read the chapter, immediately go back and scan it again. "What?!! I just read it!" Yes, you did. And the best way to determine whether you have mastered the information is once again to survey the chapter, review marginal notes, high-lighted areas, and vocabulary words, and determine whether you have any questions that have not been answered. This step will help you store and retain this information in long-term memory.

THE READ METHOD

The READ method works best for studying notes you have taken from the text or in class. It has four steps:

1. **Read the notes.** Many students take notes and never go back to read them. As we pointed out in Chapter 7, the best way to study your notes is to read them the day you take them. It is important to read your notes as soon after you write them as possible so that you can make corrections. You should also read your notes often. For example, if you took notes on Meech Lake and the Charlottetown Accord last month, you should read those notes before the lecture on the 1995 Quebec Referendum tomorrow. Doing so will refresh your memory and prepare you to participate in class discussions. Reading your notes is an important step in your success plan.

2. **Evaluate what you have read.** After you have read your notes, evaluate the information and prioritize what is most important. People often write too much when taking notes. As you read over your notes, you may find that you have included information that is not important or that you have repeated information. Evaluating will help you to make your notes more concise and to the point.

You may want to highlight your handwritten notes or to add marginal notes to your notes.

3. **Ask questions.** As you read and evaluate your notes, ask questions about what you have written: "What was meant by this?" "How does this relate to the textbook information?" "Will I have to use this information on the test or in a paper?" If you have any questions that your notes do not answer, you need to review your text or make yourself a note to ask the professor at the next class meeting. Asking questions of yourself, your notes, your text, and your professors will set you on the road to success as a student.

4. **Determine the main issues.** The last part of the READ method for studying notes is to determine the main issues of what you have written. If you can read your notes and answer the question "What were the main issues covered?" you have a grasp of the material. If you cannot determine the main issues and recite them to yourself, you will need to review your text, ask questions, and maybe rewrite your notes.

UNDERSTANDING MEMORY

By now you may be thinking that if you use the SQ3R and READ methods, you will never have time even to think about that football game or your children will be grown and married before you see them again. Both methods take time, but they are essential techniques for mastering material. The final study technique we will look at is the use of mnemonic devices. A *mnemonic* is a memory technique or trick used to trigger information from the brain. Before considering mnemonic devices, you need to understand a few basic facts about memory.

- Everyone remembers some information and forgets other information

- Your senses help you take in information

- With very little effort, you can remember some information

- With rehearsal (study), you can remember a great deal of information

- Without rehearsal or use, information is forgotten

- Incoming information needs to be filed in the brain if you are to retain it

- Information stored, or filed, in the brain must have a retrieval method

- Mnemonic devices can help you store and retrieve information

Psychologists have determined that there are three types of memory: sensory memory; short–term, or working, memory; and long-term memory.

Sensory memory stores information gathered from the five senses: taste, touch, smell, hearing, and sight. Sensory memory is usually temporary, lasting about one to three seconds, unless you decide that the information is of ultimate importance to you and make an effort to transfer it to long-term memory. Although your sensory memory bank is *very large*, sensory information does not stay with you for very long (Woolfolk, 1995). Sensory memory allows countless stimuli to come into your brain, which can be a problem when you are trying to concentrate on your professor's lecture. You need to make a conscious effort to remain focused on the words being spoken and not on competing noise. When you make an effort to concentrate on the professor's information, you are then committing this information to short-term memory.

Short-term, or working, memory holds information for a short amount of time. Your working memory bank can hold a limited amount of information, usually about five to nine separate new facts or pieces of information at once (Woolfolk, 1995). Although it is sometimes frustrating to forget information, it is also useful and necessary to do so. If you never forgot anything, you would not be able to function. Educational psychologist Anita Woolfolk suggests that most of us can hear a new phone number, walk across the room, and dial it without much trouble, but that if we heard two or three new numbers, we would not be able to dial them correctly. This is more information than our working memory can handle. If you were asked to give a person's name immediately after being introduced, you would probably be able to do so. If you had met several other new people in the meantime, unless you used some device to transfer the name into long-term memory, you would probably not be able to recall it.

As a student, you would never be able to remember all that your professor said during a 50-minute lecture. You have to take steps to help you to remember information. Taking notes, making associations, drawing pictures, and visualizing information are all techniques that can help you to commit information to your long-term memory bank.

SHORT-TERM MEMORY ASSESSMENT

Theo, Gene, and Suzanne were on their way home from class. As they drove down Highway 401 toward the subdivision, they saw a 1984 Honda Civic pull out in front of a 1990 Nissan Maxima. There was a crash as the two cars collided. Theo stopped the car. Gene and Suzanne jumped from the car to see if they could help. Suzanne yelled for someone to call 911; Jacinta, a bystander, ran to the pay phone at the corner of Mason and Long Streets. Within ten minutes, an ambulance arrived and took Margaret, the driver of the Maxima, to St. Mary's Hospital. Tim, the driver of the Honda, was not badly injured.

Cover this scenario with a piece of paper and answer the following questions.

1. Who was driving the Honda? _____

2. What highway were they driving on? _____

3. Who called 911? _____

4. What hospital was used? _____

5. What year was the Maxima? _____

How many questions did you answer correctly? If you answered four or five questions correctly, your working memory is strong. If you answered only one or two questions correctly, you will need to discover ways to commit more information to your short-term, or working, memory. Some techniques for doing this are discussed later in this chapter.

Long-term memory stores a lot of information. It is almost like a computer disk. You have to make an effort to put something in your long-term memory, but with effort and memory techniques, such as visualization and concentration, you can store anything you want to remember there. Long-term memory consists of information that you have heard often, information that you use often, information that you might see often, and information that you have determined necessary. Just as you name a file on a computer disk, you name the files in your long-term memory. Sometimes, you have to wait a moment for the information to come to you. While you are waiting, your brain disk is spinning; if the information you seek is in long-term memory, your brain will eventually find it. You may have to assist your brain in locating the information by using mnemonics and other memory devices.

LONG-TERM MEMORY ASSESSMENT

Without using any reference materials, quickly answer the following questions using your long-term memory.

1. What is your mother's maiden name? _____

2. What is the year and make of your car? _____

3. What is the capital of Manitoba? _____

4. Who wrote A Christmas Carol? _____

5. What shape is a stop sign? _____

6. What is your social insurance number? _____

7. Name one of your instructors. _____

8. Where is his or her office located? _____

9. What does the first "R" stand for in the SQ3R method? _____

10. Name one character on the TV series, "Friends." _____

Did the answers come to you quickly? If you review your answers, you will probably find that you responded quickly to those questions whose content you deal with fairly frequently, such as your instructor's name, your social insurance number, or the year and make of your car. Although you were probably able to answer all the questions, in some instances your brain had to search longer and harder to find the answer. This is how long-term memory works.

There are countless pieces of information stored in your long-term memory. Some of it is triggered by necessity, some may be triggered by the five senses, and some may be triggered by experiences. The best way to commit information into long-term memory and to retrieve it when needed can be expressed through

VCR^3

VCR^3

V—Visualizing

C—Concentrating

R—Relating

R—Repeating

R—Reviewing

VCR^3

VCR^3

To **visualize** information, try to create word pictures in your mind as you hear the information. If you are being taught anatomy, try to see a picture of the body chart in your text, try to visualize the different parts of the circulatory system, for example, or try to paint a mind picture that will help you to remember the information.

Concentrating on the information given will help you commit it to long-term memory. Don't let your mind wander. Stay focused.

Relating the information to something that you already know or understand will assist you in filing or storing the information for easy retrieval. Relating the calculation functions of spreadsheet software to the algebra you learned in high school can help you remember how to set up the spreadsheet.

Repeating the information out loud to yourself or to a study partner facilitates its transfer to long-term memory. Some people have to hear information many times before they can commit it to long-term memory.

Reviewing the information is another means of repetition. The more you see and use the information, the easier it will be to remember it when the time comes.

USING MNEMONIC DEVICES

Mnemonic devices are memory tricks, or techniques, that assist you in putting information into your long-term memory and pulling it out when you need it. I recently gave a test on the basic principles of public speaking. A student asked if she had to know the parts of the communication process in order. When I replied that she should be able to recall them in order, she became nervous and said that she had not learned them in order. Another student overheard the conversation and said, "Some men can read backwards fast." The first student asked, "What do you mean by that?" I laughed and said that the mnemonic was great! The student had created a sentence to remember source, message, channel, receiver, barriers, and feedback. The relationship worked like this:

Some	=	Source
Men	=	Message
Can	=	Channel
Read	=	Receiver
Backwards	=	Barriers
Fast	=	Feedback

The first student caught on fast; she could not believe how easy it was to remember the steps in order using this sentence. This is a perfect example of how using memory tricks can help retrieve information easily.

The following seven types of mnemonic devices may help you with your long-term memory.

■ JINGLES You can make up rhymes, songs, poems, or sayings to assist you in remembering information, for example, "Columbus sailed the ocean blue in fourteen hundred and ninety-two."

■ ASSOCIATIONS Associations put words, ideas, and symbols together for you. For instance, you might associate the following:

idea = light bulb

trillium = Ontario

$ = money

■ SENTENCES   You can make up sentences such as "Some men can read backwards fast," to help you remember information. Another example is "Please excuse my dear Aunt Sally," which corresponds to the mathematical operations: parentheses, exponents, multiplication, division, addition, and subtraction.

■ WORDS   You can create words also. For example, Roy G. Biv may help you to remember the colors of the rainbow: red, orange, yellow, green, blue, indigo, and violet.

■ VISUALIZATION   Creating an image in your mind can help you recall certain facts. Picturing Italy's boot shape, for example, may help you identify Italy on a map. Drawing pictures that you can recall when you are taking a test may also be useful. If you are trying to remember the planning process for your management course, draw a model, and then when you need to recall the steps involved in planning, close your eyes and visualize your drawing.

■ RAP   Rap songs can be a great way to remember information, and they can work for a group. For example, you could get together with your study group to create a rap song using information from biology or marketing.

■ STORY LINES   If you find it easier to remember stories than raw information, you may want to process the information into a story that you can easily tell. Weave the data and facts into a creative story that can be easily retrieved from your long-term memory. This technique can be especially beneficial if your instructor gives essay exams, because the "story" that you remember can be what was actually told in class.

Mnemonic devices have assisted millions of students for countless years. It can be very helpful to create pictures, jingles, and sentences to help you recall information. Most successful students do just that.

Create a mnemonic for the following pieces of information.

1. The parts of speech (nouns, pronouns, verbs, adverbs, adjectives, prepositions, conjunctions, interjections). _____

_____

_____

_____

_____

2. *The Great Lakes (Ontario, Huron, Superior, Erie, Michigan).* _____

_____

_____

_____

3. *The nine planets in the solar system (Mercury, Venus, Earth, Mars, Jupiter, Saturn, Uranus, Neptune, Pluto).* _____

_____

_____

_____

4. *The concepts of art (form, space, area, mass, perspective, proportion, scale).*

_____

_____

_____

5. *The cost concepts in economics (fixed cost, variable cost, total cost, marginal cost, average cost, average fixed cost, and average variable cost).* _____

_____

_____

_____

Studying with Small Children in the House

For many students, finding a place or time to study is the hardest part of studying. Some students live at home with younger siblings; some students have children of their own. If you have young children in the home, you may find the following hints helpful when it comes time to study.

- **Study at school.** Your schedule may have you running from work to school directly to home. Try to squeeze in even as little as half an hour at school for studying, perhaps immediately before or after class. A half hour of pure study time can prove more valuable than five hours at home with constant interruptions.

- **Create crafts and hobbies.** Your children need to be occupied while you study. It may help if you have available crafts and hobbies in which they can be involved while you are involved with studying. Choose projects your children can do by themselves, without your help. Depending on their ages, children could make masks from paper plates, colour, do pipe cleaner art or papier-mâché, use modeling clay or dough, or build a block city. Explain to your children that you are studying and that they can use this time to be creative; when everyone is finished, you'll share what you've done with each other.

- **Study with your children.** One of the best ways to instill the value of education in your children is to let them see you participating in your own education. Set aside one or two hours per night when you and your children study. You may be able to study in one place, or you may have separate study areas. If your children know that you are studying and you have explained to them how you value your education, you are killing two birds with one stone: you are able to study and you are providing a positive role model as your children study with you and watch you.

- **Rent movies or let your children watch TV.** Research has shown that viewing a limited amount of educational television, such as *Sesame Street*, *Polka Dot Door*, or *Mr. Dressup*, can be beneficial for children. If you do not like what is on television, you might consider renting or purchasing age-appropriate educational videos for your children. This could keep them busy while you study and it could help them learn as well.

- **Invite your children's friends over.** That's right. A child who has a friend to play or study with may create less of a distraction for you. Chances are your children would rather be occupied with someone their own age, and you will gain valuable study time.

■ **Hire a sitter or exchange sitting services with another student.** Arrange to have a sitter come to your house a couple of times a week. If you have a classmate who also has children at home, you might take turns watching the children for one another. You could each take the children for one day a week, or devise any schedule that suits you both best. Or you could study together, and let your children play together while you study, alternating homes.

Studying at any time is hard work. It is even harder when you have to attend to a partner, children, family responsibilities, work, and a social life as well. You will have to be creative in order to complete your education. You are going to have to do things and make sacrifices that you never thought possible. But if you explore the options, plan ahead, ask questions of other students with children and with other responsibilities outside the classroom, you can and will succeed.

 **for effective studying**

■ Study your hardest material first.

■ Don't cram the night before; plan your time appropriately.

■ Overlearn the material.

■ Review your classroom and textbook notes daily.

■ Set rules for studying.

■ Study in a brightly lit area.

■ Use the SQ3R method when studying texts.

■ Use the READ method when studying lecture notes.

■ Use mnemonic devices.

■ Take breaks every half hour.

■ Have a healthy snack.

■ Turn the heat down.

The one minute journal

in one minute or less, jot down one major idea you learned from this chapter

The splendid achievements

of the intellect, like the soul,

are everlasting.

The Proving Ground: Strategies for Test Taking

Fatima could tell that something was wrong with her roommate, Ellen. Ellen had been quiet and distant for the past two days. That evening, while walking to the dining hall, Fatima asked Ellen if there was something bothering her. Ellen confided that the first test in her nursing class was in one week and that if she failed the test, she would be asked to leave the nursing program.

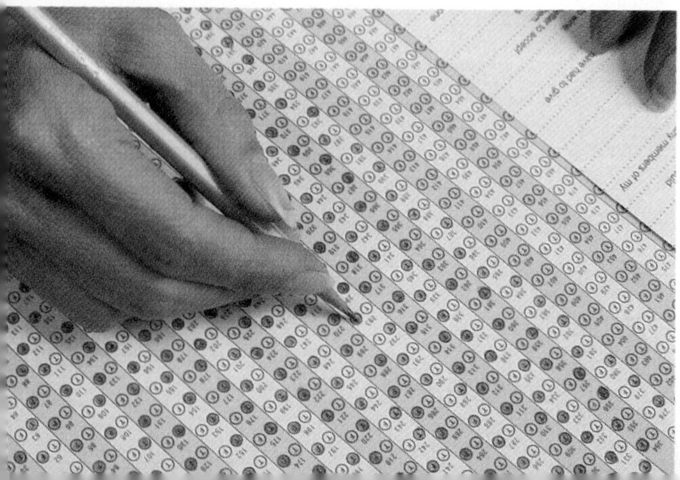

Fatima tried to tell Ellen that she had plenty of time to study the material and prepare for the test. Ellen replied that she was not worried so much about knowing the material, but that she was worried because she was a poor test taker. "I can know it from beginning to end," Ellen said, "but when she puts that test in front of me, I can't even remember my name! What am I going to do? This test is going to determine the rest of my life."

Fatima explained to Ellen that she suffered through the same type of anxiety and fear in high school until her math teacher had taught the class how to take a test and how to reduce test anxiety. "Its just a skill, Ellen, like driving a car or typing a research paper. You can learn how to take tests if you're really serious." Ellen asked if Fatima could give her some hints about test taking. As they finished eating, Fatima told Ellen that they could begin working for an hour every morning and an hour every evening to learn how to take exams and to reduce anxiety.

The week of the test rolled around, and Ellen was confident that she knew the material that she was to be tested on. She still had a degree of anxiety, but she had learned how to be in control of her emotions during a test. She had also learned how to prepare herself physically for the exam. She went to bed early the night before the exam. On exam day, she got up early, ate a healthy breakfast, had a brief

This test is going to determine the rest of my life.

review session, packed all the supplies needed for the exam, and headed to class early so that she could relax a little before the instructor arrived.

When the exam was passed out, Ellen could feel herself getting somewhat anxious, but she quickly put things into perspective. She sat back and took several deep breaths, listened carefully to the professor's instructions, read all the test instructions before beginning, told herself silently that she was going to ace the exam, and started.

After one hour and five minutes, time was called. Ellen put her pencil down, leaned back in her chair, took a deep breath, rubbed her aching fingers, and cracked the biggest smile of her life. Fatima had been right. The strategies worked. Ellen was going to be a nurse.

T-Day !

The day has finally arrived. Test day! But you are calm and collected because you have learned, as Ellen did, how to listen, take effective, useful notes, apply study habits, and reduce test anxiety. You are ready! You are a success because you planned ahead and because you have convinced yourself that taking a test is a privilege and not a prison sentence.

So, why do you think professors give tests? Do you think they are necessary? Before going any further, list some reasons that professors give tests.

_____

_____

_____

_____

_____

_____

How do you really feel about tests? Some students dislike tests and wish they weren't part of college life. Some students believe that testing is not necessary and don't see its value. Successful students, however, realize that testing is necessary and even useful, that it has several positive purposes. Testing serves to provide motivation for learning, provide feedback to the student and to the professor, and determine mastery of material.

Successful people accept testing as a fact of life. You have to be tested to drive a car, to continue in school, to join the armed forces, to become a teacher, a lawyer, a doctor, or a nurse, and often to be promoted at work. To pretend that testing is not always going to be a part of your life is to deny reality.

You may dread tests for a variety of reasons. You may be afraid of the test itself and the questions it may pose. Test anxiety can be overcome however, and this section will present several ways you can become a more confident test taker and get started on the path to success. At the end of this chapter, you should be able to

- Recognize symptoms of extreme test anxiety

- Put tests into perspective

- Determine your test-anxiety level

- Control test anxiety

- Predict certain test questions

- Identify and use strategies for taking matching tests

- Identify and use strategies for taking true–false tests

- Identify and use strategies for taking multiple choice tests

- Identify and use strategies for taking short-answer tests

- Identify and use strategies for taking essay or discussion tests

AT THIS MOMENT...

1. I have a low degree of test anxiety. *1 2 3 4 5*

2. I can control my test anxiety. *1 2 3 4 5*

3. My mind stays on the material at hand when testing. *1 2 3 4 5*

4. I seldom worry about time when testing. *1 2 3 4 5*

5. I read all the directions before beginning a test. *1 2 3 4 5*

6. I know how to relax before a test. *1 2 3 4 5*

7. I know what supplies to bring to a test. *1 2 3 4 5*

8. I read the entire test before beginning. *1 2 3 4 5*

9. I feel ready to take tests when test day arrives. *1 2 3 4 5*

10. I remember test information after the test is over. *1 2 3 4 5*

5 = Strongly Agree

4 = Agree

3 = Don't Know

2 = Disagree

1 = Strongly Disagree

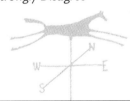

A SELF-ASSESSMENT Total your points from these ten questions. Refer to the following rating scale to determine where you stand in relation to dealing with test anxiety.

0–10 *You probably have very little test-taking training, and you usually experience extreme anxiety.*

11–20 *You may have had some test-taking training, but you still experience high anxiety and dread taking a test.*

21–30 Your test-anxiety level is average. You probably know a few techniques for reducing anxiety.

31–40 Your test-anxiety level is lower than that of most students. You know how to take a test, preread the instructions, and reduce anxiety.

41–50 You have very little test anxiety. You have learned how to properly prepare for and take a test.

Now, refer to your journal and respond in writing to your findings. Consider the following questions when writing in your journal.

1. Why are so many students uptight about testing?

2. Why do tests mean so much?

3. Describe the best testing situation in which you have been involved. Why was it the best?

Controlling Test Anxiety

Many students would do almost anything to get out of taking exams and tests. Some students have physical reactions to testing, including nausea, headaches, and blackouts. Such physical reactions may be a result of being underprepared or not knowing how to take an exam.

Why do you experience test anxiety?

Your answer to this question is more than likely negative. You may approach tests thinking

I'm going to fail

I knew I couldn't do this

There is no way I can do well, the teacher hates me

I should never have taken this class

These types of attitudes can cause you to be unsuccessful in testing, but with an attitude adjustment and some basic preparation, you can overcome a good deal of your anxiety about tests. You can reduce anxiety when you are in control of the situation, and you can gain control by convincing yourself that you *can* and *will* be successful. If you can honestly tell yourself that you have done everything possible to prepare for a test, then the results are going to be positive.

It is important to realize that a test is not an indication of who you are as a person or a mark of your worth as a human being. Not everyone can be good at all things. You will have areas of strength and of weakness. You will spare yourself a great deal of anxiety and frustration if you understand from the start that you may not get 100 on every test. If you expect absolute perfection on everything, you are setting yourself up to fail. Think positively, prepare well, and do your best, but also be prepared to receive less than a perfect mark.

TEST-ANXIETY SCALE

Check the items that apply to you when preparing for a test:

_____ I do not sleep well the night before a test.

_____ I get sick if I eat anything before a test.

_____ I am irritable and hard to be around before a test.

_____ I see the test as a measure of my worth as a student.

_____ I go blank during the test and am unable to recall information.

_____ I worry when other students are still testing and I am finished.

_____ I worry when others finish and I am still testing.

_____ I am always afraid that I will run out of time.

_____ I get frustrated during the test.

_____ I have a negative attitude about testing.

_____ I think about not taking the test.

_____ I always average my grades before a test.

_____ My body reacts negatively to testing (sweats, nervousness, butterflies).

If you checked off more than five items on this list, you experience test anxiety. It you checked off ten or more, you probably have severe test anxiety.

PREPARING FOR TESTS

You can take many steps to reduce test anxiety, but one of the most effective ways to reduce anxiety is to know what materials to study in preparation for the test.

Without looking at the answers, can you list the top ten places to find answers to test questions?

1. _____

2. _____

3. _____

4. _____

5. _____

6. _____

7. _____

8. _____

9. _____

10. _____

Answers

- Lecture notes
- Textbook notes
- Textbook highlighting
- Chapters in the textbook
- Sample tests in each chapter
- Previous tests given by the instructor
- Handouts given by the instructor
- Notes of videos watched in class
- Notes from CD-ROMs or other electronic media
- Study-group notes

Most students can name only four or five of the top ten places to find answers to test questions. One of the most common errors students make when studying for exams is forgetting about handouts and about notes taken from videos and other media. When you are reviewing for an exam, be sure to review *all* information from class, notes, texts, study groups, and media. Professors often test on information other than what they specifically talk about in class.

You can also reduce test anxiety by trying to predict what types of test questions the professor will give. Professors frequently give clues ahead of time about what they will be asking and what types of questions will be given.

Several classes before the test is scheduled, find out from your professor what type of test you can expect. This information can help you study more effectively. Some questions you might ask are

1. What type of questions will be on the test?

2. How long is the test?

3. Is there a time limit on the test?

4. Will there be any special instructions, such as use pen only or use a number 2 pencil?

5. Is there a study sheet?

6. Will there be a review session?

7. What is the weighting of the test?

Asking these simple questions will help you know what type of test will be administered, how you should prepare for it, and what supplies you will need.

PREDICTING EXAM QUESTIONS

You will want to begin predicting questions early. Listen to the professor intently. Professors use cue phrases, such as "You will see this again," and "If I were to ask you this question on the test." Pay close attention to what is written on the board, what questions are asked in class, and what areas the professor seems to be concentrating on more than others. You will begin to get a feel for what types of questions the professor might ask on the test.

It may also be beneficial for you to keep a running page of test questions that you have predicted. As you read through a chapter, ask yourself many questions at the end of each section. When it is time to study for the test, you may have already predicted many of the questions your professor will ask.

Save all quizzes and exams that your professor lets you keep (some professors take the exams back after students have had a chance to review them). These are a wonderful resource for studying for the next exam or for predicting questions for the final exam.

Take a moment to try to predict two essay test questions from Chapter 8 on studying.

Question 1. _____

_____

_____

Approach the test with an "I can" attitude.

Why do you think this question will be asked? _____

_____

_____

Question 2. _____

_____

_____

Why do you think this question will be asked? _____

_____

_____

Three Types of Responses to Test Questions

Almost every test question will elicit one of three types of responses from you as the test taker.

- Quick-time response

- Lag-time response

- No response

Your response is a **quick-time response** when you read a question and know the answer immediately. You may need to read only one key word in the test question to know the correct response. Even if you have a quick-time response, however, *always* read the entire question before answering. The question may be worded in such a way that the correct response is not what you originally expected. By reading the entire question before answering, you can avoid losing marks to careless error.

You have a **lag-time response** when you read a question and the answer does not come to you immediately. You may have to read the question several times or even move on to another question before you think of the correct response. Information in another question will sometimes trigger the response you need. Don't get nervous if you have a lag-time response. Once you've begun to answer other questions, you usually begin to remember more, and the response may come to you. You do not have to answer questions in order on most tests.

No response is the least desirable situation when you are taking a test. You may read a question two or three times and still have no response. At this point, you should move on to another question to try to find some related information. When this happens, you have some options:

1. Leave this question until the very end of the test.

2. Make an intelligent guess.

3. Try to eliminate all unreasonable answers by association.

4. Watch for modifiers within the question.

It is very difficult to use intelligent guessing with essay or fill-in-the-blank questions.

Remember these important tips about the three types of responses.

1. Don't be overly excited if your response is *quick*; read the entire question and be careful so that you don't make a mistake.

2. Don't get nervous or anxious if you have a *lag-time* response; the answer may come to you later, so just relax and move on.

3. Don't put down just anything if you have *no response;* take the remaining time and use intelligent guessing.

HELPFUL REMINDERS FOR REDUCING TEST ANXIETY

■ Approach the test with an "I can" attitude.

■ Prepare yourself emotionally for the test, control your self-talk, and be positive.

■ Overlearn the material—you can't study too much.

■ Remind yourself that you studied and that you know the material.

■ Go to bed early. Try not to pull an all-nighter before the test.

■ Chew gum or hard candy during the test if allowed, it may help you relax.

- Eat a healthy meal before the test.

- Arrive early for the test (at least 15 minutes early).

- Sit back, relax, breathe, and clear your mind if you become nervous.

- Come to the test with everything you need: pencils, calculator, and so on.

- Read the *entire* test first; read *all* the directions and highlight the directions.

- Listen to the professor before the test begins.

- Answer what you know first, the questions that are easiest for you.

- Keep an eye on the clock.

- Check your answers, but remember, your first response is usually correct.

- Find out about the test *before* it is given; ask the professor what types of questions will be on the test.

- Find out exactly what the test will cover ahead of time.

- Ask the professor for a study sheet; you may not get one, but it does not hurt to ask!

- Know the rules of the test and of the professor.

- Attend the review session if one is offered.

- Know the weighting of the test with regard to your final mark.

- Ask about extra credit or bonus questions on the test.

- When you get the test, jot down any mnemonic you might have developed on the back or at the top of a page.

- Never look at another student's test or let anyone see your test.

Test-Taking Strategies and Hints for Success

Wouldn't it be just great if every instructor gave the same type of test? Then you would have to worry about content only, and not about the test format. Unfortunately, this is not going to happen. Professors will continue to test differently and to have their own style of writing. Successful students know the differences among testing techniques and know what to look for when dealing with each type of test question. You may have a preference for one type of question over another. You may prefer multiple-choice to essay questions, whereas someone else may prefer essay to true–false questions. Whatever your preference, you are going to encounter all types of questions. To be successful, you will need to know the techniques for answering each type.

The most common types of questions are

- Matching

- True–false

- Multiple choice

- Short answer

- Essay

Before you read about the strategies for answering these different types of questions, think about this: There is no substitute for studying. You can know all the tips, ways to reduce anxiety, mnemonics, and strategies on earth, but if you have not studied, they will not help you much.

STRATEGIES FOR MATCHING QUESTIONS

Matching questions frequently involve knowledge of people, dates, places, or vocabulary. When answering matching questions, you should

- Read the directions carefully.

- Read each column before you answer.

- Determine whether there are equal numbers of items in each column.

- Match what you know first.

- Cross off information that is already used.

- Use the process of elimination for answers you might not know.

- Look for logical clues.

- Use the longer statement as a question; use the shorter statement as an answer.

SAMPLE TEST #1
Directions: Match the information in column A with the correct information in column B. Use capital letters.

LISTENING SKILLS

A	B
_____ 1. Listening	a. Within range
_____ 2. Hearing	b. Obstacle
_____ 3. Receiving	c. Voluntary
_____ 4. Objectivity	d. Origin and direction
_____ 5. Prejudging	e. Open-minded
_____ 6. Organizing	f. Involuntary
_____ 7. As a result	g. Key phrase

STRATEGIES FOR TRUE–FALSE QUESTIONS

True–false tests ask if a statement is true or not. True–false questions are some of the most tricky questions ever developed. Some students like them, some hate them. There is a 50/50 chance of getting the correct answer, but you can use the following strategies to increase your odds on true–false tests.

■ Read each statement carefully.

■ Watch for key words in each statement, for example, negatives.

■ Read each statement for double negatives, such as *not un*truthful.

■ Pay attention to words that may indicate that a statement is true, such as *some, few, many, often.*

■ Pay attention to words that may indicate that a statement is false, such as *never, all, every, only.*

■ Remember that if any *part* of a statement is false, the *entire* statement is false.

■ Answer every question unless there is a penalty for guessing.

SAMPLE TEST #2

Directions: Place a capital "T" for true or "F" for false beside each statement.

NOTE-TAKING SKILLS

_____ 1. Note taking creates a history of your course content.

_____ 2. "Most importantly" is not a key phrase.

_____ 3. You should always write down everything the instructor says.

_____ 4. You should never ask questions in class.

_____ 5. The L-STAR system is a way of studying.

_____ 6. W/O is not a piece of shorthand.

_____ 7. You should use 4-by-6-inch paper to take classroom notes.

_____ 8. The outline technique is best used with lecture notes.

_____ 9. The Cornell method should never be used with textbook notes.

_____ 10. The mapping system is done with a series of circles.

STRATEGIES FOR MULTIPLE-CHOICE QUESTIONS

Many college professors give multiple-choice tests because they are easy to grade and provide quick, precise responses. A multiple-choice question asks you to choose from among usually two to five answers to complete a sentence. Some strategies for increasing your success in answering multiple-choice questions are

■ Read the question and try to answer it *before* you read the answers provided.

■ Look for similar answers; one of them is usually the correct response.

■ Recognize that answers containing extreme modifiers, such as *always, every,* and *never,* are usually wrong.

■ Cross off answers that you know are incorrect.

- Read *all* the options before selecting your answer, even if you know that A is the correct response; read them *all*.

- Recognize that when the answers are all numbers, the highest and lowest numbers are usually incorrect.

- Recognize that a joke is usually wrong.

- Understand that the most inclusive answer is often correct.

- Understand that the longest answer is often correct.

- If you cannot answer a question, move on to the next one and continue through the test; another question may trigger the answer you missed.

- Make an educated guess if you must.

- Answer every question unless there is a penalty for guessing.

SAMPLE TEST #3

Directions: Read each statement and select the best response from the answers given below. Use capital letters.

STUDY SKILLS

_____ 1. What are the components of getting organized?

a. supplies, notebook, environment

b. environment, books, clock

c. supplies, notebook, lecture notes

d. lecture notes, computer, environment

_____ 2. The best notebook system used for lecture notes is

a. a spiral-bound composition book

b. a legal pad

c. a three-ring binder with loose-leaf paper

d. a collection of Post-it notes

_____ 3. A mnemonic is

a. a note-taking device

b. a memory trick

c. a listening tool

d. a type of harmonica

_____ 4. The first "R" in the SQ3R method stands for

a. read

b. recite

c. review

d. respond

_____ 5. Short-term, or working, memory is

a. great in capacity and lasts for almost 1 hour

b. limited in capacity and holds 5 to 9 pieces of information

c. great in capacity and holds 5 to 9 pieces of information

d. limited in capacity and lasts for almost 1 hour

STRATEGIES FOR SHORT-ANSWER QUESTIONS

Short-answer questions, also called fill-in-the-blanks, ask you to supply the answer yourself, not to select it from a list. Although short answer sounds easy, these questions are often very difficult. Short-answer questions require you to draw from your long-term memory. The following hints can help you answer this type of question successfully.

- Read each question and be sure that you know what is being asked.

- Be brief in your response.

- Give the same number of answers as there are blanks, for example, _____ and _____ would require *two* answers.

- Never assume that the length of the blank has anything to do with the length of the answer.

- Remember that your initial response is usually correct.

- Pay close attention to the word immediately preceding the blank; if the word is *an*, give a response that begins with a vowel.

- Look for key words in the sentence that may trigger a response.

STRATEGIES FOR ESSAY QUESTIONS

Most students approach essay questions with dismay because they take more time. Yet essay tests can be one of the easiest tests to write, because they give you a chance to show what you really know. An essay question requires you to supply the information. If you have studied, you will find that once you begin to answer an essay question, your answer will flow easily. Some tips for answering essay questions are

- Sometimes more is not always better—sometimes more is just *more*. Try to be as concise and informative as possible. A professor would rather see 1 page of excellent material than 5 pages of fluff.

- Pay close attention to the action word used in the question and respond with the appropriate type of answer. Key words used in questions include

discuss	illustrate	enumerate
compare	define	relate
contrast	summarize	analyze
trace	evaluate	critique
diagram	argue	justify

- Write a thesis statement for each answer.

- Outline your thoughts before you begin to write.

- Watch your spelling, grammar, and punctuation.

- Use details, such as times, dates, places, and proper names, where appropriate.

- Be sure to answer all parts of the question; some discussion questions have more than one part.

- Summarize your main ideas toward the end of your answer.

- Write neatly.

- Proofread your answer.

SAMPLE TEST #5

Directions: Answer each question completely and thoroughly.

STUDY SKILLS

1. Describe the READ study method. _____
_____
_____
_____

2. Discuss why it is important to use the SQ3R method. _____
_____
_____
_____

3. Justify your chosen notebook system. _____
_____
_____
_____

4. Compare an effective study environment with an ineffective study

environment. _____
_____
_____
_____

Learning how to take a test and reducing your anxiety are two of the most important gifts you can give yourself as a student. Although there are many tips and hints to help you, don't forget that there is no substitute for studying and knowing the material.

CORNERSTONES for test taking

- Always write your name on each page of your test.

- Write clearly.

- Check punctuation, spelling, and grammar.

- Use capital letters for true–false and multiple choice.

- Answer all questions.

- Check to see if you skipped a question or a page.

- Ignore the pace of your classmates; some may finish earlier than others.

- Check to see if one question answers another.

- Never use drugs or alcohol to get through a test.

- Watch time limits.

- Ask questions of the professor if allowed.

- Read the entire test before beginning.

- Think positively.

The one minute journal

n a minute or less, jot down one major idea you learned from this chapter.

Are You Using Good Study Skills and Time- Management Habits?

Access the study skills self-help information checklist at this Internet address: http://www.ucc.vt.edu/stdysk/stdyhlp.html. Complete the checklist to gain more detailed information about your own study habits and attitudes. The inventory will identify areas in which you are proficient as well as areas in which you could use some improvement.

Name the areas on which you need to focus to improve your study skills. _____

_____

_____

_____

_____

_____

_____

_____

What strong points relative to your study skills did you identify? _____

_____

_____

_____

_____

_____

_____

_____

For more help improving your study skills, you may want to access these additional articles on the Internet:

- Time-Scheduling Suggestions

- Time Scheduling

- Concentration—Some Rules of Thumb

- Reading and Study Skills: Note Taking—The Cornell System

- Editing Lecture Notes

- Constructive Suggestions Regarding Motivation

- Control of the Environment

UNIT

Building the Body, Mind, and Soul

■ AN INSIDER'S VIEW

Shauna Sedgewick
Age 23
University of British
Columbia
Vancouver, BC
University of Toronto

In my mind, there's really only one way to get the most out of college and to enjoy yourself along the way, and that's to manage your time well. Most people get stressed out when they've got more work to do than they have time for, so to me it's pretty simple — stay on top of your workload. And if you don't let yourself get behind, you'll have time to do a quality job on the project you're doing, so you'll do better academically.

I've always been involved in extra-curricular activities and worked part time while I've been at university. I've been involved in intramural sports and I'm on the rowing team, which has me up at 4:30 AM every day. I work between 10-15 hours every week. And because I want to do well academically, I have to manage my time well to make sure I can fit everything in.

There are a couple of things I do that help me cope with my workload. When I am given an assignment, I break it down into smaller parts. I schedule each part of the assignment into the time frame I've been given. For example, I do an outline for my papers as soon as they were assigned. Then I know how much research I have to do, and I have a pretty good idea of how long the research will take me. I make up a schedule for completing each paper, and I make a deadline for each part of the paper. I have found that this eliminates a lot of stress, because I don't get behind.

I can't afford to waste a second, so I use every minute of each day well. I even study between races during rowing practice! I've learned to group my classes together to save time, and I live close to the university so that I'm not spending too much time travelling to and from school. I never turn on the TV — unless it's Hockey Night in Canada — and I make sure that my schoolwork is done before I go out. That way, I can go and enjoy myself with a clear mind. Lastly, I associate with people who have similar goals. It's easier to stay focused on your priorities if your friends are doing the same.

The last thing I want to tell you is to make sure you keep some time for yourself. It's important to keep a healthy balance between work and leisure. I work out every day, because I find that I have more energy when I do so. By managing my time carefully, I've really enjoyed my years at university.

It's important to keep a healthy balance between work and leisure.

■ **AN INSIDER'S VIEW**
Aruna Papp
Age 45
York University
Toronto, Ontario

I came to Canada from India in 1972. I was 21, the mother of two, living in an abusive marriage. Moving to Canada meant only two things to me. One, that somehow the abuse in my life would stop, and two, that there might me educational opportunities for my daughters and me. As a child, I did not get the education that I craved. I am the eldest of seven children, six of which are girls, so I was married off at a young age.

Since my ex-husband could not find employment to his liking when we arrived in Canada, I worked at menial jobs to support my family. I felt very discouraged, because I was forced to put my dreams on hold. I got a job as a short order cook at York University, where I worked from 5 AM until 3 PM. From 4 PM until 11 PM I worked as an attendant in the athletic complex locker room. My children came to my workplace after school, and we had dinner together at the cafe. I helped them with their homework, while they taught me what they had learned at school.

Being in an educational environment but not being able to attend classes was most disheartening. One day, however, I found out that full-time university employees were entitled to tuition-free schooling. I registered for two classes: English as a Second Language, and Sociology 101. I found some students to cover for me in the locker room while I was in class, and I successfully completed the courses. In 1989 I received my Master's Degree in Sociology, and in September 1996 I will begin my Ph. D.

Looking back, I think I was able to reach my goals because I knew very clearly what I wanted. I soon realized that many of the barriers to achieving my goals were within me. My culture and socialization had taught me that I could not be a success because I was female. I had to deal with the issues that accompany this mindset, and I have come to the conclusion that I can accomplish anything I want to.

One of the biggest factors that contributed to my success was the relationships I made. I decided that I wanted to be with people I could learn from and after whom I could pattern myself. My advice is this: find people who have the traits that you would like to develop. They could be a professor, boss, or fellow student. Develop a relationship with them. Watch what they do, see what makes them successful. Ask questions of them. Observe how they organize their time, listen to them when they talk, read the books they recommend. You'll learn so much about how to be successful from them. Moreover, the roadblocks you face won't seem as huge if you've got someone to help you through it all.

Many people have helped me along the way, and I believe that I should pass this on to others. To this end, I have worked extensively with battered women. I have received seven awards for my work in this area, but my most cherished award is the YWCA's Women of Distinction Award, because it comes from women who are my colleagues and clients.

No man is an island, entire

of itself.

John Donne, poet

Getting Along with Others: The Power of Relationships

In the year 1800, one of the most fascinating cases of human identity and social relationships came to light. Early one morning, a man working in his vegetable garden in Aveyron, France, heard something making a sound. He looked for the origin of the sound and found a boy. This "wild" boy "showed no signs of behaviours one would expect in a social human" (Adler, 1989). Apparently, he had spent his early childhood without *any* human contact.

The boy could not speak a single word, but uttered only cries and moans as one would expect from an animal. Adler suggests that more significant than his lack of social skills was his total lack of identity as a social human. "He had no sense of being in the world. He had no sense of himself as a person related to other persons." Only after years of contact with a "mother" did the wild boy of Aveyron begin to behave as a human being.

This true story, referenced in the 1995 movie *Nell*, is important to us today because it proves that we learn who and what we are from our relationships with other people. It is only through contact with other humans that we know we are human. Adler says that we gain an idea of who we are from the way others define us. Our development as human beings

We learn who and what we are from our relationships with other people.

in a social world continues throughout our lives.

Relationships

Life is about relationships. Relationships between people, between people and nature, and between people and the environment. The statement "No man is an island" is true. You would literally have to be shipwrecked on an island to be free of relationships with other humans, but you would still have relationships with nature, the animals, birds, and reptiles on the island. People do not live in a vacuum. We are the sum total of all of our relationships.

You are entering a new time in your life; you may be starting college for the first time, returning to university after taking some time off, or transferring from one institution to another. Whatever the circumstances, you are in a state of transition. The relationships in which you have been involved are going to change. If you are a parent going to school, your relationship with your children will change because of your school commitments. If you are a first-year student who left home to go to college, your relationships with your parents, family, and friends at home will change. If you are still living in your community, perhaps even living at home while attending college, your relationships also will change because of college. As we noted in Chapter 1, your involvement in higher education will provoke some of the most significant changes you will experience in your life. This idea may be exciting or scary to you, but knowing how to deal with the changes in old relationships and how to build new relationships will be essential to your success in college.

This chapter is designed to help you explore some of the relationships and experiences you will have throughout your college or university career and to provide some ideas of how to grow in a positive manner from these experiences and relationships. At the end of this chapter you will be able to

- Understand the importance of relationships

- Discuss the importance of friendships

- Differentiate among the different stages of relationships

- Discuss the concept of community

- Understand how to create your own community

- Understand the importance of interpersonal communication

- Develop a healthy approach to relationships

- List the qualities of a true friend

- Understand more about your own sexuality

Before discussing relationships in further detail, take a moment to assess how you feel now about relationships.

1. Relationships are important to me right now.

   1 2 3 4 5

2. I make friends easily.

   1 2 3 4 5

3. I rarely have problems with relationships.

   1 2 3 4 5

4. I am comfortable with my sexuality.   *1 2 3 4 5*

5. I understand how to be a good friend.

   1 2 3 4 5

6. I understand the importance of communication in relation-ships.   *1 2 3 4 5*

7. I understand how to resolve social conflict.

   1 2 3 4 5

8. I understand my need for intimacy.   *1 2 3 4 5*

9. I understand how to develop a sense of community in my new environment.

   1 2 3 4 5

10. I understand the importance of personal accountability.

    1 2 3 4 5

5 = Strongly Agree

4 = Agree

3 = Don't Know

2 = Disagree

1 = Strongly Disagree

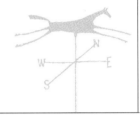

A SELF-ASSESSMENT Total your points from these ten questions. Refer to the following rating scale to determine where you stand in dealing with relationships.

0–10   *You probably have a great deal of difficulty and anxiety dealing with relationships.*

11–20   *You probably have a greater than normal amount of anxiety when dealing with relationships.*

21–30   *You probably have a considerable amount of anxiety when dealing with relationships.*

31–40   *You probably have some anxiety about dealing with relationships.*

41–50   *You deal with relationships easily and with little anxiety.*

Now, refer to your journal and respond in writing to your findings. Consider the following questions when writing in your journal.

1. Why are relationships hard (or easy) for me?

2. What makes me afraid (or unafraid) of change?

3. Why do I suffer (or not suffer) emotionally and physically from relationships?

Why Are Relationships Important?

> If there is radiance in the soul it will abound in the family.
> If there is radiance in the family it will be abundant in the community.
> If there is radiance in the community it will grow in the nation.
> If there is radiance in the nation the universe will flourish.
>
> Lao Tsu,
> Chinese philosopher

To function in a happy and healthy manner, human beings need one another. Everything we learn in this life comes through and from our relationships with others. As illustrated by the story about the wild boy from Aveyron, the very essence of our humanness depends on our interaction with other humans. We need each other to help us laugh, help us cry, help us work, help us provide for the survival of the species, and help us die when the time comes.

Throughout our lives we experience a myriad of relationships. We are someone's son or daughter, we may be someone's brother or sister, we probably will be someone's friend and someone's lover, as well as someone's helpmate through life. Each of these relationships has its own individual dynamics, but all successful relationships have some similarities.

In a recent focus group of university students, participants were asked, "What is the most important component of any relationship?" What do you think the answer was? Overwhelmingly, the group agreed that honesty was the most important component in any relationship. Loyalty, which is closely related to honesty, ranked second.

Do you agree with this focus group's emphasis on honesty? Why or why not?

_____

_____

_____

_____

_____

_____

_____

_____

_____

_____

_____

_____

_____

Communities

ost, if not all, of our relationships take place within a community. Carolyn Shaffer and Kristin Anundsen, in their book *Creating Community Anywhere* (1994), define a community as a dynamic whole that emerges when a group of people

- Participate in common practices

- Depend on one another

- Make decisions together

- Identify themselves as part of something larger than the sum of their individual relationships

- Commit themselves for the long term to their own, to one another's, and to the group's well-being

You may find yourself involved in several separate communities: a home community, a school community, a work community. There is nothing wrong with this; to the contrary, it can be rewarding. You may also find that your communities overlap at times, adding more balance to your life.

What is your current community like? Your community has most likely changed recently because of your entry into higher education. In the past, your community may have been dictated by your physical surroundings, your parents and extended family, or the school you attended. Now you have many more choices in how your community looks and feels and you also have more say about who will be a part of your community.

Describe what you think your ideal community (while you're in

school) would look like. _____

_____

_____

_____

_____

_____

_____

In class, discuss how your hypothetical community is similar to those of your classmates and how it differs.

In your new situation, you may be asking a lot of questions: What do college students do on Saturday nights? How do I build a network of friends? Will I ever feel secure in this new life? Will I ever have someone with whom I can talk and be myself?

The thought of building a new community can be extremely frightening, but the following six-step process (adapted from Shaffer, 1994) can help you.

Step 1—Assess the present

Step 2—Form a vision for the future

Step 3—Look inside out

Step 4—Tear down walls

Step 5—Get started

Step 6—Deal with failure

Step 1 involves some introspection on your part to review what you have experienced in the past and what you currently have in your life. Think about the times in your life when you have felt a part of a successful community. Write down the characteristics of the community that made it successful.

_____

_____

_____

_____

Next, in the inverted triangle, write your name in level 1. In level 2, list people with whom you are currently in close interaction. These people might be roommate(s), people in your academic program, family members, friends you have made in the short time you've been in college. In level 3, list people with whom you have a less intimate relationship. These might be professors, people with whom you commute to campus, people with whom you work. In level 4, list people with whom you have less contact, but who have some impact on your life, such as college or university administrators, and employers.

Step 2 involves determining what kind of community you would like. Your past community may have been dictated by your parents and others, but now you have the opportunity to surround yourself with a community designed to suit you. You are being given a new beginning. Develop a list of statements that describe the kind of community you

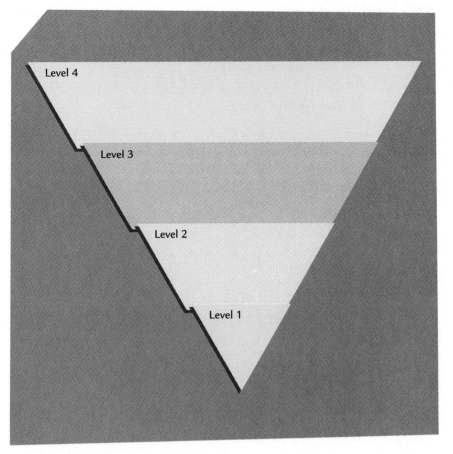

would like to have and write them in the space provided. Use the following sample statements for guidance.

I want to make new friends and develop relationships that challenge me to be the best that I can be.

I want to make new friends and develop relationships with people who have the same values that I have.

I want to make new friends and develop relationships with people who have a different background and outlook on life than I do.

_____

_____

_____

_____

_____

_____

_____

_____

Now develop a list of statements that describe the kind of community you don't want to create. Again, read the sample statements to help get you started.

I don't want a community that is filled with people who have a negative outlook on life.

I don't want a community that is filled with people who are comfortable with the status quo.

I don't want a community that is exclusive instead of inclusive.

_____

_____

_____

_____

_____

_____

By now you should be getting a clearer picture of the community and the types of relationships you would like to develop.

Step 3 addresses your personal requirements for a successful community. As your inverted pyramid shows, your community stems and grows from you. You are critical to the success of your own community, and your relationship with yourself is critical to your success. Do you have a healthy approach to taking care of yourself and improving yourself? Do you see that you are the centre of your community? Do you realize that you can control a great deal of your personal community?

List the personal qualities you feel are important for you to possess if you are to be a successful part of your community; for example, honesty, a sense of giving, devotion, and so on.

_____

_____

_____

_____

_____

_____

_____

_____

In your double-entry journal, develop some goals to help you cultivate these qualities in yourself. Use what you learned about motivation and goal setting from Chapter 2.

Step 4 deals with the walls that stand between you and your new community. Some people live their entire lives within walls that they have created to protect themselves from emotional or physical pain. Some of these walls are built out of fear of rejection: "If I ask her to be my friend and she says no, I'll be hurt"; "If I want to join a group and they don't accept me, I'll be sad." Although such walls may have served a good purpose when they were built, they may now serve to box you in and hinder your growth. Whenever you move outside the walls of your comfort zone, you risk being hurt, but this is the only way you can grow. You need to tear down the walls that keep you from creating the relationships that will make up your new community.

Most walls can be torn down simply by acknowledging that they exist. You can remove walls by developing new and different behaviours.

Describe some of the walls (fears) you have built that stand between you and the community you have been describing in this section. _____

_____

_____

_____

_____

_____

_____

_____

_____

Now that you have identified your walls, develop goals that promote changing the behaviours that keep the walls up. Talk with your classmates about ways to change these behaviours. Keep a record in your journal of your progress in tearing down your walls.

Step 5 starts the building process. As with many projects, the first step can be the most difficult step to take. To build relationships that lead to a community, the first step you need to take is with yourself. To have good friends, you must first be a good friend. Look over the goals you developed in step 3 and start working on yourself. Then look at level 2 of your pyramid. Find people with whom you would like to continue a relationship or with whom you would like to have a different relationship. Don't assume that you have to start from scratch. Your relatives and friends may like to join you in your new

> If you think you can't change the world by yourself, join some people who agree.
> **Motto of Business Partnership and Peace**

community. You may want to develop a deeper relationship with someone in your existing community. Make an effort to work on your relationship with that person. Start with what you have in your present community to see if it will work in your new one.

Continue to use your triangle to determine which of the people with whom you have contact already you would like to include in your new community, and involve them. If you meet resistance or experience failure, move on to step 6.

Step 6 involves persistence. If developing a positive sense of community were easy, we wouldn't be discussing it. We've all experienced failure in relationships. Remember the saying "If at first you don't succeed, try, try again." You may feel you want to give up, but don't. Regroup, rethink, and try again.

> A friend is one who knows you as you are, understands where you've been, accepts who you've become, and still gently invites you to grow.
>
> Pat Moody, author

Friendship

t has been said that a *very* lucky person has three to four good friends at any given time in his or her life. True friends are hard to find, and even harder to keep! Many of us approach friendship as if it just happens, and, in some cases, it does. Think about your best friend. How did you meet? Probably by chance. Unfortunately, chance can also cause you to drift apart.

List the qualities you look for in a friend. _____
_____
_____
_____
_____
_____

With a group of friends or classmates, discuss the characteristics you listed and generate a list of common characteristics you all look for in a friend.

Discuss whether you possess any, some, or all of these characteristics. _____
_____
_____

_____

_____

_____

_____

_____

You can probably tell by looking at these lists that being a good friend takes work. Remember, to have a good friend you need first to be a good friend.

Friendships in college sometimes take on dimensions that you may not have experienced in previous relationships. Your new friends may be your roommates, classmates, varsity team members, or fellow employees. They may have backgrounds very different from yours. In your new environment you will likely encounter all kinds of new situations. Read the following scenarios. Answer the questions following each scenario.

■ SCENARIO #1 Sally and Marianna were first-semester roommates. They hit it off immediately during orientation and became friends fast. The first couple of weeks of their acquaintance were wonderful. One Friday night they both had their first college date. They prepared for their dates together, eagerly anticipating the evening. Sally arrived home later than Marianna and walked into their room to find Marianna and her date lying in bed, obviously very involved with one another. Sally was embarrassed. She quickly excused herself and spent a very uncomfortable few hours in the downstairs lounge. Later, Marianna acted as if nothing out of the ordinary had transpired. Sally followed her lead, and they went about life as usual. Over the next month Marianna continued to bring dates back to the room for intimate encounters, and Sally became very familiar with the downstairs lounge. Sally was disillusioned with her new friend and angry about having to spend so much time out of her room.

If you were Sally, how would you react in this situation? _____

_____

_____

_____

If you were Marianna, how would you react? _____

_____

_____

_____

■ SCENARIO #2 José and Terry were high school friends. They went to the same school, played on the same teams, and even double-dated. After graduating from high school, José decided to attend the local community college and Terry opted to go to work for his father's company. Because of their hectic schedules and new environments they weren't able to spend as much time together as they once had. José was making a whole new circle of friends, but he didn't want to exclude his best friend Terry, so he invited Terry along whenever he could. Terry always accepted José's invitation, but once he was with José and José's new friends, he became sullen, argumentative, and difficult to deal with. Terry began to put down José's new friends, calling them uppity and warning José that he would become like them if he didn't watch out. Terry's behaviour hurt José and placed him in a difficult position. José didn't want to turn his back on his new friends because they were so much a part of his new life, but at the same time he cared deeply about his relationship with Terry.

If you were José, how would you deal with this situation? _____

_____

_____

_____

_____

If you were Terry, how would you feel about your relationship with José?

_____

_____

_____

_____

Loneliness

> The worst solitude is to be destitute of sincere friendship.
>
> Francis Bacon,
> author

Developing friends helps you to develop your sense of community and allows you to minimize the feelings of loneliness that so many college and university students experience. Having friends does not mean that you will not be lonely, but friends can help you to deal with loneliness. Loneliness is especially common among first-year students. Here are some suggestions on how to get through the periods of loneliness you may experience.

1. Join a campus club or activity that involves one of your hobbies or interests.

2. Go to the orientation activities that most colleges sponsor.

3. Volunteer at one of the organizations sponsored by your department or school.

4. Ask one of your classmates to be a study partner. You could suggest meeting after each class to discuss the day's lecture, readings, and activities.

5. Offer to serve on a college committee.

6. Get a part-time job in the field you are studying.

If these activities don't seem to work for you, if your feelings of loneliness are intensifying and causing you to become depressed, consider making an appointment with one of the counsellors on campus. You can check the student handbook for names and numbers or ask Student Services to direct you to the appropriate person. These feelings are normal; the key is not to stay in this state of loneliness, but to be proactive and deal with the situation. Counsellors are trained to help students do just that.

Love Relationships

There are many types and degrees of love relationships. The love between two old friends differs tremendously from the passion of two lovers. Love can be as relaxing and comfortable as an easy chair or as tumultuous and exhilarating as any roller-coaster ride. The way love is manifested in a relationship does not necessarily attest to the degree or intensity of the love.

For example, Charles and Harriet have been married 63 years. On the surface their relationship resembles that of the odd couple; they bicker and disagree about everything from religion to politics. Yet, if you were to take a closer look at the relationship, you would notice the way Charles' eyes follow Harriet whenever she is in the same room with him, and the way Harriet never passes within arm's reach of Charles without lightly brushing him. Asked about their lives

> Love is patient, love is kind. It does not envy, it does not boast, it is not proud. It is not rude, it is not self-seeking, it is not easily angered, it keeps no record of wrongs. Love does not delight in evil but rejoices with the truth. It always protects, always trusts, always hopes, and always perseveres.
>
> 1 Corinthians 13:4–7

together, they share that they have managed to stay together for so long because they have allowed their love to change, and as their love has changed over the years, they have not felt challenged or threatened or less loved. They accepted the fact that as they changed individually, they also needed to change as a couple.

Regardless of the kind of love relationship we are in, we need to allow that relationship to change. Change is the only constant in our world and therefore the only constant in love.

Most of you have experienced love in a relationship. Some of you have felt the strong love of a close friendship; others have experienced the dizzy exhilaration of first love; still others may have experienced the deep love that comes only after spending a great deal of time with a partner. You may have experienced many of the peaks and valleys associated with marriage. Or you may have had a very close and loving relationship with parents or siblings. All the love relationships you have experienced or hope to experience have a few things in common. Loving someone means caring about that person's happiness, trying to understand and to be understood by that person, and giving as well as receiving emotional support. Most love relationships involve intimacy to some degree. Intimacy is not synonymous with sex; it may or may not involve sexual relations. Intimacy refers to the emotional openness that usually develops over time between two people who love each other. Intimacy allows people to share hopes and dreams as well as pain and sorrows.

Some of you will meet and fall in love with your lifelong partner in college, and the ritual you will most likely use to become acquainted is dating. Keep the following tips in mind when you begin dating a person:

- Don't go out alone with a stranger; go out in a group until you are better acquainted with your date.

- Make sure someone knows with whom you are going out, where you are going, and the approximate time you'll return; call that person if your plans change.

- Have your own transportation, so that you can leave if you are uncomfortable.

- Don't go to someone's home unless you know that person very well.

- Establish a friendship before you try a relationship.

Sexuality

Today you are faced with a profusion of questions concerning human sexuality. In this section we will discuss sexual behaviour, sexual harassment, rape, sexually transmitted diseases, and birth control. These discussions will lay a foundation from which you can make your own decisions regarding sexual activity. An important component to responsible decision making is your own feelings. No one can tell you what or how to feel. No one can make decisions about sexual activity for you. You have to make them yourself. In a world that is becoming more and more sexually permissive, it's still okay to say no to something that makes you uncomfortable. It's still okay to be a virgin. Your sexuality is not dictated by societal beliefs, preferences of your family and friends, or what the media present as normal sexual behaviour. It is governed by your own heartfelt beliefs and attitudes.

> **Your sexuality is governed by your own heartfelt beliefs and attitudes.**

Sexual Behaviour

When a relationship is based on romantic interest, sexual activity generally becomes an issue (sexual activity can also be an issue when romance is not involved). The degree of sexual activity within a relationship spans the spectrum from total abstinence to intercourse. You may face situations in college or university that require you to make decisions about your sexual behaviour. It is important to evaluate where you stand on this important issue so that when you are in a situation, your course of action will be based on a solid understanding of what you believe and how you feel. You want to avoid having a situation or set of circumstances dictate your actions. Making good decisions about your sexual behaviour is critical not only to your college career but also to your life.

Students often cite increasing awareness of sexually transmitted diseases (STDs) and

AIDS as well as a sense of spirituality or adherence to religious beliefs as reasons for abstaining from intercourse. However, according to recent studies, some degree of sexual activity is almost universal among college and university students (Rathus and Fichner-Rathus, 1994). The form of sexual activity varies. Some students who want to abstain from sexual intercourse masturbate. Once associated with a terrible stigma and myths connecting it to blindness, sterility, and mental disease, masturbation is now considered a normal response to normal sexual urges. Other students who choose to abstain from intercourse use petting (touching or massaging another's genitals) as a means of obtaining sexual pleasure without engaging in intercourse. Some people consider oral-genital manipulation a form of petting.

Although many students abstain from sexual intercourse, a large percentage of students do engage in intercourse. If you are one of the many who are currently engaging in sexual intercourse or are planning to do so, you will need to be responsible for your own protection from unwanted pregnancy and sexually transmitted diseases. Don't assume that your partner will be prepared—that assumption could be dangerous. The most common methods of birth control are presented here. For more information on birth control, contact your health centre, a family practitioner, or a gynecologist. Information on STDs is given in the next section.

> Don't assume that your partner will be prepared—that assumption could be dangerous.

Celibacy—abstention from sexual activity with another individual. This form of birth control is 100 percent effective.

Outercourse—the practice of oral-genital sex and mutual masturbation. This form of birth control is 100 percent effective as long as the male does not ejaculate near the vagina. This form of birth control does not provide protection from sexually transmitted diseases. To avoid the transferral of an STD, a condom should be used on the penis or a dental dam on the vaginal opening.

The Pill—the most widely used form of birth control, the Pill is an oral preparation of the hormones estrogen and progestin prescribed by a physician. The Pill works by fooling a woman's body into believing it is pregnant, thus preventing conception. Pills are available in many different dosages and for a cycle of 21 to 28 days, depending on the type. The Pill does not prevent STDs and should be used in conjunction with a latex condom and spermicide to avoid their transmission.

Diaphragm—a round, flexible disk that is inserted into the vagina to cover the cervix and prevent the passage of sperm into the uterus. A woman must be fitted for a diaphragm by a physician. Diaphragms should be used in conjunction with a spermicide.

Intrauterine device (IUD)—a device that is inserted into the uterus by a physician and remains in place for a year or more. The IUD prevents fertilized eggs from becoming implanted after they enter the uterus. An IUD must be inserted by a physician.

Condom—a sheath, generally latex, worn over the penis to prevent the ejaculated semen from entering the vagina. Condoms also prevent the spread of STDs. Condoms are available at pharmacies.

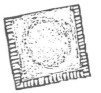

Female condom—a single-use, soft, loose-fitting polyurethane sheath. The female condom is a relatively new form of birth control currently under review in Canada. It is designed as one unit with two diaphragm-like rings. One ring, positioned inside the sheath, serves as an insertion mechanism and internal anchor. The other ring, which remains outside the vagina when the device is inserted, protects the labia and the base of the penis from infection. Female condoms are available at pharmacies.

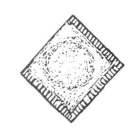

Spermicides—substances that are inserted into the vagina to kill sperm. The most common spermicides take the form of foams, suppositories, jellies, and creams. Spermicides are available at pharmacies.

Coitus interruptus—a method of birth control in which the penis is withdrawn from the vagina prior to ejaculation. This method is ineffective because many males release small amounts of semen during sexual intercourse prior to ejaculation, and impregnation can result from this small amount.

Rhythm method—abstaining from sexual intercourse during the period of the menstrual cycle when ovulation occurs. This method of birth control is unreliable because there is no foolproof way to predict ovulation.

Sexually Transmitted Diseases

Sexually transmitted diseases (STDs) are diseases that are generally transmitted through vaginal or anal intercourse or oral sex. Although they are most commonly spread through sexual contact, some can be transmitted through related nonsexual activities. (For example, human immunodeficiency virus, HIV, can be contracted by using contaminated needles, and crabs can be contracted through contact with contaminated bed linens or towels.)

It is estimated that one in five Canadians will contact an STD during his or her lifetime. The majority of these cases occur in people under the age of 25.

HUMAN IMMUNODEFICIENCY VIRUS (HIV) AND THE ACQUIRED IMMUNE DEFICIENCY SYNDROME (AIDS)

Did you know that . . .

- According to recent data, HIV, the virus suspected of causing AIDS, can strike anyone, even young, non-drug using heterosexuals

- AIDS kills by disabling the body's defenses against life-threatening illnesses

- As of April 1996, 12 670 cases of AIDS had been reported in Canada.

- Heterosexual transmission of AIDS accounts for three of four AIDS cases worldwide

- In Canada, AIDS is increasing more rapidly among women than among men

- Your behaviour, not the groups to which you belong, determines your risk of contracting HIV (Nevid, 1995)

AIDS is a syndrome of symptoms. Its symptoms may not arise for as long as ten years after a person is infected. The HIV virus invades the body and systematically breaks down the immune system, disabling the body's ability to fight off infections and diseases. AIDS itself does not kill. It is the body's inability to fight simple illnesses when the immune system has been destroyed that results in death. The disease has several stages:

- HIV positive (HIV has entered the body)

- HIV positive but asymptomatic (the person is a carrier of the virus, but shows no symptoms related to AIDS)

- AIDS symptomatic (the person suffers from several symptoms, for example, swollen glands, fatigue, fever, and diarrhea with intermittent weight loss)

- Full-blown AIDS (the person suffers from fevers; weight loss; swollen lymph glands in the neck, underarm, or groin; fatigue; diarrhea; blemishes that won't go away; weakness; dry cough; headaches; coordination problems; confusion; or infections of the skin). A person with full-blown AIDS can no longer fight off everyday illnesses, which therefore might very likely cause the person's death.

A physician first identified AIDS in 1980, yet the impact it has had in that short time has been enormous. When AIDS first hit the scene, many people labelled it the "gay plague" and dismissed it as something that didn't concern them. This approach played a large part in creating the epidemic from which we are now suffering. Consider these words: AIDS is an equal opportunity killer; it knows no boundaries; it cares not about race, money, age, gender, sexual orientation, marriage, or love. AIDS does not discriminate.

HIV can be transmitted by

- Sharing needles, syringes, cookers, eyedroppers, water, or cotton when shooting drugs

- Having anal, vaginal, or oral sex without the protection of a barrier such as a condom

- Receiving a transfusion of infected blood (chances of this happening are very slim)

- An infected mother to her unborn child

HIV is not contracted by

- Having everyday contact with infected people—in school, at work, or socializing

- Swimming in a pool where a person who is HIV positive is swimming

- Being bitten by a mosquito that has previously bitten an infected person

- Clothes, telephones, toilet seats, or eating utensils that have previously been used by a person with AIDS

- Hugging, kissing, or touching a person with AIDS

HIV/AIDS is a very complex syndrome, and discoveries about the syndrome are made daily. It is our fervent wish that by the time you read this section, a cure will have been found. Unfortunately, as we write it, many of our students are suffering from the impact of AIDS on our community. You can help stop this plague by following some guidelines.

1. Abstain from risky activities.

2. Practise safer sex.

   - Use latex condoms during vaginal, anal, or oral sex. Be sure the condoms do not have an expired date of use and are not yellowed or in any way damaged.

   - Do not use petroleum jelly (Vaseline) for lubrication—it breaks down latex condoms.

   - Use a spermicide containing nonoxynol-9, and insist on latex barriers when engaging in vaginal, anal, or oral sex.

   - Avoid having multiple or anonymous sex partners.

   - Avoid having sex with a partner who you know has had multiple or anonymous sex partners.

   - Do not mix alcohol or drugs with sex; they can lead to irresponsible behaviour.

3. Don't use intravenous drugs. If you are addicted, are not in a recovery program, and are "shooting" drugs, use the following guidelines.

   - Don't share needles or syringes.

   - Don't share cookers.

   - Don't share cotton, water, or eyedroppers.

   - Don't use needles or syringes passed around in shooting galleries.

4. If you are scheduled for surgery, donate your own blood prior to the operation.

5. If your job places you at risk for coming in contact with the body fluids of a person who is HIV positive, follow safety practices to avoid contamination.

OTHER STDS

Although AIDS has received widespread attention, other STDs, such as gonorrhea, syphilis, chlamydia (nongonococcal urethritis), and genital herpes, are extremely prevalent among college and university students. The following paragraphs present a preliminary discussion of these diseases. For a more comprehensive overview of STDs, you might want to consult your local health centre or your library for a book on sexually transmitted diseases.

■ GONORRHEA Also referred to as "the clap" and "the drip," gonorrhea is one of the most commonly diagnosed STDs in Canada. It is caused by the gonococcus bacterium. Gonorrhea is extremely contagious and is transmitted primarily through unprotected vaginal, oral, and anal sexual activity or from an infected mother to a newborn during delivery.

Symptoms of a gonorrheal infection for men are a thick, yellow-white penile discharge and a burning sensation during urination that develops two to nine days after sexual contact with an infected person. Symptoms are likely to be similar for women who have them—a discharge and a burning sensation during urination. However, it is estimated that as many as nine out of ten infected women have no symptoms at all. Undetected, the gonococcus can live in the vagina, cervix, and fallopian tubes for years and continue to infect a woman's sexual partners.

Treatment with the antibiotic Ceftriaxone is very successful and usually results in full recovery. Untreated, the bacteria spread through the genital and urinary tracts and can cause infertility, pelvic inflammatory disease, abdominal pain, fever, headaches, and nausea.

■ SYPHILIS Syphilis is transmitted primarily through unprotected vaginal, oral, and anal sexual activity or from an infected mother to her fetus. Syphilis has four developmental stages. In the first stage, primary syphilis, the infected individual suffers from a lesion, often referred to as a *chancre*. The second stage, secondary syphilis, develops one month to a year following primary syphilis. Many people exhibit no symptoms during this stage; others may develop a skin rash, whitish patches in the mouth or throat, temporary baldness, a low-grade fever, headaches, swollen glands, or large, moist sores around the mouth and genitals.

Latent syphilis produces no signs or symptoms, although the disease is still very active. During this third stage of syphilis, the spirochetes are slowly invading organs in the infected person's body. For the first two to four years of this stage there may be recurring, highly contagious lesions of the skin and mucous membranes. After two years, the infected person no longer transmits the disease to his or her sexual partners. The final stage of syphilis, late syphilis, occurs 10 to 20 years after the beginning of the latent period. Syphilis that reaches this stage causes the most harm. Late syphilis can result in death from heart damage or a ruptured aorta, or it can cause progressive brain or spinal cord damage leading to blindness, insanity, or paralysis.

Penicillin is the treatment of choice for syphilis. In the early stages, a small dose of penicillin will kill the disease. In later stages, a more intense therapy is needed.

■ CHLAMYDIA Although most people are less familiar with chlamydia than with gonorrhea or syphilis, chlamydia is more prevalent than these other diseases. It is the most common cause of non-gonococcal urethritis, an inflammation of the urethra. Chlamydia is transmitted through unprotected vaginal, oral, and anal sexual activity. Chlamydia may also cause eye infections if the parasite comes in contact with the eye. The symptoms of chlamydia are pain during urination, tenderness in the genitals, and a mild vaginal or penile discharge. If untreated in women, chlamydia can lead to pelvic inflammatory disease and scarring of the fallopian tubes, which in turn result in infertility. The antibiotics doxycycline, tetracycline, and erythromycin provide effective treatment.

■ GENITAL HERPES Genital, or type 2, herpes is a form of herpes simplex that causes lesions or blisters on the skin and mucous membranes. In Canada it is transmitted almost exclusively through sexual contact. People infected with genital herpes develop itching lesions on the genitals and sometimes in the pubic area or on the buttocks. Participation in oral-genital manipulation with an infected person can cause blisters to develop in the throat and mouth. The initial attack lasts two to four weeks and then the lesions disappear.

Genital herpes has no cure—flare-ups of blisters and lesions can occur throughout a person's life. Because irritating attacks reoccur for years, people infected with genital herpes may suffer more emotionally and psychologically than do people infected with curable STDs. Treatment is symptomatic and aimed at alleviating the discomfort associated with the blisters. Treatment includes anesthetic cream, cold compresses, cool baths with skim milk or salt water, avoidance of hot showers or baths, topical ointments, exposure to light and ultrasonic waves, and wearing cotton instead of nylon underwear. Although genital herpes never goes away, the frequency and severity of attacks lessen over time.

Read the following scenarios. Answer the questions following each scenario.

■ SCENARIO #3 Yumiko and Larry are both 19, and they have been in a relationship for eight months. They have decided that they are committed to one another, and they want to have sexual relations. They are having trouble coming to an agreement about being tested for HIV, the virus that is suspected of causing AIDS. Both have been sexually active in the past, and both are concerned about what the other might be bringing, albeit unknowingly, to the relationship. Yumiko does not feel comfortable with merely practising safer sex. Larry is insulted that Yumiko feels this way. Still, he wants to stay in the relationship, so he is considering the test.

What you would do if you were Larry? If you were Yumiko? _____

_____

_____

_____

_____

_____

_____

■ SCENARIO #4 Jessica and Saul have had a sexually active relationship for six months. Both have been moderately sexually active for the past three years. They practise safer sex most of the time. Recently, Saul experienced a burning sensation while urinating, which he discussed with Jessica. When the burning sensation subsided a few days later, they decided that it must have been a bug and that they did not need to worry about it.

What would you do if you were Jessica? If you were Saul? _____

_____

_____

_____

_____

_____

_____

■ SCENARIO #5 Beth has genital herpes. She contracted the disease from a relationship she had in high school two years ago. Since the initial outbreak, she has been symptom-free. Although Beth understands that genital herpes is incurable, she has continued to have sexually intimate relationships with a number of men. She has not discussed her condition with her lovers, because she fears that they will reject her.

_____

_____

_____

_____

_____

_____

_____

Discuss your answers with your classmates. Although many of you may know what you need to do to make socially responsible decisions regarding your sexual behaviour, others may find it difficult to put responsible decision making into practice.

Sexual Harassment

It would be nice if colleges and universities were immune to problems of sexual harassment, and we fostered an atmosphere in which such behaviour is not tolerated. But the cold, hard facts prove otherwise. At many colleges, sexual harassment takes place among students, between students and faculty, among faculty, and between faculty and administration. The federal government defines sexual harassment as deliberate or repeated unsolicited verbal comments, gestures, or physical contact of a sexual nature that is considered to be unwelcome by the recipient. The Ontario Human Rights Commission adopted a policy in 1983 which describes sexual harassment as including

- verbal abuse or threats

- unwelcome remarks, jokes, innuendos or taunting

- practical jokes which cause awkwardness or embarrassment

- unwelcome invitations or requests, whether indirect or explicit, or intimidation

- leering or other gestures

- unnecessary physical contact such as touching, patting, pinching

- physical assault

Consider the following scenario.

■ SCENARIO #6 Damian, a basketball player, is taking a class from Professor Maxine Moore. Professor Moore has repeatedly asked Damian to stay after class to discuss his grades. During several of those conferences she has made a reference to her sex life or to Damian's. Because she is his teacher, Damian's response has been to laugh about the remarks and go along with her joking. Recently, Professor Moore has begun to touch Damian and to allude to a possible relationship between them. Damian is not interested in a personal relationship, but he is fearful of putting his grade in jeopardy. He needs a good grade in this class to maintain his eligibility to play basketball.

Is Professor Moore sexually harassing Damian? What should he do?

_____

_____

_____

_____

_____

_____

In a classroom discussion, find out how others in your class feel about this situation. Do they agree with you about how Damian should react? If not, why do their suggestions differ from yours?

If you are faced with a situation that you believe is sexual harassment, you can take several steps to protect yourself.

1. Make a conscious effort to keep interactions between you and the person harassing you as impersonal as possible.

2. Avoid being alone with the person harassing you. If that person is your professor, bring a friend with you to meetings and arrange to meet in a classroom either right before or right after class.

3. Keep a record of the harassment in case you have to bring formal charges.

4. Tell the harasser that you believe he or she is harassing you and you want the behaviour to stop. Be very specific, so that the person knows what you perceive as harassment.

5. Tell your academic advisor or a campus counsellor about the events. Seek their counsel.

6. See a lawyer. Sexual harassment is against the law, and you may need to bring formal charges.

Sexual Assault

The most severe form of sexual harassment is rape. The term *rape* refers to sexual penetration by means of intimidation, force, or fraud for aggressive and/or sexual reasons. Rape is a cause of fear and concern among college students, and date, or acquaintance, rape has become as much a concern as rape by strangers. You can take steps to lessen the possibility of rape. To decrease the chances of sexual assault by a stranger:

1. Know where campus security is located and be familiar with campus security procedures; keep emergency phone numbers handy.

2. Travel with a friend if you are at the college after dark.

3. If you're staying late, move your car close to the building before it gets dark.

4. List only your first initials in the phone book or on your mailbox.

5. Be aware of yourself and of your surroundings; have a plan for what to do if you are attacked.

6. Vary your route and walk in groups whenever possible.

7. Stay on well-lighted paths, sidewalks, and streets.

8. If a car pulls up beside you, stay at least an arm's length away; *never* get into the car.

9. If you are afraid, yell "No!" or "Call 911." "No" makes it clear that there is a problem, and makes it more likely that a passerby will intervene; "911" alerts people to call for help.

10. Use dead-bolt locks on your doors.

11. Keep windows locked.

12. Have your keys ready when you approach your car door or home.

13. Drive with your doors locked and windows up. If you are driving alone, try to time your approach to lights to avoid having to come to a complete stop. It is more difficult for someone to get into a moving car.

14. Always check the identification of people such as utility workers, security officers, or salespeople who come to your door. Keep your door locked and ask for the phone number of their dispatcher, so that you can check on them. If they refuse to provide the number, do not let them in.

You can take steps to lessen the possibility of rape.

15. Check the backseat of your car before getting in.

To decrease the chances of acquaintance or date rape:

1. Until you are very familiar with your date, avoid being alone together or going to secluded places; double-date, group date, or frequent familiar places.

2. Stay sober. It is important to remain clear-headed about your sexual encounters. It is also considered rape if a man has sexual intercourse with a woman who has passed out.

3. Be very clear about your sexual intentions.

4. Understand that when your partner says no, it means no!

5. Tell a friend whom you are out with, where you are going and when you expect to return home.

6. Use your own transportation until you are comfortable with your date. If you don't have transportation, carry the number of a cab company and cab fare with you.

Consider the following scenario:

■ SCENARIO #7 Chantal and Steve meet on the first day of class. During the next couple of weeks they sit together. One day Chantal invites Steve out for an evening of fun. During the evening both have too much to drink. Chantal becomes aroused and starts kissing Steve and dancing seductively with him. She invites him back to her room for a nightcap. When they get there, Steve is sexually aggressive and takes off Chantal's clothes. She protests. He coaxes. She acquiesces. They lie on the bed together kissing. He moves toward intercourse. She says no. She says no a number of times, but in his excitement, he doesn't pay any attention to what she is saying.

How would you have reacted if you were Chantal? If you were Steve?

_____

_____

_____

_____

_____

_____

_____

In class, discuss the reactions of your classmates to this scenario.

College is an experience fraught with new situations, new relationships, and new behaviours. It is our hope that this chapter will help you think about the circumstances you may find yourself in and prompt you to make responsible decisions.

CORNERSTONES for getting along with others

- Learn to recognize and develop the important components of relationships with individuals and with communities.

- Understand the importance of maintaining close friendships.

- Combat feelings of loneliness by getting involved with an organization or talking with a friend.

- Understand how you feel about your sexuality and about sexual relationships.

- Learn about STDs so that you can protect yourself from them.

- Know how to recognize and stop sexual harassment.

- Know what rape is and take steps to protect yourself from rape and sexual assault.

The one minute journal

n a minute or less, jot down one major idea you learned
from this chapter.

11

Look to this day!

For it is life, the very life of life.

In its brief course

Lie all the verities and realities

of your existence:

The bliss of growth;

The glory of action;

The splendor of achievement;

For yesterday is but a dream,

And tomorrow is only a vision,

But today, well lived, makes every

yesterday

a dream of happiness, And every

tomorrow a vision of hope.

Look well, therefore, to this

day!

Kalidasa, *ancient Sanskrit poem*

Staying Fit: A Personal Plan for Wellness

onathan was the typical college student. He was a full-time student, worked part-time at a small restaurant on weekends, and was a member of the student association, among other commitments. Despite his busy schedule, he maintained a decent grade point average (GPA). When I first met Jonathan, I was impressed by his ability to keep so many balls in the air successfully. As I got to know him, I learned that his busy life

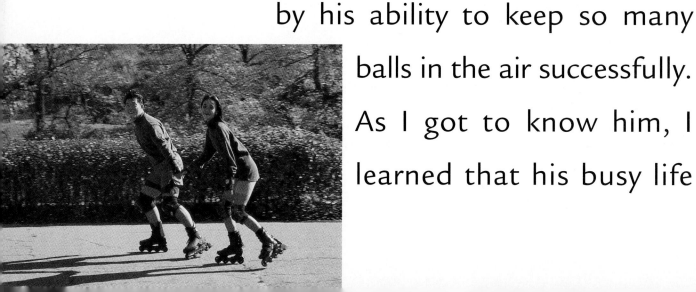

left no time for any fitness activity and led to many fast food meals on the go. He tried to cope with stress by being the life of the party whenever he went out with his friends. Jonathan had no serious problems.

The problems he did have were related to his frequent illnesses, not serious illnesses, but a constant battle with the flu, or a cold, or strep throat. It seemed that Jonathan would no sooner get over one illness than another would come along. Jonathan's illnesses affected his life negatively. When he was not sick he could manage quite well, but when he was ill it was difficult for him to juggle his many activities. If you've ever been caught in a juggling act with your own schedule, you understand what happens when one ball drops—they all drop. Jonathan's life was a series of ups and downs. When he was healthy, everything was great, but the moment he got sick, his house of cards would crumble and he would fall into a downward spiral from which he had difficulty recovering.

When he was healthy, everything was great.

Probably many of you can relate to Jonathan's saga; he is a perfect example of the average student. Most of you maintain a schedule designed to kill a horse, don't always take care of yourselves, and then end up behind the eight ball when you become ill. It seems that the pace of the '90s sets us up for this vicious cycle.

If you are always vowing to start eating right, if you have every intention of making use of your college's exercise facility but haven't gotten around to it, if you've been fighting a cold or flu recently, sit back, prop your feet up, and we'll take a journey together down the wellness highway to see if we can come up with a few suggestions that will help you on your quest for wellness.

What Does It Mean to Be Healthy?

Most people consider themselves healthy. They believe that if they are not sick, they are healthy. However, the absence of illness does not mean that you are healthy, it simply means that you are temporarily without illness.

The World Health Organization defines health as "not merely the absence of disease or infirmity, but a state of complete physical, mental, and social well-being." Realistically, health is a continuum: on one end you have death, and on the other you have excellent health. Most students are somewhere in the middle of the continuum, experiencing neither excellent health nor debilitating diseases. Often students slip slowly into a state of unhealthiness, which, if ignored, could lead to serious health problems. Most of us take our health for granted. We place undue stress on ourselves and assume that our bodies will continue to take this abuse. This chapter will afford you the opportunity to review your own health status and to explore some issues that might help you to lead a healthier lifestyle. At the end of this chapter you should be able to

- Determine your own health status

- Understand the key issues to developing a healthy diet

- Develop a personal plan for wellness

- Understand the importance of activity in your life

- Develop an activity schedule for your college years

- Determine your own mental state and recognize the warning signs that require professional help

A Holistic Approach to Wellness

You cannot divide your approach to wellness into specific categories because all aspects of your health are interrelated. You cannot address your mental health without taking into account your physical well-being; you cannot talk about fitness without including nutrition in your discussion. If your body, mind, and soul are to function in a healthy manner, then your approach to wellness should be balanced. You need a holistic approach to wellness; that is, you need to look at yourself as a whole rather than as parts. The holistic view of wellness focuses on self-responsibility in all areas of health. You will find in this chapter specific exercises designed to help you take a proactive stance on your own health and to make some changes that will give you the best chance for a healthy and successful college experience.

1. My health is important to me right now. *1 2 3 4 5*

2. The state of my health is important to my future plans. *1 2 3 4 5*

3. I find it easy to take care of myself. *1 2 3 4 5*

4. I can recognize the signs of getting myself run down. *1 2 3 4 5*

5. I know what to do to take care of myself physically. *1 2 3 4 5*

6. I know how to take care of my mental well-being. *1 2 3 4 5*

7. I understand about a spiritual component to my wellness. *1 2 3 4 5*

8. Taking time to nurture my soul is important. *1 2 3 4 5*

9. I know where to turn to for help if I'm mentally or physically sick. *1 2 3 4 5*

10. I have a wellness plan. *1 2 3 4 5*

5 = Strongly Agree

4 = Agree

3 = Don't Know

2 = Disagree

1 = Strongly Disagree

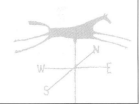

A SELF-ASSESSMENT Total your points from these ten questions. Refer to the following rating scale to determine where you stand in relation to dealing with wellness.

0–10   You have a great deal of difficulty with personal issues of wellness.

11–20   You have a greater than normal number of problems with wellness issues.

21–30   You have a considerable number of problems with wellness issues.

31–40   You have some problems with wellness issues.

41–50   You have a healthy approach to personal wellness issues.

Now, refer to your journal and respond in writing to your findings. Consider the following questions when writing in your journal.

1. Why am I experiencing difficulty with wellness issues?

2. With what areas in particular am I especially having difficulty?

3. I suffer (or do not suffer) from poor health.

The Mind

The mind is an incredibly complex organ. The health industry has not begun to tap the awesome power the mind has over a person's physical health. Very basic studies have shown that the mind has a vital link to physical health. For example, when patients were given placebos instead of medication, patients who trusted their doctors and their prescribed treatments were more likely to report positive results from the placebos than were patients who did not trust their doctors or their prescribed treatment. There are thousands of anecdotal reports of people who have overcome tremendous physical illnesses through positive thinking and believing that they could overcome the illness. There is no question that the mind has power over the body, but just how and why are still a mystery.

Many of us tend to ignore mental health unless there is a serious problem. We are quick to visit a doctor if we have a broken bone, but we are much less willing to seek professional help if we are experiencing emotional distress. There is still a stigma attached to seeking professional counselling in regard to our mental well-being; yet mental health is often more important than physical health because of the important part it plays in maintaining physical well-being.

Mental health, like physical health, is not simply the absence of mental illness. People who are psychologically healthy

- Have a positive sense of self-worth

- Are determined to make an effort to be healthy

- Can love and have meaningful relationships

- Understand reality and the limitations placed on them

- Have compassion for others

- Understand that the world does not revolve around them

Mental health, too, should be viewed as a continuum, ranging from excellent mental health, to suffering from minor mental illness, to life-threatening illnesses. Psychiatrist Karl Menninger developed a continuum to represent the range of psychological states, from optimal mental health to severe mental illness.

The keys to mental wellness are to understand what reality is, to be able to change and to adapt to that reality, and to be able to cope with changes over which you have no control. To be mentally healthy you must be in touch with your feelings, you must be able to understand what you are feeling and why you are feeling it, and you must

Level of Dysfunction	
Optimal Mental Health	Normal coping devices and ego control
Level 1	Hyperreactions; Anxiety; Nervousness; Minor physical symptoms
Level 2	Personality disorder; Phobias
Level 3	Social offenses; Open aggression; Violent acts
Level 4	Severe depression and despondency; Psychotic and bizarre behavior
Level 5	Severe psychological deterioration; Loss of will to live

be able to read your physical responses and trace them to mental thoughts and images.

1. Find a mirror in a place where you will not be disturbed for a few minutes. Determine whether your face is relaxed and smiling or fixed and tight. Pay attention to your heartbeat and to other muscles in your body.

2. Think of an incident in your life that made you angry, perhaps something a friend said or did or an injustice you experienced. Carefully think through the entire incident.

3. Now, look in the mirror again. Have your facial features changed? Has your heartbeat accelerated? Are your muscles tense?

List the physical changes you experienced while reliving this angry experience.

1. _____

2. _____

3. _____

4. _____

As you discuss these changes with your classmates, you will discover that many experienced the same physical changes. We all share similar physical responses to difficult situations: our muscles become tense, our heartbeat accelerates, our breathing becomes shallow and rapid, and our body temperature rises. It is important to understand that these changes take place and that if they remain undetected and ignored for long periods, they can lead to health problems.

I must love this miserable state I'm in, because I've chosen to stay there since a quarter past ten. I know my mind can only think of one thing at a time so I keep focusing on making misery mine. But what if I choose to find a better space, could imagination find peace in a private place?
Barbara Gray, *Life's Instruction Book for Women*, Vol. 2

Our physical feelings are a measure of our psychological well-being. Feelings of anxiety often lead us away from difficult or scary situations, just as feelings of warmth and security draw us into situations that provide comfort and love. Frequently, people who have suffered an emotional trauma cut themselves off from their feelings and refuse to acknowledge hurt, fear, sadness, or anger because of what these feelings will remind them of. Although ignoring such feelings may provide temporary relief, it leads to deeper psychological trauma in the long run.

As you learned in Chapter 3, one of the best ways to monitor your emotional well-being is to listen to your self-talk. Almost everyone keeps a running conversation going on in his or her head. What are you saying to yourself? Are you saying loving and affirming things? Are you beating yourself up emotionally? Over the next week, keep a list in your journal of things you hear yourself saying to you. Monitor what actions or surroundings elicit negative thoughts and self-degrading talk.

Once you have written a couple of days of conversations in your journal, decide to change the recording in your head. Make a list of positive things you can say about yourself.

_____

_____

_____

_____

_____

_____

_____

Copy this list, put it where you will see it often, and practise giving yourself a pep talk. If you're not good to yourself, why should anyone else be?

Depression

epression is used to describe feelings ranging from feeling blue to utter hopelessness. The use of "I'm depressed" to mean "I'm sad" or "I'm down" is a far cry from the illness of clinical depression. Depression is a sickness that can creep up on an individual and render that person helplessly lost if it is not detected and properly treated. Signs of depression include the following (Donatelle and Davis, 1994):

- lingering sadness

- inability to find joy in pleasure-giving activities

- loss of interest in work or school

- unexplainable fatigue

- sleep disorders, including insomnia or early-morning awakenings

- loss of sex drive

- withdrawal from friends and family

- feelings of hopelessness and worthlessness

- desire to die

If you are feeling depressed, but your depression seems minor or probably temporary, try some of these helpful hints for picking yourself up out of the blues.

1. Exercise. Exercise causes the release of endorphins, which help to stimulate you and give you a personal high.

2. Spend time talking with a good friend; share your thoughts and feelings.

3. Control your self-talk. If you're playing a negative tune, change to a positive song.

4. Do something special for yourself: Take a long walk in the park, watch a favourite movie, listen to a special CD, or eat a hot fudge sundae. It doesn't really matter what you do as long as it's something special.

5. Nurture yourself.

List special activities you could use to treat yourself when you are down or feeling

blue. _____

_____

_____

_____

_____

_____

_____

_____

Most students experience a slump from time to time, but if you suffer depression for an extended period or if you are having trouble pulling yourself out of a depression, you should seek professional counselling. Remember, we would all be better off if we sought help for our minds as quickly as we do for our bodies.

Make a list of the names and phone numbers of college resources that help students with psychological problems. _____

_____

_____

_____

_____

_____

Spirituality

> I believe in the sun—even when it does not shine; I believe in love—even when it is not shown; I believe in God—even when he does not speak.
>
> *Scratched on the wall of a house in Germany by a victim of the Holocaust*

The human being is an incredibly, insatiably inquisitive creature. Our quest for the greater meaning of life is equalled only by our quest for eternal life. For some, these two quests become one in the search for spiritual meaning. Some people find the true meaning of life in the teachings of Jesus Christ; others study the Koran or the teachings of Buddha or worship the wonder of Nature. Whether they follow a formal religion or not, people have their own beliefs about the universe, human nature, and the significance of life. How we approach our beliefs is related to our perception of our own spiritual nature, or the state of our soul.

Your time in higher education provides an outstanding opportunity for you to explore the true meaning of life. Many campus organizations can help you in your quest for spirituality. Take this opportunity to explore your spirituality and to provide food for your soul. To ignore this aspect of yourself is to shut off a potentially rich and wonderful source of joy.

Make a list of the campus organizations that are designed to help students in their spiritual quest. _____

_____

_____

_____

_____

_____

_____

Go with someone from your class to one of these places to talk with the members. Take some time to reflect in your journal on what you learned.

 **for mental health**

- Learn to recognize signs of depression.

- Make use of counselling services if you are suffering from depression.

- Make a practice of monitoring your self-talk.

- Learn to redirect negative thoughts.

- Develop your sense of spirituality.

What Influences Your Eating Habits?

Eating has become one of Canadians' favourite hobbies. Rather than eating to live, many of us live to eat. We socialize around food—dinner and a movie, pizza and a beer with friends, and so on. Virtually every holiday or celebration we observe has a food focus. Marketing firms have made millions of dollars from our preoccupation with food and its effect on our bodies. They understand that we eat for reasons far different than mere fulfillment of a biological need for nutrients.

Your personal food choices are derived from a blending of culture, religion, and family habits. As you start your life in university or college,

your eating habits may change dramatically. If you eat at the cafeteria, you may encounter familiar foods with different tastes; for example, your cafeteria's interpretation of turkey and dressing may differ greatly from what you knew at home. You may encounter other foods you've never tried. You may find yourself eating alone among strangers, when you were used to sitting down with parents or siblings. Or you may be used to eating solitary meals because of your family's hectic schedule, and now find yourself eating with hundreds of others.

At most colleges you can find things to eat 24 hours a day, and your new environment and friends will probably encourage a variety of new experiences with eating times and food choices. Just as college provides an opportunity to expand your mind, it provides an opportunity to expand your culinary repertoire.

Discuss some of the changes that have already occurred in your eating habits.

_____

_____

_____

_____

Do you see these changes as positive or negative? Discuss with fellow classmates their perceptions of their new dining habits.

As you enter into this new stage of your life, you need to understand that your body will be undergoing tremendous biological stress. The hormonal changes that tend to coincide with the traditional university age, 18 to 22, will cause many of you to experience an alteration in your basal metabolic rate; you will no longer be able to eat like a horse and not gain a pound. At the same time, your lifestyle in college is likely to be more sedentary than your lifestyle prior to college. As a result, you may well end up gaining additional weight you weren't planning on.

If you are a nontraditional student, you'll find that entering college places new demands on your body as well. Perhaps in your effort to juggle family, work, friends, and classes you spend more time eating on the run (if the staff at the local fast-food restaurant know you by name, chances are you are eating on the run a lot). You may munch while you are studying. It is common for nontraditional as well as traditional students to experience a change in their eating habits and consequently in their weight on entering college or university.

Unfortunately, students, particularly female students, tend to react to this weight gain in an unhealthy way. If you try to diet away those pounds, you'll only place added wear and tear on yourself both emotionally and physically. The only way to take proper care of yourself is to eat the right kinds of foods and the right amount of food and not get caught in the "thin is in" movement that has swept the nation.

Most Canadians have an unrealistic notion of their optimum weight. The average female who appears on television or in magazines wears a size 6. Only 15 percent of the female population is physically capable of ever being a size 6, yet this is the standard that most women hold themselves up to. According to Health Canada's 1991 report on the health of Canada's youth, 81 percent of 10-year-old girls were on a diet because they thought they were too fat. Our society is slowly creating a population of weight-neurotic people consumed with maintaining a certain size because of the unrealistic demands placed on them by the media.

Learn to eat right by listening to your body. First of all, understand why you are eating. Are you eating because you are hungry?

List the time of day and events associated with when you eat. _____

_____

_____

_____

_____

_____

_____

Do you see some trends? Start responding to what your body is telling you. Eat only when your body tells you to. And try to eat things that are good for you.

You eat to provide your body with nutrients—proteins, fats, carbohydrates, vitamins, and minerals. These nutrients enable your body to function. Of the many guides available to help you make the correct choices of foods, probably the most widely used is Canada's Food Guide to Healthy Eating published by Health Canada. It is an excellent guide because it tells and *shows* you how many servings of foods to eat.

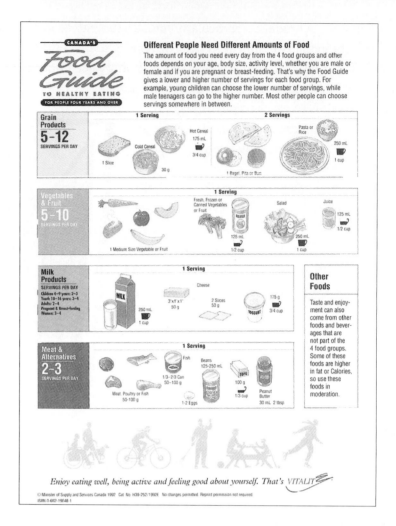

Canada's Food Guide was designed with the following five goals in mind.

1. To address current nutrition issues.

2. To provide consumers with updated information.

3. To recognize changes Canadians are already making in their eating patterns.

4. To provide consumers with practical, realistic guidance in selecting foods.

5. To present a new design to reflect newer healthy eating messages.

Remember, you don't have to be a fanatic to eat healthily. Try to balance your food intake. This does not mean that you can't eat fast food—it simply means you shouldn't have a steady diet of fast food. If you know you're going to be on the run from class to meetings and back to class with very little time for a healthy meal, pack a piece of fruit or a box of juice in your backpack. If you carry some healthy choices for snacks with you, you will be less likely to stop by the vending machine for a bag of chips and a can of pop. But if you do go for the chips and pop, don't beat yourself up—enjoy it, and then try to balance it out with an apple or juice later on. The key to healthy eating is education. If you understand what constitutes healthy dining, then you will be able to make the right choices to balance your eating habits.

Based on the information you have read about nutrition, establish four goals for improving your eating habits.

1. _____

2. _____

3. _____

4. _____

CORNERSTONES for a better diet

- Limit your fat intake to less than 30 percent of your total calories.

- Eat a diet high in complex carbohydrates.

- Limit your protein intake to 15 percent of your total calories.

- Eat a variety of foods.

- Avoid eating too many empty calories (chocolate bars, pop, alcohol).

- Limit your sodium (salt) intake to no more than 3,000 milligrams per day.

- Get your vitamins and minerals from foods, not from supplements.

- If you drink alcohol, do so in moderation.

Activity

What does it mean to be physically fit? Basically, physical fitness means being physically capable of meeting life's daily demands without impairing your health. Physical fitness, using this definition, is different for everyone.

Why is physical fitness important? The list of reasons for maintaining an activity level that will keep you physically fit is lengthy.

Among other benefits, physical fitness

- Helps you have more energy
- Gives you increased confidence
- Helps you deal with stress
- Improves the health of your skin
- Helps prevent insomnia
- Reduces your risk of heart disease
- Helps control blood-serum cholesterol levels
- Helps control high blood pressure and diabetes
- Increases longevity of bone structure
- Helps maintain your quality of life

There is no universal fitness plan or program that suits everyone, but there are universal components of fitness. Cardiovascular fitness, flexibility, muscular strength, and muscular endurance are the four components of fitness. Cardiovascular fitness is by far the most important component. Cardiovascular fitness means that your heart is able to pump oxygen-carrying blood to your cells and carry waste away from your cells. Excellent cardiovascular fitness is ensured by maintaining a level of aerobic exercise that conditions your body to be able to carry larger amounts of oxygen to working muscles. Some aerobic activities are walking, jogging, biking, swimming, jumping rope, dancing, and cross-country skiing. The benefits of aerobic exercise include reducing the risk of heart disease, keeping blood pressure down, increasing the level of HDL (good cholesterol), and helping control weight in addition to such psychological benefits as increased self-esteem, reduced stress, and decreased anxiety.

Flexibility is the ability of joints to move through the full range of their motion. Good flexibility is believed to prevent pulls, tears, and other damage to your muscles and is particularly important in preventing back pain. The key to flexibility is stretching correctly. You should stretch in a slow relaxed movement.

Muscular strength is the muscles' ability to exert force in one motion, such as a jump or lift. Muscular endurance is the muscles' ability to perform repeated muscular contractions. These two components are interrelated in that most muscular contractions use some degree of muscular strength. You can increase both strength and endurance by doing exercises that involve resistance, usually weights. You gain strength by conditioning your body to more and more weight; you improve endurance by increasing repetitions at the same weight.

could spend time with her children. She attended classes while they were in school, went home and took a nap, and then got up to do homework with the children and help her mother with chores around the house.

Amanda came to my office two weeks after the fall semester began to tell me that she would not be in class because her mother had passed away. We worked out a plan for her to make up her assignments and to take her test at a later date. She was unable to return as quickly as we had hoped because she had trouble finding someone to help her care for her children. Finally, she arranged for her sister to care for the children, and she returned to school.

Amanda made up her assignments and earned one of the highest grades on the exam. Several weeks later, she returned to my office in tears— she had just learned that her son was diagnosed with diabetes. She was devastated, but decided not to drop out of school because it was too late in the semester for her to be reimbursed for the tuition she had paid. She had to take her son to a hospital in another city. After her return, she worked diligently to complete her assignments on time.

In spite of all this stress, Amanda completed the fall semester and with very high marks. She continued

In spite of all this stress, Amanda completed the fall semester and with very high marks.

through the spring semester and eventually graduated from her program.

ew students ever have to face this type of adversity or stress. Amanda's story is an example of how some people handle stress. Amanda was able to achieve despite the stress of death, and illness in her life; others might not have responded to this much stress in nearly as positive a manner. Everyone handles stress differently.

Negative stress can rob you of serenity, peace, and quality of life. In some cases, it can rob you of life itself. Stress is not exclusive to the college experience. You may have endured a great amount of stress already, on many different levels. You may have experienced terrible events—major stressors such as the loss of a parent, grandparent, sibling, lover, or classmate. You have no doubt experienced failure in school, athletics, personal relationships, or achieving your own goals. You may have suffered or may still be suffering from a physical or mental illness. Stress is not likely to be a stranger to you.

We have written this chapter because many of the students we have counselled during our years in higher education have sought help for stress-related problems, with a course, a test, an instructor, or some nonacademic area of their lives. Regardless of the source, students are under incredible stress. We want to share with you some suggestions for dealing successfully with stress.

By the end of this chapter, you should be able to

- Distinguish the different types of stressors

- Determine your own stress level

- Understand how stress is related to your overall health

- Develop a personal stress-management program

Stress is an important issue for you, because for the first time you will be dealing with stress without your usual support mechanisms. For some of you this is a positive situation, because your home or school has been a negative influence on your own health and well-being. Others of you have left warm and caring environments that have nurtured you and protected you from many hardships. For all of you, stress will be difficult to handle. If you have been leading a stressful life, you will be bringing some of that stress to your college or university experience, and new problems will add to it. If you have been leading a more protected life, you will be facing stress without the safety net once provided by your family and friends.

Before discussing stress in further detail, take a moment to assess how you feel now about stress in your life.

1. Controlling my stress level is important to me now.
   1 2 3 4 5

2. I can define stress.
   1 2 3 4 5

3. I know what situations cause me stress.   *1 2 3 4 5*

4. I can recognize the signs when I am getting stressed out.
   1 2 3 4 5

5. I understand how to relieve stress.   *1 2 3 4 5*

6. I know how to avoid stress.
   1 2 3 4 5

7. I understand that stress affects all areas of my life.
   1 2 3 4 5

8. I take time out of busy days to take care of myself.
   1 2 3 4 5

9. I practise stress-relief techniques.   *1 2 3 4 5*

10. I have a stress-management plan.   *1 2 3 4 5*

5 = Strongly Agree

4 = Agree

3 = Don't Know

2 = Disagree

1 = Strongly Disagree

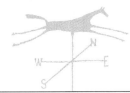

A SELF-ASSESSMENT Total your points from these ten questions. Refer to the following rating scale to determine where you stand in relation to dealing with stress.

0–10   You have great difficulty dealing with stress.

11–20   You have greater than normal difficulty dealing with stress.

21–30   You have considerable difficulty dealing with stress.

31–40   You have some difficulty dealing with stress.

41–50   You are not negatively impacted by stress.

Now, refer to your journal and respond in writing to your findings. Consider the following questions when writing in your journal.

1. What stressors am I dealing with right now in my life?

2. How am I handling those stressors?

3. Do I want to change how I deal with stress in my life?

What Is Stress?

he word *stress* is derived from the Latin word *strictus,* meaning "to draw tight." Stress is your body's response to people and events in your life; it is the mental and physical wear

and tear on your body as a result of everyday life. Stress is inevitable, and it is not in itself bad. It is your response to stress that determines whether it is good stress (eustress) or bad stress (distress). The same event can provoke eustress or distress, depending on the person experiencing the event; just as "one person's trash is another's treasure" (or so you know if you shop at used-clothing stores), so one person's eustress may be another person's distress. For example, if you know that you are going to be evaluated on oral presentations only in one course, you may experience eustress, while another student may perceive the situation as a fate worse than death and be deeply distressed.

The primary difference between eustress and distress is in your body's response. It is impossible to exist in a totally stress-free environment, in fact, some stress is important to your health and well-being. Only when the stress gets out of hand does your body become distressed. Some physical signs of distress are

Headaches	Abdominal pain and diarrhea
Dry mouth	Impotence
Muscular tension and pain	Menstrual disorders
Hypertension and chest pain	Insomnia
Coughs	Depression
Heartburn and indigestion	Suicidal tendencies
Loss of appetite	Fatigue

If you are suffering from distress, you may have one or more of these physical signs. You may also have problems with your relationships, feel increasingly negative about yourself, and engage in more bad habits.

Three Types of Stressors

SITUATIONAL STRESSORS

There are two categories of situational stressors—physical environmental and social environmental. A change in your physical environment can be a tremendous source of distress even if you are prepared for it. When you come to college, physical environmental stressors will abound. You may feel a moment of anxiety when you realize that you can't remember how to get from the cafeteria to your next class, or you lose the outline you prepared for your research paper, or you have trouble dealing with living in a crowded environment. The place where you live may change from a warm, quiet, and homey environment to a noisy, impersonal environment. At home you might have been able to count on finding a quiet place to curl up with a good book or to study for a test. Your new home, whether a residence or a boarding house, may not provide such an environment. You may be faced with the added pressures of taking care of children while trying to study, or trying to find time to spend with your spouse and still meet the demands of studying and going to class. Whatever your place in life, your age, or your economic status, you can't avoid facing added stressors when you attend college or university.

You have probably already found that your new social environment is somewhat stressful. New friends, classes, study time, recreational activities, and work-related activities may make conflicting demands on your time and attention. Parents may place added stress on you by expecting you to be home for certain weekends, or they may place great emphasis on marks. You may feel the pressure of trying to maintain a GPA that will enable you to stay in school while you are also juggling family responsibilities and work commitments. The social culture at your college is probably different from what you are accustomed to. This difference is not necessarily bad, but it is nonetheless the source of some distress. List three examples of situational stressors that affect you.

1. _____

2. _____

3. _____

Later in this chapter you will come back to these situational stressors and develop coping strategies for handling them.

PSYCHOLOGICAL STRESSORS

Psychological stressors have to do with how you perceive and respond to the world around you. If you have to travel a long way to a university, for example, dealing with travel arrangements, tickets, luggage, and train stations may all contribute to your level of stress.

Unrealistic expectations can also add to your psychological stressors. Many first-year students are excited about going away to college, but are at the same time confused and upset about the overwhelming sense of homesickness they experience. The expectation that you will

not become homesick is probably unrealistic; your new life will be exciting, challenging, frightening, and exhilarating, sometimes all at the same time. When faced with all these new feelings, it is completely natural to experience feelings of homesickness and fear. Don't be afraid to pick up the phone and call your parents or a good friend to talk about your feelings. And don't be afraid to voice your fears to some of your new friends at college. If they aren't experiencing the same feelings at the same time you are, they have no doubt felt them before; they will be able to lend a sympathetic ear to your thoughts and perhaps help you get through a difficult time.

Another source of stress for new students comes from trying to do everything. Many students place unrealistic demands on their time by trying to burn the candle at both ends—studying and going to classes all day and partying all night; then, when their grades are not what they expect, they become stressed out.

List three examples of psychological stressors that you are facing.

1. _____

2. _____

3. _____

Later, you'll develop coping strategies for these stressors, too.

BIOLOGICAL STRESSORS

Psychological stressors are closely linked with the third category of stressors, biological stressors. Every stage of your life brings new biological stressors. How you deal with them determines how stressful that period of your life will be. Everyone handles life stages differently.

Your college years put new demands on your body. For many students, going to college coincides with major hormonal changes as well as changes in lifestyle. Physical activity may be replaced by lethargy. The walk to the corner store may seem so far, even if it is only two blocks away, that you drive to pick up milk. Your physical activity is likely to be decreasing while your metabolic rate is dropping because of your age. It is possible to gain weight without even realizing it. Many college students do not understand how all these biological changes affect them until they have gained the weight; then they place unrealistic demands on their bodies as they try to lose it.

List some examples of biological changes you may be dealing with now.

1. _____

2. _____

3. _____

4. _____

You should expect a certain amount of distress during your transition into college life. For example, if you are living with a roommate, it can be a highly stressful situation. You have to get used to one another's idiosyncrasies. You may be neat, and your roommate may be a slob; you may be a morning person, and your roommate may be a night owl; you may have come to college to prepare for your career, and your roommate may have come to college to party. Regardless of differences or commonalities, the following suggestions may help you keep the stress level down in your new living quarters.

- Respect your roommate(s).

- Establish some ground rules regarding quiet times.

- Don't infringe on one another by borrowing without asking.

- Do your share.

- Establish an open line of communication so that you can discuss differences when they arise.

- Take time out of your busy schedule to do something nice for your roommate(s).

Take a moment now to draw up a list of specific ground rules that you would like to implement, and then ask your roommate(s) to do likewise. Schedule a time to sit down together to discuss the ground rules and reach a consensus. You'll be thankful in the long run that you did this.

1. _____

2. _____

3. _____

4. _____

5. _____

Meeting New People

Your high school friends will still be a part of your life, but now you have an opportunity to expand your circle of friends by gathering new friends who can offer new experiences. Think of meeting new people not as a chore, but as a positive challenge, and remember that no matter how different people appear to be, they all respond to the same basic things. People want to be respected and listened to. You will experience much less distress in life if you have a network of friends and acquaintances among whom there is a high level of respect that enables you to be totally honest with each other. The following are some helpful hints for meeting new people.

1. Keep an open mind.

2. Remember that everyone has something to share.

3. Be friendly.

4. Approach every relationship with trust.

5. Show interest in other people.

6. Be a good listener.

7. Study with people.

8. Be the one to initiate things.

9. Remember you have to be a friend to have friends.

10. Remember that not everyone will be your friend.

Other Worrisome Things

Finances are a source of stress for most students. Whether you've learned it yet or not, money doesn't grow on trees. The key to alleviating distress caused by finances is planning. Create a budget for each semester. First, total your projected earnings or monthly allowance. Then determine what you will have to pay for tuition, room and board, and other standard fees and subtract it from your total. This will tell you how much disposable income you will have. Work very hard to stick to your budget, because financial worries can constitute a huge stressor, and poor budgeting could result in your having to leave school.

Many students have to work to be able to afford to go to school. If you work, you have to deal with some stressors that do not affect non-working students. You need to take some time to prioritize your commitments. Obviously work will have to be rather high on your priority list, since most colleges and universities won't allow you to attend if you don't pay the bills. But determine whether you are working for necessities, such as room and board, tuition, and books, or for luxuries, such as eating out, new clothes, and social functions. If you seem to be struggling under a tremendous financial burden, find out how much of that burden was incurred for luxury items. If attending school and getting good marks is important to you, you will probably have to make some sacrifices. Determine your priorities, then explore your options and work out a plan that enables you to lead a life that is in sync with your priorities.

Your value system may turn out to be the focus of a great deal of stress when you go to college. Values that you may never have questioned will be challenged. You will meet people in classes or at social events who hold beliefs very different from yours. What is taboo for you may be acceptable for them. When you encounter people with different beliefs, listen to their points of view—you may learn something. Don't be afraid to share your own beliefs and to stand firmly by them, but always remember to respect the opinions of others. Everyone does not have to have the same beliefs as you; diversity makes this a much more interesting world to live in.

Unfortunately, recognizing that you will face major stressors when you go to college or university may not be enough to keep you from suffering from distress. Don't let this get you down. Most people let stress interfere with their lives at some point. The truly happy and healthy people in the world learn how to cope with this stress and how to make stress work for them.

Building a Stress Management Program

Learning how to manage stress has become a national hobby. How-to books, audiotapes, videotapes, and self-help seminars are advertised everywhere. Most libraries and bookstores have sections dedicated to stress. People have made fortunes expounding on stress. However, there is no one way of handling stress that is 100 percent effective. Each individual has a unique need and ability to manage stress. To help you manage the stress you will encounter during your college years and for the rest of your life, we offer a variety of techniques and suggestions that you can adapt to your own needs.

Your approach to managing stress should address all three types of stressors—situational, psychological, and biological.

MANAGING SITUATIONAL STRESSORS

To manage situational stressors, you need to understand what it is in your environment that is causing stress for you. If your living arrange-ments, either the physical facilities or the people around you, are creating stress and you have been unable to work things out, take the necessary steps to change your resi-dence. Since this may take some time, do what you can in the interim to remove stress from the environment. For example, if you are having trouble with the noise level at your dorm, find a quiet place elsewhere to study.

For another example of situational stress, consider one student, who complained that she just couldn't study in her room. It wasn't that she didn't like her roommate or that the dorm was too noisy for her; the problem was that her friends were constantly stopping by and keeping her from studying. The student needs to tell her friends that she is studying and cannot spend time talking with them, or she needs to study in a quiet place where her friends are unlikely to drop by. Both options may be difficult; no doubt the student enjoys talking with her friends and does not want to alienate them by being less available.

A change of environment can help with stress. We are often so involved in the hustle and bustle of everyday liv-ing that we don't even realize how the fast pace is stressing us out. Be aware of your environment. If you find you are becoming stressed, do an environment check. Look around. Is the stress coming from the obnoxious music your next-door neighbour is playing? Are there too many people walking in and around the room you are in? Are people in your classroom annoying you by constantly coughing, scratching, or clicking a pen? Keep your options open—if your environment gets to you, change it.

If you are feeling stressed, try taking a walk in a quiet part of the campus, going to the library and reading, or searching out an empty classroom for a quiet time of prayer, meditation, or self-reflection. One of these options may provide a big enough environmental change to decrease your stress. Since music has a therapeutic effect on many people, adding some soothing music to your environment may be just the change you need.

Another way to reduce situational stress is to arrange a class schedule that fits your needs and ability to accomplish tasks. If you function better in the morning, try to schedule your classes and study time for early in the day. If you are a night owl, try to avoid early morning classes and use the evening hours to your best advantage.

The key to controlling situational stressors is the ability to diagnose the situation, to determine just what it is about the environment that is causing the distress, and then to make a change. Essentially, you have three choices: *You can learn to live with the situation; you can adjust the situation; or you can change the situation.* Remember, it's easier to make a change if you have scouted out some peaceful and relaxing areas ahead of time; know where you can go.

Now, take some time to review the situational stressors you listed earlier in this chapter and come up with some coping strategies you might implement the next time you face them.

1. _____

   _____

   _____

2. _____

   _____

   _____

3. _____

   _____

   _____

MANAGING PSYCHOLOGICAL STRESSORS

Psychological stressors are probably the most prevalent as well as the most difficult to handle. Again, you need first to be able to pinpoint what is causing you stress and then to develop a coping technique to get you through the situation. It is crucial that you do not ignore the stress! You cannot afford to let yourself get run down. Since you may not be in the best position to recognize exactly what your stressors are when you are in the middle of a stressful time, talk with a good friend about your feelings and ask for feedback about the situation. Choose someone who is positive; someone who tends to be negative can hurt the situation more than help it. You might also talk with a professor with whom you have developed a special relationship. Instructors and mentors can provide insight and compassion. These are people who probably understand your feelings and needed someone to listen to them at one time or another. They are also intimately familiar with the pressures of academia and might be able to offer some concrete suggestions to help you cope with your distress.

Every school has a network of support services. Most colleges and universities provide easy access to counsellors, therapists, and psychiatrists at no charge or at a reduced rate. These people are trained to deal with students and are aware of the kinds of stresses you may be experiencing. Remember, talking about your problems is key to relieving stress and these individuals are trained listeners.

Review the psychological stressors you named earlier in this chapter and list some strategies that might help you deal with these stressors. Why did you choose the strategies you did?

1. _____

_____

_____

2. _____

_____

_____

3. _____

_____

_____

MANAGING BIOLOGICAL STRESSORS

You will have to deal with biological stressors for the rest of your life, as your body ages and changes. You may feel invincible now, but this will change. The physical changes that will take place in your body are not something to dread or despise. There is no one more beautiful or appealing or sexy than a person who is comfortable with his or her body, regardless of age, weight, size, or shape. Still, biological stressors exist and you have to be prepared to deal with them. Learn to eat right by listening to your body. Understand why you are eating. Are you hungry? Many Canadians do not allow themselves to feel hunger; they eat not because they are hungry, but because they are happy, sad, nervous, tired, or stressed out and because eating is a social event. Stress can make you ravenous or disinterested in food. Although both extremes are bad, the former may be preferable. The physical changes brought on by stress cause your body to burn calories; thus your body needs more energy when you are stressed.

Learn to eat right by eating foods such as fresh fruits, vegetables, whole-grain breads, and cereals. Eat adequate amounts of protein and drink lots of water—at least eight glasses per day. Your body will feel better and you will be more capable of handling stressful events.

Exercising is a wonderful coping activity for stress. Exercise releases endorphins, which cause a natural high and help relieve all types of stresses. Aerobic exercises are the best stress reducers. According to Herbert Benson, a physician and author of *The Relaxation Response* (1992), you should exercise vigorously for at least 20 minutes at least three times per week to enable your body to release the pent-up energy caused by stress. You might want to avoid competitive exercises, because they may cause additional stress. Have a friend join you in your exercise program; you can socialize while doing something good for yourselves, rather than share stories over pizza and beer. Exercise prepares your body for stressful situations while it helps you to relieve stress.

Physical activity will also help you avoid the insomnia that is sometimes associated with stress. Adequate sleep is extremely important, although what counts as adequate is different for everyone.

List the types of activities you enjoy. The next time you feel stress, take the time to do one of these activities. _____

_____

_____

Write down some ideas for dealing with the biological stressors you listed earlier in the chapter.

1. _____

_____

2. _____

_____

_____

3. _____

_____

_____

Dealing with Stress on a Personal Level

As you start your journey through college, be aware that this is a stressful event, so don't try to tackle too many changes at once. Develop a schedule that includes stress-relieving activities. If you enjoy athletics, schedule athletic activities once a day. If you enjoy music, reading, or the theatre, make time in your schedule for enjoying the beauty that is found in the arts. And make time for talking with a good friend, playing a game of cards, or watching television, all of which can help relieve stress too.

 **for handling stress**

- Don't procrastinate.

- Set aside time each day to organize your day.

- Tackle your most difficult and important work first.

- Learn to say no!

- Take time out to be with friends or family.

- Surround yourself with people who are upbeat, kind, sympathetic, funny, and caring.

- Work at your relationships.

The one minute journal

In a minute or less, jot down one major idea you learned from this chapter.

Sex, Drugs, and Rock 'n' Roll: Social and Personal Responsibility

Erica was a first-year stud-ent at a university in British Columbia. She came from a small, rural town in Ontario and was finding it difficult to make new friends. She was shy and had never had an active social life. One day, a classmate invited her to a party at an apart-ment near the campus. Erica was apprehensive about going to a party with people she barely knew, but she

decided she ought to go if she ever wanted to make any friends. At the party, she was introduced to several people, and one of them handed her a beer. Erica had drunk a couple of times in high school, but she wasn't accustomed to drinking. She didn't want to appear rude, so she took the beer and drank it. During the course of the evening Erica drank several beers. She was amazed at what a good time she was having. She felt that her conversation was funnier and more alive. The next morning she felt a little rough, but overall, she was extremely pleased with how the evening had turned out and she was looking forward to the party she had been invited to the next night.

At the next party, Erica didn't wait for someone to offer her a beer; she went directly to the keg and helped herself. Again she had a great time. As the semester wore on, Erica was surprised at how popular she was becoming. She grew accustomed to drinking, and routinely had a couple of drinks before leaving for a party or a date.

Toward the end of the semester, Erica was partying six nights out of seven and her marks were suffering. Exam week was a blur, because she was so far behind in her classes. She went home dreading the arrival of her grades; she knew her parents weren't going to be happy. The day came, and Erica held her worst dreams in her hand; she had

Erica was partying six nights out of seven and her marks were suffering.

received two F's, a D, a C, and a B. A letter accompanying her grade report informed her that she had been placed on academic probation.

rica's story is not unusual. Many students come to college or university prepared to test their wings. The freedoms associated with college, the very thing they all have been waiting for, often prove to be their undoing. One of the most fundamental lessons first-year students must learn is self-restraint. You may be thinking "Oh no, here comes the lecture." But the purpose of this chapter is to present information and to discuss personal accountability, not to lecture you. At the end of this chapter, you will be able to

- Discuss the reasons that people use drugs

- Describe how drugs affect your body

- Identify the signs of drug addiction

- Describe the support systems your campus makes available to help people who have drug addictions

- Put into practice the cornerstones for drinking at a social function

Before discussing drug use and personal responsibility, take a moment to assess how you feel about drug use.

AT THIS MOMENT...

5 = Strongly Agree

4 = Agree

3 = Don't Know

2 = Disagree

1 = Strongly Disagree

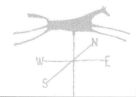

1. I know what drugs are.
    1 2 3 4 5

2. I understand how different drugs affect the body.
    1 2 3 4 5

3. I understand the impact of drug abuse on the body.
    1 2 3 4 5

4. I am comfortable with my own use of drugs or druglike substances.   1 2 3 4 5

5. I recognize the signs of drug abuse.   1 2 3 4 5

6. I know where to turn for help if I experience problems with drugs.   1 2 3 4 5

7. I know what the penalties are for the illegal use of drugs.
    1 2 3 4 5

8. I know what to do if a friend is experiencing problems with drugs.   1 2 3 4 5

9. I know what programs the college has on drugs and drug use.   1 2 3 4 5

10. I feel comfortable talking with my family about drug use.
    1 2 3 4 5

A SELF-ASSESSMENT Total your points from these ten questions. Refer to the following rating scale to determine the level of your knowledge of drugs and drug abuse.

0–10 You have very little knowledge about drugs and drug abuse.

11–20 You have below-average knowledge about drugs and drug abuse.

21–30   Your knowledge about drugs and drug abuse is average.

31–40   Your knowledge about drugs and drug abuse is above average.

41–50   You have an excellent knowledge about drugs and drug abuse.

Now, refer to your journal and respond in writing to your findings. Consider the following questions when writing in your journal.

1. Do you agree or disagree with the results of the assessment? Why?

2. Are you comfortable with the amount of knowledge you have regarding drugs and the abuse of drugs? Why?

3. Do you have a problem with drugs? Do any of your friends have a problem with drugs?

Drugs

The word *drug* describes a substance, legal or illegal, that interacts with your body chemistry. Examples of drugs are caffeine, nicotine, alcohol, amphetamines, anabolic steroids, cocaine, marijuana, and crack. The misuse or abuse of drugs takes place for many reasons.

Why do you or some of the people you know take drugs? _____

_____

_____

_____

As you may have noted, many people wander into drug use because they are curious, and once they have briefly experienced drugs they move on. Others continue the use of drugs for a variety of reasons. Some people are recreational drug users; they see getting stoned as a form of entertainment. Unfortunately, recreational users often become abusers, and drug abuse is not a recreational activity. Many young people try drugs because their friends, siblings, or parents are using drugs; young people are often pressured by their peers to conform with their social crowd. Some people view drugs as a panacea for psychological needs.

Drug Dependency

A person can be physically or psychologically addicted to a drug. In physical dependency, physiological changes to cell structure cause a person to crave a certain chemical; if the chemical is denied, the person experiences withdrawal. Withdrawal causes nausea, anxiety, and an intense craving for the chemical, which continues until the drug is given or withdrawal is complete.

In psychological dependency, a person craves a drug for its pleasurable effects. People often become psychologically addicted to drugs that enable them to relax, as with Erica in the opening story. Marijuana is an example of a drug that does not cause physical dependency but that frequently gives rise to psychological dependency.

Some Common Legal Drugs

CAFFEINE

Caffeine is America's favorite drug and a staple in the average college student's life. It is found in many forms; some of the most common are coffee, tea, colas, and caffeine pills. Caffeine is a stimulant. It enables a person to stay alert and may in some cases increase a person's capacity for work and ability to perform repetitive tasks. The negative side effects of caffeine include increased anxiety, insomnia, accelerated breathing, upset stomach, dizziness, and headaches. Caffeine is an addictive drug; when its use is stopped, withdrawal symptoms such as headaches, irritability, and fatigue occur.

OVER-THE-COUNTER DRUGS

Over-the-counter drugs are drugs that you can purchase without a prescription, such as antihistamines and sedatives. These drugs provide relief from many common ailments and are widely used in North America. Many of these drugs can be abused if they are not taken in the proper usage or for the symptom for which they are intended. For example, many bulimics become addicted to the laxatives they use in an attempt to lose weight. Although less dangerous than prescription drugs, over-the-counter drugs can cause side effects that have a negative impact on the quality of life.

PRESCRIPTION DRUGS

Prescription drugs, drugs prescribed by a doctor, are some of the most abused substances in our society. Amphetamines, opiates, and sedatives can induce physical dependency if used for an extended period of time. Some of the most common prescription drugs associated with addiction are Valium, Librium, Xanax, Percodan, Demerol, morphine, and Ativan. Usage of these drugs must be closely monitored by a physician. If you have cause to use any of these drugs, it is important for you to take them exactly as directed and to contact your physician if you experience changes in your lifestyle or in other prescriptions you are taking. Most people probably think of illegal drug use when they hear "drug abuse," but the abuse of prescription drugs is prevalent and something to be mindful of.

ALCOHOL

Alcoholic beverages have been a part of culture for as long as records have been kept: wines have been used in religious ceremonies and served at feasts; liquor has been used for medicinal purposes. Today the consumption of alcohol is associated with many celebrations. People consume alcohol because they enjoy the taste, they like its physical side effects, they think it helps them relax, and it makes them feel less inhibited. There are as many reasons for enjoying alcohol as there are people. Despite the enjoyment alcohol may provide, it is important to remember that it is a drug, and it reacts in our bodies as a very powerful drug.

You may think of alcohol as something that makes you feel happy, relaxed, and at peace, but these feelings are side effects of the initial stages of alcohol consumption only. Alcohol acts on the body as a depressant. It is a toxic substance that your body metabolizes as quickly as possible into harmless by-products. These by-products are disposed of naturally by your lungs and kidneys, which is why Breathalyzer or urine tests are used to determine a person's level of alcohol consumption. Alcohol acts as an anesthetic on the nervous system in the following way:

1. Small amounts of alcohol affect the forebrain, causing feelings of happiness and a sense of being relaxed and less inhibited and impairing judgment.

2. Moderate amounts of alcohol affect the midbrain, resulting in some loss of muscular coordination, slowing of reflexes, and slurred speech.

3. Large amounts of alcohol affect the hindbrain, causing a dulling of the senses and eventually resulting in a stupor.

4. Very large amounts of alcohol can affect the part of the brain responsible for controlling vital functions, resulting in loss of consciousness and eventual death.

Very general terms are used to describe the amount of alcohol that brings on these reactions because people metabolize alcohol at very different rates. Alcohol absorption actually begins in the stomach, where the small ethanol molecules are easily absorbed into the bloodstream and then carried to the brain within minutes. The effect is more noticeable on an empty stomach. Eating while drinking alcohol can slow the rate of absorption and thus affect, to a very mild extent, the time it takes to get high from the alcohol. Once the contents of the stomach are emptied into the intestine, however, food has no effect on the absorption of alcohol. Hence, eating has little long-term effect on the amount of alcohol you can consume.

TIPS FOR DRINKING ON SOCIAL OCCASIONS

- Eat something before you start drinking.

- Pace your drinking; drink no more than one drink every one and a half hours.

- Drink plenty of water to counteract the dehydrating effect of alcohol.

- Set a limit and stick to it. Learn to say no.

- Always have a designated driver who abstains from all alcohol.

- Don't drink by yourself.

- Don't drink at home *before* you go out to drink.

If your best intentions did not work, and you are suffering from the dreaded hangover, try these suggestions for relieving your discomfort.

- Take aspirin or acetaminophen for headaches.

- Eat a bland diet if you are nauseous.

- Drink lots of liquids, preferably clear liquids such as water, ginger ale, or apple juice.

- Drink orange juice to replace the potassium you lost through frequent urination.

- Get some extra sleep, but don't sleep the day away or you will feel worse.

DO YOU HAVE A DRINKING PROBLEM? You have probably been told that if you are going to drink, you should drink in moderation. But what does that mean? For the average person, moderation can be defined as one drink or less at least once a week, or two to four drinks three or four times a month. Moderate drinkers are not at risk for any of the health problems associated with drinking in excess.

Many drinkers do not drink in moderation, however. Although legal, alcohol is a drug, and a very addictive one. In North America, alcohol is the drug of choice for many people, and drinking, even in excess at times, is considered socially acceptable. The media often portray alcohol as glamorous and drinking the thing to do if you want to be popular. Rarely are the negative aspects of alcohol shown or discussed. Although we may prefer to think that the only alcoholics are the skid-row bums shown on TV and in the movies, alcoholism is as prevalent on college and university campuses and in upper- and middle-class communities as it is anywhere else. As a society, we are starting to face up to this fact and trying to help people addicted to alcohol.

People who have drinking problems tend to have one of the following drinking patterns.

1. They drink large amounts of alcohol every day.

2. They drink large amounts of alcohol on weekends only.

3. They binge drink.

The following alcohol dependency questionnaire was developed by the U.S. National Council on Alcoholism.

1. Do you occasionally drink heavily after a disappointment or a quarrel, or when your parents give you a hard time?

2. When you have trouble or feel pressured at school, do you always drink more heavily than usual?

3. Have you noticed that you are able to handle more liquor than you did when you were first drinking?

4. Did you ever wake up on the "morning after" and discover that you could not remember part of the evening before, even though your friends tell you that you did not pass out?

5. When drinking with other people, do you try to have a few extra drinks that others don't notice?

6. Are there certain occasions when you feel uncomfortable if alcohol is not available?

7. Have you recently noticed that when you begin drinking you are in more of a hurry to get the first drink than you used to be?

8. Do you sometimes feel a little guilty about your drinking?

9. Are you secretly irritated when your family or friends discuss your drinking?

10. Have you recently noticed an increase in the frequency of your memory blackouts?

11. Do you often find that you wish to continue drinking after your friends say that they have had enough?

12. Do you usually have a reason for the occasions when you drink heavily?

13. When you are sober, do you often regret things you did or said while drinking?

14. Have you tried switching brands or following different plans for controlling your drinking?

15. Have you often failed to keep the promises you've made to yourself about controlling or cutting down on your drinking?

16. Have you ever tried to control your drinking by changing jobs or moving to a new location?

17. Do you try to avoid family or close friends while you are drinking?

18. Are you having an increasing number of financial and academic problems?

19. Do more people seem to be treating you unfairly without good reason?

20. Do you eat very little or irregularly when you are drinking?

21. Do you sometimes have the shakes in the morning and find that it helps to have a little drink?

22. Have you recently noticed that you cannot drink as much as you once did?

23. Do you sometimes stay drunk for several days at a time?

24. Do you sometimes feel very depressed and wonder whether life is worth living?

25. Sometimes after periods of drinking, do you see or hear things that aren't there?

26. Do you get terribly frightened after you have been drinking heavily

Now look over the questions to which you responded yes and refer to the following rating scale. Several yes answers within one of these groups indicates that stage of alcoholism.

Questions 1–8	Early stage. Drinking is a regular part of your life.
Questions 9–21	Middle stage. You are having trouble controlling when, where, and how much you drink.
Questions 22–26	Beginning of the final stage. You can no longer control your desire to drink.

The Addiction Research Foundation (ARF), in their report *Drugs in Ontario*, narrowed their questionnaire down to four questions:

1. Have you felt you should reduce your drinking?

2. Have others bothered you by complaining about your drinking?

3. Have you felt bad or guilty because of your drinking?

4. Have you drunk in the early morning to get rid of a hangover?

Two or more yes answers indicate a possible alcohol problem.

The ARF also highlighted an interesting statistic with regard to heavy drinking. In answer to the question "Who had five or more drinks at one time on a weekly basis?" it was reported that in 1994, 10 percent of all adult drinkers did; 15 percent of adult male drinkers, 5 percent of adult female drinkers, and 31 percent of student drinkers had five or more drinks at one time during the four weeks prior to the survey.

Many people tend to drink more than usual during their college or university years. You need to understand that an addiction developed during college may not be easy to get rid of later on. If, after answering the questionnaire, you found that you are at risk, here are some suggestions for seeking help.

- Call your provincial drug and alcohol department

- Ask a trusted instructor, perhaps the one you have for this course, to refer you to a specialist

- Call your local chapter of Alcoholics Anonymous

- If you have a good relationship with your parents, call them

■ Call your local Drug and Alcohol Treatment Centre

Read the following case and respond to the questions that follow.

Driving home from a party, a first-year university student, who has had too much to drink, lets his car drift over the centre line and runs head on into a father and his three young children. The father and one of the children are killed instantly. The other two children are severely injured, and one will be disabled for life. The student driver has had no previous convictions for driving while under the influence.

What criminal action should be taken against the driver? If you were his friend, how would you feel? How would you feel if you were the wife and mother of the victims? _____

_____

_____

_____

_____

_____

In class, discuss the answers of your classmates. What were their opinions?

To ignore the negative consequences of alcohol on society is to live in a make-believe world. We hope that this information will give you an opportunity to think about your approach to drinking.

TOBACCO

"Cigarettes are the single greatest cause of disease and disability in Canada" (Collisaw and Myers, 1984). More deaths are associated with tobacco than drugs and alcohol combined. The use of tobacco is a highly addictive practice, and it may be more difficult to overcome addiction to tobacco than it is to overcome alcohol or drug addictions.

People start smoking for many of the same reasons they try or start using drugs: curiosity, peer pressure, the perceived calming affect of the drug on their system, or the taste. Nicotine, the addictive ingredient in tobacco, is extremely addictive, and because the withdrawal symptoms, anxiety and irritability, interfere so much with everyday life, smokers find kicking the habit is difficult. In addition, nicotine withdrawal causes cravings for the drug long after other withdrawal symptoms have disappeared. The negative health effects of nicotine include

■ Increased risk of heart disease and stroke

■ Increased risk of lung and oral cancer

- Increased risk of respiratory diseases
- Yellowing of the teeth
- Bad breath from trench mouth

If you want to stop smoking, try these suggestions from the Canadian Cancer Society.

1. Set a date to quit.

2. Prepare for 'quit' day by:

   - Listing the reasons you want to quit and reviewing them nightly.

   - Bet a friend you can quit on your target day.

   - List what you like and dislike about smoking.

   - Ask a friend or relative to quit smoking with you.

   - Smoke only half a cigarette.

   - Wait until your pack is empty before buying another pack.

   - Change your smoking circumstances. If you like to smoke with others, smoke alone.

   - Drink juice instead of smoking for a pick-me-up.

   - Don't empty your ashtrays. They will remind you of how much you smoke and how bad stale butts smell.

3. Quit. There are only two ways to kick the smoking habit: cold turkey and tapering off slowly. Select the method which seems most comfortable for you.

Here are some helpful hints that will assist you in sticking with your commitment to quit smoking:

- On 'quit' day, throw out all cigarettes, matches, lighters, and ashtrays.

- Spend as much time as possible in places where smoking is prohibited.

- Avoid situations you associate with smoking (e.g., after-dinner coffee).

- Associate with non-smokers at parties, work, and school.

- Increase your physical activity.

- Get plenty of rest.

- Keep healthy substitutes handy such as carrots, pickles, sunflower seeds, and oranges.

- Add up the money you have saved by not smoking. Buy yourself something special.

■ Don't believe that "one won't hurt." It will.

If you are a nonsmoker, try some of these helpful hints for maintaining a smoke-free environment.

1. Post no smoking signs in your office, residence room, or apartment.

2. Request seating in the nonsmoking area of restaurants.

3. Ask that meetings be smoke-free and that the group take breaks to allow smokers the chance to leave and smoke.

4. Ask smokers to refrain from smoking in your house.

5. Suggest to friends who are hosting a party that they designate an area or a room for smoking.

6. If someone lights up in your presence, don't be afraid to say, in a courteous way, "Smoking bothers me."

You have as much right to have a smoke-free environment as smokers have to smoke. You just have to be willing to take the steps to find a solution for both groups.

Illegal Drugs

According to the Addiction Research Foundation, worldwide production of opium, cocaine, hashish, and marijuana is on the rise. Thus, the availability and use of illegal drugs is expected to increase despite continued pressure on growers, developers, sellers, and users (Sciolino, 1990). More than ever, colleges and universities need to be prepared to help students deal with drug-abuse problems.

Hales (1991) describes four stages of drug dependency:

Stage 1—The user begins to do drugs.

Stage 2—The user is no longer happy to wait for recreational use, but wants the high to help cope with everyday anxieties.

Stage 3—The user has to work harder and harder to acquire drugs, because he or she is using increased amounts.

Stage 4—The user is controlled by the substance abuse.

The Addiction Research Foundation lists the following behaviours as indications of a drug problem.

- Abrupt change in attitude, including a lack of interest in activities once enjoyed
- Frequent vague and withdrawn moods
- Sudden decline in performance at work or school
- Sudden resistance to discipline or criticism
- Secret phone calls and meetings
- Increased levels of frustration
- Changes in sleeping and eating habits
- Sudden weight loss
- Evidence of drug use
- Frequent borrowing of money
- Stealing
- Disregard for personal appearance
- Impaired relationships with family and friends
- Disregard for deadlines, curfews, or other regulations
- Unusual flare-ups of temper
- New friends, especially known drug users, and strong allegiance to these friends

It is easy for drug users to believe that drug abuse is a problem suffered by others and that they can control their own usage. But drugs are powerful substances, and they can create a dependency that is difficult to control. If you or a friend is having trouble with drugs, it is extremely important for you to seek help. Most colleges and universities have personnel who are trained to help people suffering from drug dependencies.

As you read through the brief descriptions of some of the illegal drugs found on many campuses, think about your own experiences with drugs and drug abuse and consider the following questions.

1. Are drugs accessible in your circle of friends?

2. Is the use of drugs a common practice among your friends?

3. Do you or any of your friends exhibit some of the characteristics associated with drug abuse?

4. Do you think there is a drug problem on your campus? If so, what can you do to help your college deal with this problem?

MARIJUANA

A mild hallucinogenic or psychedelic (mind-expanding, -manifesting, -clarifying, or -revealing) drug, marijuana is used extensively on college and university campuses. It is derived from the plant *Cannabis sativa,* which is grown in many areas of the world. Marijuana is usually smoked, but can be ingested. Most users report that marijuana relaxes them and gives them the sense that time has been slowed down; many claim that it is a mood elevator. People may experience mild hallucinations when using marijuana. Although marijuana is used primarily as a recreational drug, it has medicinal uses as well. It decreases nausea in cancer patients undergoing chemotherapy and reduces the fluid pressure in the eyes of people who suffer from glaucoma.

Students use marijuana for many of the same reasons they use alcohol. They claim that the drug helps them to relax, lowers inhibitions, and helps them to socialize. Although research continues, marijuana is currently believed to be non-addictive. Users do not appear to develop tolerance; rather, frequent users claim that they can get high on lesser amounts. There is scientific proof for this phenomenon, but it may be that because the drug takes a long time to metabolize, doses amplify one another.

COCAINE

Cocaine is a stimulant extracted from the leaves of the coca plant. It is ingested in many ways. Most commonly, users snort in the powder form; they can also inject the liquid or brew a tea from the leaves of the coca plant. Cocaine generates feelings of euphoria, deadens pain, reduces hunger, and boosts self-confidence. Like marijuana, cocaine is used primarily for recreation, but has medicinal uses as well. Cocaine was not believed to be addictive or seriously harmful until recently. The use of cocaine is extremely dangerous because of the frequency of contamination from foreign substances. Intravenous use has been closely linked with increased risk of contracting HIV because of the unsanitary practice of sharing needles. Cocaine use causes blood pressure to increase and blood vessels to constrict, which can result in cardiovascular collapse. Crack is the street name given to freebase cocaine that has been processed from the cocaine hydrochloride using ammonia or baking soda and water. Crack use has been linked to strokes and grand mal seizures. Although researchers disagree on just how addictive cocaine is, studies show that users quickly come to crave the drug.

AMPHETAMINES

These stimulants were until recently routinely prescribed to help students stay awake for all-nighters, keep truck drivers alert during long hauls, and help dieters lose weight. Amphetamines also boost self-confidence and help alleviate depression. Because of their negative physiological effects, they are no longer commonly prescribed to alleviate depression. In large doses, amphetamines cause a euphoric high, which can last for days if the dose is large enough. This high is followed by a crash, which can be quite painful. Amphetamine users quickly develop tolerance for the drug, and therefore need to keep increasing their dosage to maintain their accustomed high, but amphetamines are not considered addictive.

OPIATES

Opiates are depressants derived from the opium poppy. Common opiates include morphine, heroin, codeine, and meperidine. Doctors prescribe opiates as analgesics, that is, to deaden pain. Most users report a euphoric rush. Opiates are extremely addictive, and a high rate of overdosing, which often ends in death, is associated with their use.

PSYCHEDELICS

Psychedelic drugs alter the feelings, perceptions, and thoughts of those using them. The most widely used psychedelics are LSD, mescaline, psilocybin. These drugs affect the reticular formation, located in the brain stem. The reticular formation is responsible for receiving messages from outside the brain, interpreting those messages, and relaying them to other parts of the brain. When psychedelics are present, the reticular formation has trouble decoding the messages and sends out wrong messages, which cause the senses to become confused. Thus, people using psychedelics may report smelling colours and hearing tastes. Some psychedelics are hallucinogens, which cause the brain to produce hallucinations.

DESIGNER DRUGS

Substances created in the laboratory to mimic other drugs are called designer drugs. Amphetamines and methamphetamines are the most common designer drugs found on college campuses. Designer drugs mimic not only the effects of the drug, but also the addictive nature of the drug, and they carry the same risk of overdose.

Drugs are powerful substances, and they can create a dependency that is difficult to control.

Anabolic steroids are an artificial form of testosterone, the male hormone that promotes muscle growth and strength. Their increased popularity is an outgrowth of our obsession with looking good. They are used primarily by young men trying to bulk up to improve their athletic performance or their physical appearance and are procured through the black market. The negative side effects of steroids include severe mood swings, acne, liver tumours, high cholesterol levels, hypertension, and kidney disease. Male users of the drug may experience increased breast size as well as testicle atrophy. Female users may experience increased body hair, baldness, enlarged clitoris, and decreased breast size. Steroid users develop a psychological dependency on the drug and experience difficulty when trying to stop its use.

Personal Responsibility

The issues of drug use raise many thought-provoking questions. We want to encourage you to think through various situations. College provides infinite new freedom, but with freedom comes responsibility. You are the only one responsible for your actions. Don't be a victim of your own bad choices.

The one minute journal

In a minute or less, jot down one major idea you learned from this chapter.

Date Rape—
Fact or Fiction

Access the article "Friends Raping Friends-Could It Happen to You?" by Jean O. Gorman Hughes and Bernice R. Sandler at the Internet address: http://www.cs.utk.edu./~bartley/acquaintRape.html) After you have read the article, respond to the following questions.

Define date rape. _____

_____

_____

_____

_____

Women in what age group are most likely to experience date rape? _____

_____

What roles do alcohol and drugs play in date rape? _____

_____

_____

_____

_____

What are four major causes of date rape? _____

_____

_____

_____

_____

Using suggestions from this article, what advice would you give someone relative to avoiding date rape? _____

_____

_____

_____

_____

Discuss the responsibility of males in avoiding date rape. _____

_____

_____

_____

_____

Discuss the danger signals that could alert women to men who might rape. _____

_____

_____

_____

_____

What would you advise someone to do if he or she is raped? _____

_____

_____

_____

_____

Note: Men can be raped and have the same rights to counselling and legal action that women have.

The Nuts and Bolts of College Life

■ AN INSIDER'S VIEW

Andrea Carnegie
Age 26
Georgian College
Barrie, Ontario

When I started university, I was en route to a degree in the social sciences. I had always wanted to pursue a career that would allow me to help others, and I was thought that this was the route to take.

Reality set in when the first semester got under way. University was a lot more work than I'd counted on, and though I worked hard, I didn't always get the marks I wanted. I was pretty discouraged, so I dropped out in my second year to reevaluate my career plans.

I spent the next year exploring career options. During the year, I went on an outward bound program. I got so much out of the experience that I thought I'd like to become an outdoor program leader. I spent some time talking with a college counsellor, and it became clear that although outdoor programming was an area I enjoyed, the field offered limited job opportunities. After much reflection, I set my sights on finding a rewarding career that would also be practical.

I decided that helping others was still an important goal of mine. The volunteer work I had done at my local hospital led me to consider a profession in the medical field. I went to Georgian College to get a copy of their college calendar so that I could research possible career opportunities. The curriculum of the nursing program appealed to me, so I spoke to a professor at the college to find out more about the program. I also talked to a number of nurses to see how they felt about their jobs. I found that my personal strengths would be well suited to a career in nursing. The research and planning I'd invested had led me to a career that was right for me. I have since graduated from Georgian's nursing program, and I am now working in the oncology unit of a hospital in Dallas, Texas. My career search has resulted in a job that I love.

■ **AN INSIDER'S VIEW**
Siamak Saleki
Age 24
Dawson College
Montreal, Quebec

When I was in my first semester of college, a representative from the Student Association came in to one of our classes and made a presentation about the Association's activities. Then he asked for a class representative to sit on the executive. Everyone sat there in silence for what seemed like forever. I don't know what made me put up my hand, but I finally volunteered. I thought I might get some time off class.

Looking back, it was one of the best things I've ever done. I learned so much by getting involved in college life! I met a great group of people, I developed my organizational skills, I made a lot of job contacts, and I had a much more fulfilling college experience because I got involved. I am now a member of the college's board of governors as a student representative. This is the highest position that any student can achieve and it holds a lot of responsibility. I believe that education without extra-curricular activities means nothing. I'm happy that I did what I did and I encourage others to do the same. College wouldn't have been half the experience if I hadn't joined the Student Association.

College wouldn't have been half the experience if I hadn't joined the Student Association.

114

Most of the luxuries and many of

the so-called comforts of life are

not only not indispensable, but

positive hindrances to the elevation

of mankind.

Henry David Thoreau, author

To Join or Not to Join—That Is the Question: Campus Activities

Eric was one of the most shy and introverted individuals in the incoming class. When asked his name during orientation, he could barely utter a sound. He held his head down most of the time and was basically a loner. Most people would have thought that Eric would not make it through the first week, but they would have been wrong.

Eric was required to

take a new-student orientation class his first semester. As the weeks grew into months, Eric began to open up a little more in class. About halfway through the semester, the professor of the orientation class asked each student to research at least one club or activity on campus. The students were to interview the advisor and at least two members of the club or other organization.

Eric chose to interview the advisor to the Student Government Association (SGA), because the SGA was responsible for all student programming and activities on campus. After meeting with the advisor, Eric met with two students involved in the SGA.

His intention was to complete his project and never look back. But that did not happen. One of the students he interviewed asked Eric to join the SGA to help with campus activities. Eric was so thrilled to be asked to do something that he agreed to help out with one dance to see if he liked it. Things could not have turned out better for Eric.

By the end of the semester, Eric was the program chair for social functions for the entire college. At the beginning of the next semester, he ran for an executive position and won the election. Although still somewhat shy and reserved, Eric made many new friends and began to experience the college life he had always dreamed of. Toward the end of his first year, Eric became interested in the

Eric made many new friends and began to experience the college life he had always dreamed of.

Student Media Association. He began to write articles about the SGA and its activities. Before long, his work was appearing in the paper weekly. At the beginning of his second year, Eric applied for the position of editor of the small newspaper and was appointed to that position by the Media Committee. With this appointment came an honorarium that paid for an entire semester's tuition; the SGA executive position paid for the other semester. Because of Eric's involvement in student activities, he had grown as a student, a leader, an individual, and a friend, and his tuition was paid for.

When Eric entered college, he wasn't sure that the business administration program he'd enrolled in was the right choice for him. Shortly after the beginning of his second year in the program, he realized he was very good with personnel matters and contract negotiations. He became committed to excelling in the business program, and chose human resources as his option.

Today, Eric flies across Canada in his capacity as a training manager for one of the largest restaurant chains in the country. He deals with people on an hourly basis, conducts workshops and training sessions, hires managers and staff, and signs off on every new restaurant in the chain. Eric attributes his success to his early days as a player in the SGA and the Media Association. "They gave me the leadership and communication skills that I needed to become a confident, self-assured professional."

Eric's story is neither unusual nor far-fetched. Student activities and organizations can give you the tools to make you successful for the rest of your life. Although academics are the most important aspect of college life, cocurricular and extracurricular activities play a major role in helping you to develop leadership, communication, interpersonal, and managerial skills. These tools will prove invaluable when you face the stiff competition of the job market.

The purpose of this chapter is to help you learn about the student functions, activities, and organizations on your campus. At the end of this chapter, you should be able to

- Discuss the difference between cocurricular and extracurricular activities

- List the benefits of becoming involved

- Explain the function of clubs and organizations

- Describe the Greek system of fraternities and sororities

- Research an organization

Take a moment to test your knowledge of student activities, the Greek system, and organizations on campus.

1. I consider myself a people person. *1 2 3 4 5*

2. I want to be involved in a campus organization. *1 2 3 4 5*

3. I understand the Greek system. *1 2 3 4 5*

4. I consider myself a leader. *1 2 3 4 5*

5. I am a good communicator. *1 2 3 4 5*

6. I like to have responsibility. *1 2 3 4 5*

7. My friends are involved in student activities. *1 2 3 4 5*

8. I feel that involvement is important to my career. *1 2 3 4 5*

9. I would join a club or organization alone. *1 2 3 4 5*

10. I am aware of the services available on campus. *1 2 3 4 5*

5 = Strongly Agree

4 = Agree

3 = Don't Know

2 = Disagree

1 = Strongly Disagree

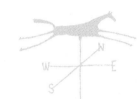

A SELF-ASSESSMENT Total your points from these ten questions. Refer to the following rating scale to determine where you stand in relation to extra- and cocurricular activities.

0–10   *You probably have not thought much about getting involved and you don't know exactly how to get involved. You do not consider activities a priority while in college.*

11–20   *You may have thought about getting involved, but you have not made any effort to do so. You think that some degree of involvement might be important to your career.*

21–30   *Your knowledge about active involvement is average. You have considered getting involved and may have thought about what activity you would like to join.*

31–40   *You have probably given some serious thought to getting involved. You understand how important involvement is to your collegiate success.*

41–50   *You have more than likely joined a club, organization, or Greek fraternity or sorority. You know the importance of getting involved in activities.*

Now, refer to your journal and respond in writing to your findings. Consider the following questions when writing in your journal.

1. Why are extracurricular activities important?

2. What club or organization are you interested in joining?

3. How could this club or organization help you in your career?

Why Get Involved?

You might be saying to yourself, "I don't have the time," or "There is nothing that really interests me," or "I'm not going to that meeting by myself!" Such thoughts are valid on the surface, but when you consider the number of activities available to you and the benefits of getting involved, you might just change your mind. If there is one piece of advice that almost every student affairs professional, professor, administrator, and former student would give, it is *Get involved!* "I'm here for an education, not a party," you might say. Well, again, academics are indeed the most important aspect of college life, but your education will be greatly enhanced if you participate in organizations and activities. Study after study suggests that "students who join social fraternities or sororities or participate in extracurricular activities of almost *any* type are less likely to drop out" (Astin, 1985).

Get involved!

Asked what advice he would give students who wanted to get the most out of college, David, a former student, replied, "First of all, get involved. . . . I remember sitting over in the student union with somebody standing up on the stage preaching to me about getting involved. It went in one ear and out the other. But it is the truth. Find yourself a niche, a group, or something. *Just get involved.* You meet more people. You have more fun. You'll have something to put on your résumé that says, 'I did more than just go to class'" (Chickering and Schlossberg, 1995).

Another student, Susan, had a similar suggestion: "Do everything you can do. Don't ever think anything is going to be boring or worthless. Get involved. Don't sit back, because the organization is not going to come to you . . . you have to go out there and sign up. . . . If you just go to class and don't get involved in other things, it is awfully depressing. And you are not enriching what you have learned in classes with the real world, real events" (Chickering and Schlossberg, 1995).

Cocurricular and Extracurricular Activities

ost student activities are referred to as extracurricular activities, but some of the activities in which you might be involved will actually be cocurricular. Cocurricular suggests that the activity goes hand in hand with your academic studies. Such organizations as the Computer Club, the Nurse's Association, and the Business Students' Association are considered cocurricular because they enhance academic classes.

Extracurricular activities involve interests and hobbies apart from your studies. Examples of extracurricular organizations include the Chess Club, the Snowboarding Club, the Tennis Club, or the Young Liberals Association. What is extracurricular for one person might be cocurricular for another. What is important is to find a club, organization, or society that allows you to learn, become involved, and grow as a leader.

just get involved.

Types of Organizations and Activities

ave you heard of the underwater basket-weaving club or the GTL (go-to-lunch) society? Well, your campus might not have these two clubs, but almost every college has organizations, clubs, and activities that can enhance your college experience.

SPECIAL STUDENT SERVICES

Special student services are designed for students who have special needs or who are underrepresented on campus. These organizations seek to meet the academic, social, cultural, and physical needs of the students.

■ SERVICES FOR PHYSICALLY IMPAIRED STU-DENTS These services try to ensure that students who have physical limitations can participate in the same types of academic, social, and cultural experiences that are available to nonimpaired students. These services may help students who are mobility impaired, hearing impaired, visually impaired, or emotionally impaired.

■ SERVICES FOR NONTRADITIONAL STU-DENTS Mature students often have special needs that can be met only by administrators, professors, and peers who understand their circumstances. These services may provide assistance with housing, day care, tutorial services, or tutoring.

■ SERVICES FOR INTERNATIONAL STUDENTS Many colleges enroll large numbers of students from abroad. These services provide support and social and cultural activities for international students.

GREEK SOCIETIES

Some universities in Canada house a form of Greek society (fraternities and sororities) on campus. Greek societies provide a wide range of services to the university and the community; they provide opportunities for leadership and developing interpersonal skills and allow men and women to grow and experience different situations in a supportive atmosphere. You may associate the Greek system with the movie *Animal House* and in the past the system has been under fire for hazing, drinking, and drug abuse. Recently, these organizations have worked hard to dispel this negative image. Many fraternities and sororities have now required study time; honour local, provincial, and national drinking and hazing policies; and have implemented community service programs.

Greek societies sponsor rush. During rush, fraternities and sororities openly recruit new members through parties, socials, open houses, and invitations to meetings.

MEDIA ASSOCIATIONS

Some of the most visible organizations on campus are those that deal with and produce various student media, such as the newspaper, yearbook, radio shows, or campus television shows. If you are planning to major in journalism, English, mass media, communications, or another media-related subject, these organizations will be invaluable to you. They provide opportunities to write, produce, research, publish, and showcase your work. Active participation in a media organization could provide you with an entrance into a career in journalism or a related field.

SPECIAL-INTEREST CLUBS

Special-interest clubs and organizations are popular on campuses across the nation. They serve the needs of students from every walk of life and with interests that vary from flower arranging to speaking German. Most academic and social clubs fall into this category. Among the variety of special-interest clubs on your campus you may find the following:

Astronomy Club

Gay and Lesbian Student Union

German, Spanish, or Chinese Club

Green/Environmental Club

Hiking Club

Macintosh Users' Group

National Student Exchange Association

Student–Alumni Association

Travel Club

Women Students' Association

PROFESSIONAL ORGANIZATIONS

The professional organizations found on most large campuses are student wings of larger organizations that serve professionals, such as pharmacists, educators, engineers, accountants, retailers, lawyers, doctors, librarians, social workers, and so on. If a professional organization is represented at your college, *get involved*. Your participation will generate contacts that can help you for the rest of your life. You will make friends and job contacts, be able to attend professional conferences, and become involved in activities that support your academic classes. Some organizations you may find on campus are

> Canadian Association for Public Relations Professionals
>
> Canadian Marketing Association
>
> Criminology Students Federation
>
> Economics Students Association
>
> Financial Management Association
>
> Institute of Electrical and Electronics Engineers
>
> Medical Students' Association
>
> Political Science Council
>
> Society for Human Resource Management
>
> Society for Journalism Students
>
> Student Bar Association
>
> Student Nurses' Association

RELIGIOUS ORGANIZATIONS

Your campus may offer organizations devoted to religion or a variety of worship services. Religious organizations are intended to give students an outlet for the practice of specific religions. Your campus may have such organizations as

> Baha'i Association
>
> Buddhist Student Association
>
> Campus Crusade for Christ
>
> Catholic Student Association
>
> Christian Fellowship Club
>
> Jewish Student Union

Hindu Student Council

Muslim Students' Association

Religious Studies Federation

MULTICULTURAL ORGANIZATIONS

Many multicultural groups have formed student support groups. Organizations such as the Sri Lankan Student Association, the First Nations Aboriginal Students' Association and the East Asian Society provide support, encouragement, opportunities and cultural events tailored to the needs of specific minorities on campus.

POLITICAL ORGANIZATIONS

Political organizations allow students to get involved in many social and political activities. Participation in a political organization can open doors for students in law, criminal justice, public administration, history, government, and business. Some of the campus organizations related to these fields are

Amnesty International

New Democratic Youth

Progressive Conservative Youth Association

Young Liberals

Young Reformers

FINE ARTS CLUBS

Fine arts clubs offer opportunities for showcasing talent in the visual and performing arts; they offer participation in plays, debates, dance, choral and instrumental performances, and bands; they allow experimentation with watercolour, oils, pastels, and sculpting. If you are interested in one of the fine arts, you may find that your club activities can lead to employment during school and after graduation.

ATHLETICS

College athletics are popular events at many schools. But if you are not a star athlete, or your college does not have a football, golf, basketball, or baseball team, you will still find plenty of opportunities to participate in sports. Some of the options available to you may be

Bowling

Bodybuilding

Fitness

Hockey

Horseback riding

Karate

Mountain climbing

Soccer

Tae Kwon Do

Tennis

Volleyball

White-water rafting

Organization Exploration Activity

Name of organization _____

Advisor to organization _____

President of the organization _____

Are officers elected or appointed? _____

Are elections held each semester or yearly? _____

What leadership opportunities are available? _____

_____

_____

What are the plans of the organization for the year? _____

_____

_____

What were the two major activities of the organization last year? _____

_____

_____

_____

Are scholarship activities available? _____

How many people are involved in the organization? _____

When do they meet? _____

Where do they meet? _____

Are there any social or help projects for the community? _____

What is the organization's philosophy? _____

_____

_____

_____

_____

What is the major goal of the organization? _____

_____

_____

_____

_____

_____

hen all is said and done, what you will remember most about your college years will be the experiences you had and the people you met. Sure, you'll remember a great deal about your studies, but long after you have forgotten who Frederick Taylor was, you will remember the night you scored the winning point in that tennis match. You'll remember the day you were elected president of the Student Government Association. You'll remember the trip you took to a provincial park with the Biology Club. You'll remember the closing night of your college musical.

In no way and under no circumstances should cocurricular and extracurricular activities be your crowning achievement in college. We do not mean to suggest that you should spend the majority of your time involved in activities other than studying. We do want to stress, however, that your college experience will be greatly enhanced by your involvement in activities that will give you a lifetime of memories, experiences, and professional contacts.

Your college experience will be greatly enhanced by your involvement in activities that will give you a lifetime of memories, experiences, and professional contacts.

The one minute journal

In a minute or less, jot down one major idea you learned from this chapter.

What Are You Doing for the Rest of Your Life?: Career Planning

I met Wilma when she was a first-year student in college. I was director of student activities and of the Student Government Association and she was her class representative. Her drive and enthusiasm distinguished her from other new students. She wanted to be a teacher. She had not gone to college immediately after high school; instead, she had taken some time off before entering

the workforce. During this time, Wilma had given her career a great deal of thought. She told me one day, "I've had many jobs in my life, but I've never had a career."

In the upcoming semesters, Wilma was named to the president's list and the dean's list, won several academic scholarships, was elected to the Student Government Association, and placed second in a squash tournament. She was the envy of her peers and colleagues. In addition to energy and drive, she had a desire to have a career, to do something that she loved—to teach. She studied hard, tutored others, and graduated with honours. She received her ECE diploma and transferred to a university and became what she had planned for so many years to be. Today, she teaches small children near her hometown.

Wilma's story does not seem extraordinary until you learn that Wilma began her career pursuit in her mid-forties. Today, in her sixties, she still teaches. She is

I've had many jobs in my life, but I've never had a career.

an inspiration to all her students and colleagues who learn from her and love her dearly.

Although most of us do not delay our career decisions for more than 20 years, as did Wilma, many students do have a hard time deciding what they want to do for their life's work. Entering the job market often helps people decide what they do not want to do, but people seldom have a clear vision of their career path. Many people search their whole lives to find that certain something that will make them feel worthy, useful, productive, and needed. Yet research suggests that we spend less than 20 hours of our lives in actual career planning (Ellis et al., 1990).

Few people realize that there are 13.5 million workers in Canada. Even fewer realize that by the year 2000, 58 percent of all new jobs will require more than 12 years of training and 40 percent will require at least 17 years of education (Colin Campbell, 1994).

This chapter is intended to guide you through a series of questions and thoughts that will start you on the road to thinking about your future.

At the end of this chapter, you will be able to

- Determine the difference between doing and being

- Define the difference between a job and a career

- Identify personal traits that affect job selection and performance

- Use the seven-step plan to decide on a career

- Develop a personal success plan

- Research a career path

- Identify resources for future career study

Take a moment to assess where you are right now in deciding on your life's work.

AT THIS MOMENT...

5 = Strongly Agree

4 = Agree

3 = Don't Know

2 = Disagree

1 = Strongly Disagree

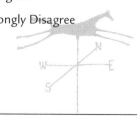

1. I have decided on a career.
   1 2 3 4 5

2. I know the difference between jobs and careers.
   1 2 3 4 5

3. I have researched a career before. *1 2 3 4 5*

4. I know how to research a career. *1 2 3 4 5*

5. I know where the career centre is located.
   1 2 3 4 5

6. I have been to an employment agency. *1 2 3 4 5*

7. I know my personality type.
   1 2 3 4 5

8. I know how my personal interests can affect my career decisions. *1 2 3 4 5*

9. I know how to use the *National Occupational Classification, Occupational Descriptions.*
   1 2 3 4 5

10. I know how to develop a success plan. *1 2 3 4 5*

A SELF-ASSESSMENT Total your points from these ten questions. Refer to the following rating scale to determine where you stand in relation to your career-planning efforts.

0–10 You have given little or no consideration to career planning.

11–20 You have given some thought to career planning.

21–30 You have given a moderate amount of thought to career planning.

31–40 You have given considerable thought to career planning.

41–50 You have given a great deal of consideration to career planning.

Now, refer to your journal and respond in writing to your findings. Consider the following questions when writing in your journal.

1. Have I made a career decision?

2. Have I researched a career?

3. How much thought have I actually put into my career plans?

Do You Want to Do Something or Be Something?

I f you were to ask most people on the street the simple question "What do you do for a living?" they would respond, "I'm a welder" or "I'm an engineer" or "I'm a teacher." Most people answer the question without thinking about what is really being asked.

One of the first questions that you need ask yourself when deciding on a career is "Do I want to *do* something or do I want to *be* something?" The title "welder," or "engineer," or "teacher" does not by itself make you be a welder or engineer or teacher. The art of *being* is a mind-set that you have to develop on your own. There are many people who teach for a living, but there are very few teachers. There are people who do social work, but few are social workers. To be something, you have to make a philosophical decision regarding your future. The questions you have to ask are "How do I want to spend my time?" and "What is my purpose in life?" As an individual, you can do almost anything. You can *do* the work of medicine, you can *do* the work of upholding the law, you can *do* the work of instruction; but in

> I went into the woods because I wished to live deliberately, to front only the essential facts of life, and see if I could not learn what it had to teach, and not, when I came to die, discover that I had not lived.
>
> Henry David Thoreau, author

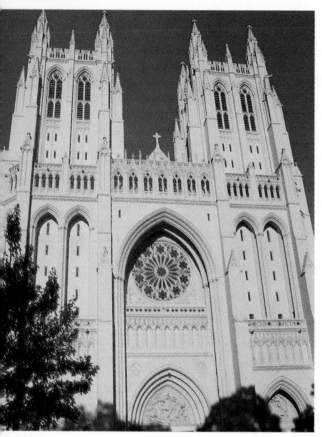

order to *be* a doctor, lawyer, or teacher, you have to want to *become* the ideal for which those professions stand. Doing is the easy part, but doing the work is not enough to bring fulfillment to your life; it is being the person who heals, protects justice, or teaches that can bring you joy.

There is an old story about a stranger walking down a road. He came upon a man cutting stone and stopped to ask what he was doing. "I'm cutting these rocks in half, can't you see that?" The stranger continued on his way until he encountered a second man cutting stone. Again he stopped and asked the man what he was doing. "I'm shaping these stones into blocks, can't you see?" Finally, the stranger came upon a third man cutting stone and stopped to ask him what he was doing. The stonecutter replied, "I'm building a cathedral, can't you see?"

Whereas it takes only physical strength to *do* something, it takes vision to *be* something. So, what do you want to *be?* Take a moment to reflect on your dreams for a career.

1. When you were a child, what was the first thing you ever wanted to be? _____

_____

_____

_____

2. Are you considering this same career now? Why or why not? _____

_____

_____

_____

3. Money aside, what would you do if you had the chance to do anything in this world? _____

_____

_____

_____

4. Who is the person in your life who has the career that you want? _____

_____

_____

_____

5. Why do you admire that person and his or her career? _____

_____

_____

_____

_____

6. How do you best like to spend your time? _____

_____

_____

_____

_____

_____

7. Write a statement detailing what you perceive as your purpose in life. _____

_____

_____

_____

_____

_____

_____

The discovery of your statement may very well lead you to a career choice. So often people choose careers with the purpose of making money or making others happy, and these decisions go against the grain of their perceived life's purpose. The hardest question to answer in this chapter is "Does my career choice complement my life's purpose?" Only you can answer this question.

Deepak Chopra, in his book *The Seven Spiritual Laws of Success* (1994), refers to this situation as the Law of Dharma. "Dharma is a Sanskrit word that means 'purpose in life.' According to this law, you have a unique talent and a unique way of expressing it. There is something that you can do better than anyone else in the whole world. . . ." Have you found that something? Have you put your finger on your purpose? If not, don't worry right now. Read on. Maybe we can help.

You've Got a Job, Now You Want a Career

Everyone at some time faces the age-old question "Should I be what others think I should be or should I be what I want to be?" The life's work for many people turns out to be what other people think it should be. Well into the latter half of the twentieth century, women were expected to have traditional female careers, such as teaching, nursing, or homemaking. They had little opportunity to select a profession that suited them; society selected their professions for them. It was uncommon for women to enter the fields of engineering, construction, management, public safety, or politics; the avenues to such choices were not open.

College students, male and female, still face pressures to be what others want them to be. Parents actively guide their children toward professions that suit their ideas of what their children should do. Some students have little choice in deciding what they will do for the rest of their lives.

For nontraditional students, spouses, time, and finances may dictate a profession. Many choose courses of study that can be completed quickly because finances and family considerations pressure them in that direction. Money is often another consideration when choosing a profession. Regardless of the pressures you have in your life, be careful to research your choices, talk with people already in the profession you are considering, and consider the long-term effects of your decisions. You want your career decisions to be well thought out, well planned, and carefully executed.

Webster's New Collegiate Dictionary defines a job as "An action that needs to be done, an act performed in exchange for money, a piece of

work to be accomplished, a duty or responsibility." The same dictionary defines a career as "The general course of one's life, a chosen pursuit, a path." *There is a great difference between a job and a career.* If you enter a profession under pressure of another person, you are likely to find yourself in a job, but if you make the decision on your own after careful planning and consideration, you will probably find yourself with a career, a chosen pursuit, a path for life.

James seemed to have it all—a good, solid education, a home, a nice car, and a career, but James hated his job as an accountant. He was physically sick each morning knowing that he had to look at numbers all day. His friends were shocked when they found out, because they all had thought he was happy. After all, why would he spend four years in university studying something that he did not like? Later, James told his friends that his parents had pressured him to study accounting because they knew that he would always be able to find a job in that field.

James is not alone. Countless thousands of people go to their jobs every day and wish they had jobs they loved—careers. James became so unhappy in his job that he began to go to school part time to become a physical therapist. In less than three years, he had quit his job as an accountant and had embarked on his career in the field of medicine. Today, he is happy with his *career* and very pleased that he decided to return to school for additional training.

You are the only person who will ever be able to determine the answers to the questions "How do I want to spend my time?" and "What is my purpose in life?" No parent, teacher, partner, counsellor, or therapist will ever be able to fully answer these questions for you. Another person may be able to provide information that can help you make the decision, but ultimately, you will be the person in charge of your career path, your life's work.

What Do You Want to Be When You Grow Up?

More people than you would imagine have trouble deciding what they want to be when they grow up. Studies indicate that more than 20 percent of all first-year college and university students do not know what their careers or majors will be. That's all right for the time being, but before long you will need to make a decision.

The questions that follow are designed to help you make that decision regarding what you want to do with the rest of your life— your career.

After you have answered these questions, you need to look for a pattern. If you want to work outdoors, love people, enjoy leading, and like to dress casually, then accounting is probably not the profession for you. However, if you like to dress up daily, enjoy working with numbers, work well under limited supervision, and enjoy the indoors,

> Find a job you like and you'll never have to work a day in your life.
>
> Unknown

then accounting or banking might be right for you. Be sure that your answers are *yours*. Don't let your fears or anything else influence you. You are the one who will ultimately have to live with your decisions, not someone else.

YOUR CAREER SELF-STUDY

■ WHAT IS YOUR PERSONALITY TYPE? You can best answer this question by taking a personality inventory, such as the Myers–Briggs Type Indicator or the Teiger Personality Test. This question is important, because your personality may very well indicate the type of work in which you will be successful and happy. If you are a real people person, for example, in a job with minimal human contact and interaction, you probably will not be very happy. Make an appointment with the career centre or a career counsellor to learn about your personality type.

After your appointment, describe your personality type. ____

_____

_____

_____

How will your personality type affect your career path? _____

_____

_____

_____

■ WHAT ARE YOUR INTERESTS? Understanding your specific interests may help you decide on a career. If you love working with cars, you might consider being a mechanic for a living. If you love to draw or build things, you might be interested in architecture or sculpting as a career.

What are your major interests? _____

_____

_____

_____

How can these interests be transferred to a career choice? _____

_____

■ DO YOU ENJOY PHYSICAL OR MENTAL WORK? Many people would go crazy if they had to spend so much as one hour per day in an office. Others would be unhappy if they had to work in the sun all day or use a great deal of physical strength. The answer to this question will greatly narrow down your career choices. For example, if you are an outdoor person who loves being outside in all kinds of weather, then you should probably avoid careers that are limited to indoor work. You should also consider whether you have any physical limitations that might affect your career choice.

Do you enjoy physical or mental work or both? Why? _____

_____

_____

_____

What does this mean to your career path? _____

_____

_____

_____

■ DO YOU WANT TO MAKE A LOT OF MONEY? Most people, if asked, "Why do you work?" would respond, "For the money." There is nothing wrong with wanting to make money in your profession, but not all professions, regardless of their worth, pay well. Some of the hardest and most rewarding work pays the least. You have to decide whether to go for the money or to do something that is personally challenging to you. *Many* times, you can find both!

Is your major goal in choosing a profession money or something else? What?

_____

_____

_____

What does your goal mean to your career path? _____

_____

_____

_____

WHAT ARE YOU DOING FOR THE REST OF YOUR LIFE?   343

■ WHERE DO YOU WANT TO LIVE? Although this question may sound strange, many careers are limited by geography. If you are interested in oceanography, you would be hard-pressed to live in Saskatchewan; if you love farming, Toronto would be an improbable place for you to live. Some people simply prefer certain parts of Canada (or the world) to others. You need to ask yourself, "Where do I eventually want to live?" "What climate do I really enjoy?" "In what size city or town do I want to work?" "Where would I be the happiest?" "Do I want to live near my family or away from them?"

Where do you eventually want to live? Why? _____

_____

_____

_____

_____

What does your preference mean to your career path? _____

_____

_____

_____

■ DO YOU WANT TO TRAVEL? Some jobs require travel; some people love to travel, some hate it. Ask yourself whether you want to be away from your home and family four nights per week or whether you want a job that does not require travel at all.

Do you enjoy travel? Do you want to do a lot of travelling? _____

_____

_____

_____

What does this mean to your career path? _____

_____

_____

_____

■ HOW DO YOU LIKE TO DRESS? Some people enjoy dressing up and welcome the opportunity to put on a new suit and go to work. Others prefer to throw on an old pair of blue jeans and head out the door. Jobs have different requirements in terms of dress, and you will be affected by them every workday, so you will want to consider your own preferences.

How do you like to dress? Why? _____

_____

_____

_____

What does this mean to your career path? _____

_____

_____

_____

■ WHAT MOTIVATES YOU? What are the one or two things in your life that motivate you? Money? Power? Helping other people? The answer to this question is an essential element to choosing a career. You have to find that certain something that gives you energy and then find a profession that allows you to pursue it with fervour and intensity.

What is your motivational force and why? _____

_____

_____

_____

How could this help you in deciding on a career path? _____

_____

_____

_____

■ WHAT DO YOU VALUE? Do you value relationships, possessions, money, love, security, challenges, or power? Once you have identified what you value in your life, you can identify careers that closely match your personal value system and eliminate careers that don't. If you have to constantly compromise your values just to get a paycheck you will be miserable.

What do you truly value in your life? _____

_____

_____

_____

How might these values affect your career decisions? _____

_____

_____

_____

■ WHAT ARE YOUR SKILLS? Are you very good at one or two things?
Are you a good typist, a good manager of money, a good carpenter, a
good communicator? Your skills will play a powerful part in selecting a
career. If you are not good or skilled at using numbers, then you will
probably want to avoid careers that require their constant use. If you are
not a good communicator, then you probably do not want a career that
requires you to give daily presentations. Employers still stress the
importance of three basic skills: writing, speaking, and listening. If you
have these skills, you are ahead of the pack. If not, you need to work on
developing them to make you more employable.

What are your skills? What do you do well? _____

_____

_____

_____

How could your strongest skills help you make a career decision? _____

_____

_____

_____

■ DO YOU LIKE ROUTINE? The answer to this question will narrow
down your choices tremendously. If you like routine, you will want a
career that is conducive to routine and provides structure. If you do
not like routine and enjoy doing different things each day, certain
careers will be unrealistic for you.

Do you like routine or do you prefer variety? Why? _____

_____

_____

_____

How does this affect your career path? _____

_____

_____

_____

■ ARE YOU A LEADER? One of the most important questions you must ask yourself is "Do I enjoy leading, teaching, or guiding people?" If you prefer to be a part of the crowd and do not like to stand out as a leader or manager, some careers may not suit you. If you like to take charge and get things done when you are with other people, you will find certain careers better than others. How you relate to leadership will be a part of your personality inventory.

Do you consider yourself a leader? Are you comfortable in a leadership role?

Why or why not? _____

_____

_____

_____

How will your feelings about leadership affect your career path? _____

_____

_____

_____

Deciding on a Career

o, it isn't a fatal disease. You're not dying. Being undecided is not a disgrace, nor a weakness. It is a temporary state of mind, and the best way to deal with it is to stop and think. You should not decide upon a career because you are ashamed to be undecided, and you shouldn't allow yourself to be pressured into doing so. Instead, you can take measures to work toward making your career decision and being satisfied with your choice.

> Not all who wander are lost.
>
> J. R. R. Tolkien, author

SEVEN STEPS TO CAREER DECISION MAKING

Step 1—Dream! If money were not a problem or concern, what would you do for the rest of your life? If you could do anything in the world, what would you do? Where would you do it? These are the types of questions you must ask yourself as you try to select a major and career. Go outside, lie on the grass, and look up at the sky; think silently for a little while. Let your mind wander, and let the sky be the

limit. Write your dreams down. These dreams may be closer to reality than you think. In the words of Don Quixote, "Let us dream, my soul, let us dream" (Unamuno).

Step 2—Talk to your advisor. Academic advisors are there to help you. But don't be surprised if their doors are sometimes closed. They teach, conduct research, perform community service, and sometimes advise in excess of 100 students. Always call in advance; make an appointment to see an advisor. When you have that appointment, make your advisor work for you. Take your calendar and ask questions, hard questions. Your advisor will not make a career decision for you, but if you ask the proper questions, he or she can be of monumental help to you and your career decisions.

Use students in your program as advisors, too. They will be invaluable to you as you work your way through the daily routine of the college. Experienced students can assist you in making decisions about your courses, programs, and work–study programs. They can even help you join and become an active member of a career-related organization.

Step 3—Use electives. Most universities and some colleges allow you to take at least one elective. Some programs allow many more. Use your electives wisely! Do not take courses just to get the hours. The wisest students use their electives to delve into new areas of interest or to take a block of courses in an area that might enhance their career decisions. If you are interested in business, you might want to use your first elective to take an introduction to business course. Perhaps you want to use your first elective to take a course in art, music, or psychology. Be creative, be courageous, be wild, but don't play it safe. Take a chance. It can be the best thing that ever happened to you. One of these electives might be the key to choosing your career.

Step 4—Choose your coop placement carefully. If your program has a field work or coop component, research possible organizations thoroughly. It's important to make the most of this opportunity; field work is a great opportunity to "try out" a career. Since you'll be spending a good number of hours at your coop workplace, make sure you don't just take the first placement that comes along. If you explore a number of organizations, you'll find a placement that best matches your career aspirations.

Step 5—Go to the career centre. Even the smallest colleges have some type of career centre or a career counsellor. *Use them!* Campus career centres usually provide services for free. The same types of services in the community could cost from $200 to $2,000. The professionals in the career centre can provide information on a variety of careers and fields, and they can administer interest and personality inventories that can help you make career and other major decisions.

Step 6—Read, read, read! Nothing will help you more than reading about careers and programs. Ask your advisor or counsellor to help you locate information on your areas of interest. Gather information from colleges, agencies, associations, and places of employment. Then *read it!*

Step 7—Shadowing. No, this is not what vampires do when the moon is full! *Shadowing* describes the process of following someone around on the job. For example, if you have an interest in dental assisting, but you don't know exactly what a dental assistant does all day, you might be able to ask your dentist to let you spend the day shadowing his or her assistant. If you are wondering what engineers do on the job, try calling an engineering office to see whether you can sit with several of their engineers for a day over spring break. Shadowing is the very best way to get firsthand, honest information regarding a profession in which you might be interested. Some of the questions you might ask when shadowing someone include "Why do you do this for a living?" "What training do you have?" "How long did you go to school in order to get this job?" "What is your salary range?" "Is there room for growth?" "What is your greatest achievement on this job?" "What was your weakest moment?"

Step 8—Join career-related professional associations. One of the most important steps you can take as a college student is to become involved in campus organizations and clubs that offer educational opportunities, social interaction, and hands-on experience in your chosen field. Professional organizations can open doors that will help you make a career decision, grow in your field, meet professionals already working in your field, and, eventually, get a job. You can review Chapter 14 for more information about professional organizations.

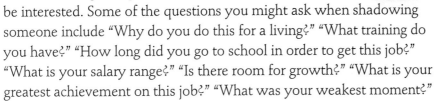

You can take measures to work toward making your career decision and being satisfied with your choice.

■ DISCOVER YOUR INTERESTS Take two minutes to fill in as many circles in the cluster chart as you can with occupations, interests, hobbies, and skills that you feel relate to you. Work quickly. Do not write

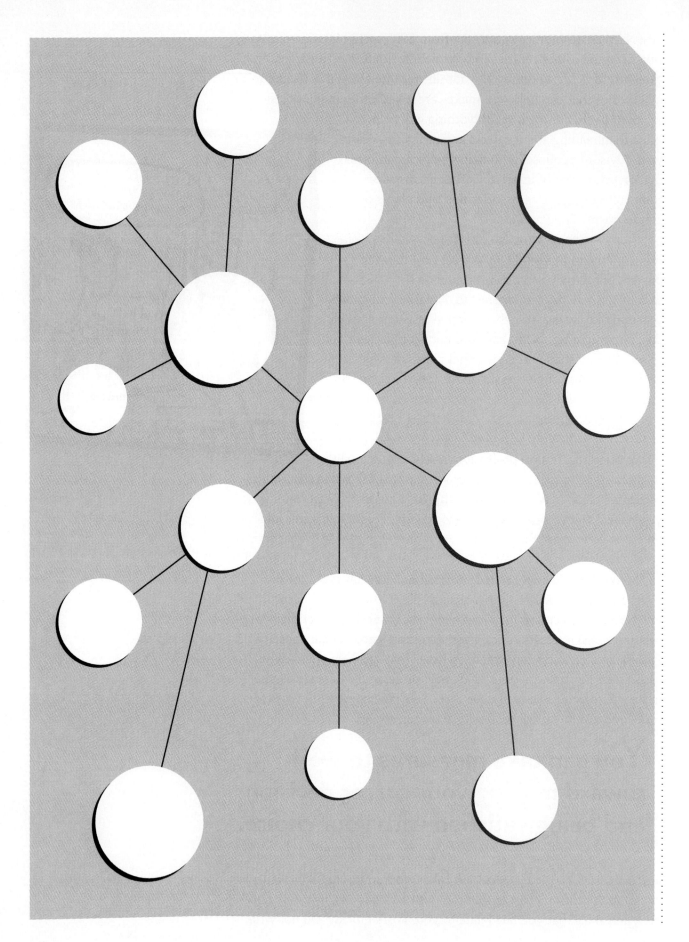

down anything that does not interest you or that you do not want to do with your life. One circle may spur you to continue on to another circle.

Now look at the cluster chart. Is there a pattern? Is a health profession or a public service profession listed in more than one circle?

Rank your responses in relation to your career interests.

1. _____

2. _____

3. _____

4. _____

5. _____

Where to Learn More About

Careers, Programs, and Work

I n your search for opportunity, pursue every avenue that is open to you. So often, we choose only the most obvious paths, unlike the poet Robert Frost, who chose "the road less traveled."

Information regarding careers, majors, and work that you might not have considered can be found in the following resources.

College or community career center

National Occupational Classification, Occupational Descriptions (Employment and Immigration Canada)

Human Resources Development Canada publications (such as *Career Directions, Career Moves, Canada Prospects*)

Canada Employment Centres

Myers-Briggs Personality Indicator

Where the Jobs Are, Colin Campbell

Job Futures - Occupational Outlooks (Human Resources Development Canada)

The Best Jobs for the 1990's and into the 21st Century, Robert Krannich

The 100 Best Careers for the Year 2000, Sally Field

Excelerations and Shifting Gears: Thriving in the New Economy, Nuala Beck

Megatrends 2000 - Ten New Directions for the 1990's, John Naisbitt, Patricia Aburdene

Financial Post 100 Best Companies to Work For

What Color is Your Parachute, Richard Bolles

Magazines career directory

Co-op program directory

Directory of Associations in Canada

Canadian Key Business Directory

Computer databases, such as InterOptions

Networking: The Overlooked
Source for Career Development

W e are often so concerned with books, computerized databases, and interest inventories that we forget to look in our own backyards when thinking about careers. Networking is one of the most important aspects of career development. Look at the person sitting beside you in your orientation class. That person could be a future leader in your field of study. You might be thinking, "No way," but you'd be surprised at how many people lose out on networking opportunities because they do not think ahead. The person sitting beside you is important. You never know where or when you may see this person again—he may be interviewing you for a job in 10 years, or she may be the person with whom you will start a business in 15 years. "Too far down the road," you say? Don't close your eyes—15 years will be here before you can blink.

You've all heard the expression "It's not *what* you know, but *who* you know." Well, few statements could be more true, and college is the perfect place for making many personal and professional contacts. At this moment, you are building a network of people on whom you can call for the rest of your life. Your network may include people you know from

High school and college or university

Clubs and professional organizations

Student government

Newspaper staff

College committees

Sporting teams and events

Fraternities and sororities

Family connections

Community organizations

Volunteer work

> Friends do business with friends.
>
> J. W. Marriott, Jr.,
> founder of
> Marriott Hotels

As you begin to develop your network, remember that you can't meet everyone or participate in every activity. Choose your activities carefully. It is important to maintain high standards when you are involved in activities, clubs, committee work, and volunteer work because your reputation will follow you. Your network of friends will remember your performance.

Mentors

A mentor is someone who can help open doors for you, who will take a personal and professional interest in your development and success. Often a mentor will help you do something that you might have trouble doing on your own. It may be too soon for you to determine now whether you have found a mentor, and you may not find that person until you begin to take courses in your field of study.

The student–mentor relationship is unique. You help one another. Your mentor may provide you with opportunities that you might otherwise not have. You may have to do some grunt work, but the experience will usually help you in the long run. While you are helping your mentor, your mentor is helping you by giving you experience and responsibility.

As a young, uncertain first-year college student, Derrick applied for and was awarded a work-study position with Professor Griffon. His job was to help Professor Griffon prepare mailings and other advertising materials for the public lecture series. The work was monumental, the pay minimal, and Professor Griffon was not always in the best of spirits. On some days Derrick left the office swearing that he would never return. But he had little choice—the job paid more than unemployment. Derrick stayed with the job, and before too long, Professor Griffon began to give him more challenging work.

One day, an important member of the community came to the office. Derrick and the professor were both working at their desks. As the professor and the guest discussed a lucrative contract for a guest lecturer, Derrick overheard Professor Griffon tell the guest he could "bring the contract by tomorrow and leave it with Derrick, my assistant." "Assistant," Derrick thought, "that's interesting."

Before Derrick graduated with his two-year diploma, he had a wealth of experience, knowledge, and, most important, contacts! He had learned how to run the audio-visual equipment in the lecture hall, he had managed the ticket sales, he had developed a marketing plan for one of the events, and he had been able to shadow many of the lecturers who came to the college to speak. All this was possible because of his relationship with Professor Griffon. This student–mentor situation was rewarding for both of them. They helped each other, and both profited.

BENEFITS OF HAVING A MENTOR

- Mentors teach, advise, and coach.

- Mentors serve as a sounding board for ideas.

- Mentors serve as constructive critics.

- Mentors can promote you among their peers and contacts.

- Mentors provide information to help with career development.

- Mentors can increase your visibility on campus and in the work arena.

- Mentors introduce you to people who can advance your career.

HOW TO FIND A MENTOR

You can't go shopping for a mentor; you don't advertise; you can't use someone else's mentor. You find a mentor through preparation, work, emotion, and a feeling of being comfortable. The following suggestions may help you find a mentor.

- Arrive at class early and work hard

- Develop an outstanding work ethic

- Seek advice from many professors and staff members

- Ask intelligent, thoughtful questions

- Offer to help with projects

- Convey the impression that you are committed, competent, and hardworking

- Look for opportunities to shadow

- If a professor or staff member gives you an opportunity, take it

- Look at grunt work as glory work

CORNERSTONES for career development

- Always make educated and researched decisions.

- Never be afraid to change your mind.

- Make your own decisions.

- Know your personality type before making major decisions.

- Pinpoint your interests.

- Identify your physical and emotional limitations.

- Know how important salary is to your future aspirations.

- Determine whether you would like to live in a specific geographic region.

- Know whether you want to travel.

- Identify what motivates you to succeed.

- Know your own value and moral system.

- Identify your best skills and sharpen and promote them.

- Shadow and do volunteer work before deciding on a career.

- Determine whether you enjoy leadership roles.

- Find a mentor.

As a mature, rational, caring human being, you should realize that you are a part of a bigger picture. This world does not belong to you, you are only borrowing it for a while. Everything you do affects someone else in some way. You must realize that what you do—not just what you do for your career, but your daily actions—matters to someone. There is value in every job, and there is honour in all professions performed well and honestly. When making career decisions, you need to take into account the fact that other people, strangers and friends, will eventually be looking to you as a mentor, and a role model. This is a major responsibility that you cannot avoid; rather, you should relish the opportunity to inspire and teach. Embrace the moment. Finally, you must realize that unless you are out there, daily, creating a better future for yourself, you have no right to complain about the one that is handed to you.

1. The career that you have chosen to research is _____

2. Why are you interested in this career? _____

_____

_____

3. What personality type is best suited for this career? _____

_____

4. Does this career require physical or mental work or both? Why? _____

_____

_____

5. What is the average salary for this career? _____

_____

6. Where do most professionals in this occupation live? Is it region-specific? _____

_____

_____

_____

7. Does this career require travel? _____

_____

8. What type of dress is required of people who work in this profession? _____

_____

9. How much training and education are required to work in this career? _____

_____

10. What skills are required to do work in this job? _____

_____

11. Does this career involve routine? _____

_____

12. Does this career require you to be a leader or a participant? _____

_____

13. Does this career require you to work indoors or outdoors? _____

_____

14. What is the code for this profession in the *National Occupational Classification Index of Titles*? _____

_____

15. What are the most positive aspects of this career? _____

_____

_____

_____

_____

16. What is the worst thing about this career? _____

_____

_____

_____

17. Are you still interested in this career? _____

18. Who is a person whom you might be able to shadow in this profession? _____

_____

_____

19. What sources did you use to research this career? _____

_____

_____

_____

20. Whom did you interview to research this career? _____

_____

_____

_____

The one minute journal

n a minute or less, jot down one major idea you learned from this chapter.

UNIT

INTERNET

ACTIVITY

Great Idea!

Many first-year college students are a little lost when it comes to choosing an academic program or deciding what kind of career they want after they graduate. The Internet is a great resource for locating career information.

Use the Internet to research a potential career interest. Using the home page for Career Mosaic (Internet address: http:// www.career-mosaic.com:80/cm/cc), find a list of company names. Select a company name that interests you. Find information about the company and print it. Locate a list of the jobs the company has open.

Do you see a job that interests you? What is it? _____

_____

_____

_____

What major do you think this job requires? _____

_____

_____

_____

Are there summer internships that might give you a taste of what working for this company is like? _____

_____

_____

_____

Write to the company and request information and an application for a summer internship position.

Appendix

Things You Need to Know but Probably Will Never Ask

This appendix provides advice, suggestions, and hints for coping with some of the common problems and situations that you may face in college and university.

THE ACADEMIC ADVISOR

If you have an academic advisor, he or she may be one of the most important people you will meet at college and university. You may never have your advisor for a class or even see your advisor except at registration time each semester, but he or she can be of ultimate assistance to you throughout your academic career.

Advisors are usually appointed by the university or college, although a few schools allow students to select their own advisors. A good advisor will be of tremendous value to you; a poor advisor is one of the worst things that could happen to you. If you find that you and your advisor are completely incompatible, do not hesitate to ask for a reassignment.

Recognize that *you* are the person most responsible for the completion of your degree. You should know as much as your advisor about your degree or diploma.

Your roommates, friends, and peers can help you in the advising and registration process, but the last word should always come from your advisor. Your decisions about classes and scheduling should be made with the advice of faculty, staff, and the administration.

If you do not know why you have to take certain courses or in what sequence courses should be taken, don't leave your advisor's office until you find out. Lack of understanding of your course sequence, your course calendar, or the requirements for graduation could mean the difference between graduating or not graduating.

Academic advisors are not counsellors or psychological counsellors. They are assigned to assist students in completing their academic programs of study. They may offer advice on personal or career matters, but they are not trained to assist with psychological and emotional matters. However, if you are having problems not related to your academic studies, your academic advisor may be able to direct you to the professional on campus who can best help you address certain issues and problems. Your academic advisor may be the first person to contact in times of crisis.

 **CORNERSTONES** for making the most of the student–advisor relationship

- Locate your advisor as soon as you arrive on campus and introduce yourself. Begin your relationship on a positive note.

- Stop by to say hello if you see your advisor in his or her office. Don't stay for a long time without an appointment, but a brief hello can help you build your relationship.

- Prepare a list of questions before you go to your advisor. This will help ensure that you have all the answers you need when you leave.

- Call your advisor if you have a problem that can be dealt with over the phone.

- Don't go to your advisor unprepared. You should have an idea of which classes you would like to take or need to take for the upcoming semester.

THE COURSE CALENDAR

Every college and university in the nation has a different calendar. Don't make the mistake of thinking that these calendars are advertising tools and not that important. Your course calendar is one of the most important publications you will read as a student. It describes the rules, regulations, policies, procedures, and requirements of the institution and your academic degree. It is imperative for you to keep the course calendar that was issued during your first year. Because academic degree/diploma requirements can change from year to year, most post-secondary schools require that you graduate under the rules and requirements published in the calendar issued during your first year. This policy is sometimes referred to as the grandfather clause.

The course calendar includes information about adding and dropping classes, auditing, probation, plagiarism, attendance, honours, course descriptions, graduation requirements, faculty credentials, and accreditation and usually includes a campus map. It is an important tool.

PREREGISTRATION

Sounds simple: preregister, "to register beforehand." Preregistration is a process by which you reserve your seat in classes for the upcoming semester. Although it sounds simple, a large number of students fail to preregister or pay fees. If you are at a large institution, preregistration is a must. If 300 people want to take a class that has 45 seats, logic will tell you that you can't walk in on the first day of class and expect to get a seat. Your graduation may hinge on preregistration; if you are not able to enrol in certain classes, your course sequence could be thrown off and you may have to wait an entire year before a prerequisite class is offered again.

It is equally important to pay your fees on time to ensure that your seat is held until the semester begins. Many institutions have a purge date. If you do not pay your fees by the end of fall term exams, for instance, your schedule of classes and your seats in those classes are purged from the computer and another student will get your seat. You may have to pay a late fee and go through the registration process again. More important, the classes you need may be full, and you will have to wait another year to take them. Preregister and pay your fees! Consult your schedule of classes to determine registration dates and fee payment dates.

CORNERSTONES for developing a schedule and preregistering

- Never wait until the last day of preregistration to begin the process.

- Think ahead. If preregistration begins on August 15, you should review the course calendar before that date to begin planning your schedule.

- Make an appointment with your advisor early. Keep the appointment and be on time.

- When developing your schedule, work with several plans. If one class happens to be full, what are your alternatives? The students who graduate on time are the students who know how to plan alternatives.

- Present your advisor with options. Don't suggest only one class or time. You may have to rearrange your life to get the course you need. Do it!

■ There is no need to pay your fees on the first day of fee payment, but make sure that you do not miss the deadline.

INDEPENDENT STUDY AND DISTANCE-LEARNING COURSES

Independent study courses or courses taught by distance learning are great for students who work or have families and small children. These courses have flexible hours and few, if any, class meetings, and allow you to work at your own pace. Do not let anyone try to tell you that these courses are easier than regular classroom offerings; they are not. Independent study and distance-learning courses are usually more difficult for the average student. Some colleges and universities reserve independent study and distance-learning courses for students with GPAs of 3.0 or higher. You need to be a self-starter and highly motivated to complete and do well in these courses.

for succeeding in independent study and distance-learning courses

■ If at all possible, review the material for the course *before* you register. This may help you in making the decision to enroll.

■ Begin before the beginning! If at all possible, obtain the independent study packet or distance-learning tape before the semester begins and start working. You may think you have the whole semester, but time will quickly slip by.

■ Make an appointment to meet the professor as soon as possible. Some colleges will schedule a meeting for you. If it is not possible to meet, at least phone the professor and introduce yourself.

■ Communicate with your advisor from time to time via E-mail if your campus is equipped for you to do so.

■ Develop a schedule for completing each assignment and stick to it! Don't let time steal away from you. This is the biggest problem with these courses.

- Keep a copy of all work mailed to the professor or the school. When possible, send your materials by registered mail to ensure their delivery.

- Always mail or deliver your assignment on time or even early if possible. Remember that you have deadlines and the mail system can be slow. Allow time in your schedule for revisions.

- Try to find someone who is registered for the same course so that you can work together or at least have a phone number to call if you run into a problem.

SUMMER SCHOOL

Some students can think of nothing worse than summer school. Others see it as a chance to get ahead or repeat a class in which they might have received a poor grade. Whether you attend summer school by choice or necessity, it can be a rough experience if you do not pace yourself and prepare from day one. Although you will have an instructor in summer classes, summer school is similar to independent study or distance-learning courses in that you must begin your studies, projects, and activities from day one! Most summer sessions last only a few weeks, and you will not have time to put things off until later. You will be exposed to the same amount of information and the same amount of work involved in courses offered during the regular semester.

Some academic programs require students to attend for at least one summer session during a four-year degree program. Some degrees cannot be completed in four years without taking a course during the summer or an overload during the fall or spring semesters. If this is your situation, a few courses in summer school may be an option for you.

You may want to save your more difficult courses for the summer session when you can take only one course at a time. Many students take courses with labs during the summer, because they can devote more time to them then than is possible during the traditional semester.

If you are attending a college far from home, you might consider taking a class locally during the summer. Most post-secondary schools require you to get permission from your registrar or department head before enrolling in a summer program at another school if you want credit for your work. Check your course calendar for details and rules regarding status as a *transient* student.

DROPPING CLASSES, DROPPING OUT, AND STOPPING OUT

Sometimes students have to drop a class or their entire schedule because of family problems, medical reasons, work, or other reasons.

We mention this because some students simply "leave" college, thinking that if they do not come back, their classes will automatically be dropped and everything will be fine. Then, when they return or transfer to another institution, they are horrified to see five F's on their transcript. Never assume that your classes have been dropped from your records. At most schools, classes are *not* automatically dropped. *You* must take care of this process. To make matters worse, some colleges and universities *never* remove grades from your transcript, even if you repeat the course a thousand times and get an A every time. If you leave your classes without taking care of the paperwork, your grade of F can be with you *and* be calculated in your GPA for the rest of your academic years.

If you have to drop all your courses, it is best to talk with each professor and explain why you are leaving. An open and honest relationship with your professors could help you when you return. Leaving your program for an entire semester is called dropping out; if you decide not to return, the same term applies. Leaving school for one semester because of problems, work, or personal reasons and planning to return is sometimes called stopping out. Whether you drop a class, drop out for the semester, or stop out for a year, make sure that your records are in order *before* you go. This will save you money, time, effort, energy, and frustration upon your return to school. Consult your course calendar for information dealing with dropping out, dropping courses, or stopping out.

THE PROFESSORATE

In high school, if a teacher is out because of illness or for some other reason, a substitute teaches the class. In college and university, substitutes are rarely used. When a professor is absent because of illness, a conference, or another commitment, the class is usually cancelled. Occasionally, guest lecturers substitute for an absent professor. Do not assume that you can cut class or give less than your full attention to a guest professor. Information provided by a guest professor often appears on tests and quizzes.

■ WHEN THE PROFESSOR DOESN'T SHOW At times during your academic career a professor will not show up for class. This will be rare, but it will happen. Sometimes, a note on the board or door will explain the circumstances of the professor's absence. If there is no note, assume that the professor is running late. Do not leave class just because the professor is not there on time. Use common sense and wait long enough to see whether the professor is just running late or is truly not going to show for the class.

You might consider starting a roster for students to sign before they leave so that you all have proof that you attended the class. You can present the list to the professor if there is a question about attendance.

Consult your course calendar or your course syllabus for details regarding a policy for waiting when a professor does not arrive.

■ WHEN PROFESSORS DON'T SPEAK ENGLISH WELL Yes, you will have professors who do not speak English well. Universities often hire professors from around the world because of their expertise in their subjects. You may be shocked to find that it is difficult to understand a professor's dialect or pronunciation. If you have a professor with a foreign dialect remember these hints:

- Sit near the front of the room

- Watch the professor's mouth when you can

- Follow the professor's nonverbal communication patterns

- Use a tape recorder if allowed

- Read the material beforehand so that you will have a general understanding of what is being discussed

- Ask questions when you do not understand the material

- Research and obtain a copy of the previous year's course notes

■ UNDERSTANDING WHAT PROFESSORS WANT Professors are unique. They all value and appreciate different things. What makes one professor the happiest person on earth will upset another. One professor may love students who ask questions and another professor will think these students are trying to be difficult. One instructor may enjoy students who have opposing points of view, while the next may consider them troublemakers. One professor may be stimulated when students stop by the office to chat, while another may consider this an infringement on his or her time.

The best way to deal with your professors is as individuals, on a one-to-one, class-by-class basis. Take some time at the beginning of the semester to make notes about what you see in class, how students are treated who do certain things, and how the professor reacts in certain situations. This exercise will assist you in decoding your professors and in making the most out of your relationship with them.

There are, of course, certain characteristics that all professors cherish in students, so keep in mind that all professors like students who

- Read the text

- Come to class and come on time

- Hand in assignments on time

You may feel that it is crazy to talk about financial aid at this point. After all, you had to have found the money to enroll in college or you would not be in this orientation class. Still, financial aid comes in many forms, and there may be some sources of aid you have not yet thought about that can help you through the rest of your education.

Applications for Canada's Student Loans Program are available at your post secondary institution, or from your province's student aid office. Some provinces require you to submit your financial aid application directly to your institution, while others require that the application be submitted to the student aid office. Details are available at your institution's financial aid office, or you can consult the federal government's Canada Student Loans Program Student Guide publication, which is produced by Human Resources Development Canada. The guide also outlines eligibility, amount of assistance available, payment terms, interest rates, and sources that provide additional information.

Each provincial government publishes an application and guide to its financial aid program. These guides are available in your college or university's financial aid office.

Some students may be confused about the difference between loans, grants and work-study. They are defined as follows:

- Grants — Monies that you don't have to repay

- Work-Study — Money earned for working at college or university; this money does not have to be repaid.

- Loans — Borrowed money that must be repaid *with* interest.

As you apply for financial aid, keep these guidelines in mind.

STUDENT ELIGIBILITY FOR FINANCIAL AID

To receive aid from Canada's Student Loans Program, you must:

- Be a Canadian citizen or permanent resident of Canada;

- Be a resident of a province or territory that participates in the Canada Student Loans Program. The province of Quebec and the Northwest Territories operate their own student assistance plans;

- Satisfy the appropriate provincial or territorial authority that financial resources available to you are not enough to cover your education costs by completing an application form for student assistance;

- Enroll or be qualified to enroll in at least 60% of full-time course load at a designated post-secondary educational institution. Students with permanent disabilities are required to enroll in 40% of a full-time course load; and

- Enroll or be qualified to enroll, in a program leading to a degree, diploma or certificate. The program must be at least 12 weeks in length within a period of 15 consecutive weeks.

To continue to be eligible for a full-time Canada Student Loan in subsequent years:

- You must successfully complete at least 60% of full-time post-secondary course load for which you have received a Canada Student Loan. This means, for example, passing three out of five courses.

- There is a limit to the number of weeks of assistance, depending on your program and depending on when you started studying.

- You must complete the program within the number of periods of study normally specified by the school for completion of that program plus one additional period.

- You can't have been denied further assistance for reasons such as failing to make payments on your Canada Student Loan for 60 days or more.

Source: Canada Student Loans Program Student Guide, Human Resources Development Canada

The Canada Student Loans Program Student Guide also cites the following sources for student assistance:

- Your own money from work and savings

- Financial help from your family

- Scholarships and bursaries

Other sources include child care bursaries, bursaries for students with disabilities, and work study programs.

You will also want to research

- Your course calendar (for scholarships at your school)

- Your place of employment

- Your parents' or spouse's place of employment

- Social and civic groups within your community or hometown

CORNERSTONES for applying for financial aid

- *Do not miss a deadline.* There are *no* exceptions for making up deadlines for financial aid!

- *Read* all instructions before beginning the process.

- Always fill out the application completely and have someone proof your work.

- If documentation is required, submit it according to the instructions. Do not fail to do all that the application asks you to do.

- Never lie about your financial status.

- Begin the application process as soon as possible. Do not wait until the last moment. Some aid is given on a first come, first served basis. Income tax preparation time is usually financial aid application time.

- Talk to the financial aid officer at the institution you will attend or to your high school guidance counsellor. Person-to-person contact is always best. Never assume anything until you get it in writing.

- Take copies of flyers and brochures that are available from the financial aid office. Private companies and civic groups will often notify the financial aid office if they have funds available.

- Always apply for admission as well as financial aid. Many awards are given by colleges or universities to students who are already accepted.

- If you are running late with an application, find out if there are electronic means of filing.

- Always keep a copy of your tax returns for each year!

- Apply for everything possible. You will get nothing if you do not apply.

WORK–STUDY PROGRAMS

A part of your financial aid package could include work–study. In this program you work a few hours each week and earn a paycheque at the end of each month to help defray the cost of your education. A work–study program confers several secondary benefits that can make this a vital aspect of financing your tuition.

A work–study position provides additional experiences that may allow you to explore jobs and activities that you may not previously have considered. Work–study jobs are often connected to the department or discipline of your major or program, and the knowledge and experience you can gain are immeasurable.

Work–study can also provide the opportunity for you to meet people who may eventually help you get a job, help you get into graduate school, or assist you through difficult times in your diploma or degree program. Work–study is more than earning money; it is a chance to explore new options, meet exciting people, and gain experience in your discipline. Work–study money is taxed, and counts against your earned income when applying for financial aid for the next year.

PAYING TUITION

Paying tuition is another process that *sounds* simple, and it is if you do it. Yet each semester, countless students for one reason or another do not pay their tuition on time, or at all, and lose their spots in classes for which they were preregistered. Painful as it may be, you *must* observe the deadlines for payment dates. Paying tuition on time can save you $25 to $50 in late fees, not to mention the hassle and frustration of having to reregister. Take this seriously. If you can pay your tuition by mail, you can avoid wasting valuable time standing in long lines. However, never send cash in the mail. Keep your paid receipts from tuition payments.

BUYING A MEAL PLAN

Some colleges and universities offer a meal plan, some do not. Some schools require on-campus students to purchase some variation of a meal plan, others do not. You will need to consult your student handbook for details. Be careful about purchasing something that you may not use. If you purchase a three meal-a-day plan, but never get up early enough to eat breakfast, you have wasted a great deal of money. If you have pizza delivered to your room a lot and don't eat dinner at the dining hall or cafeteria, again, *you* have wasted money. Purchase a meal plan that matches your habits!

CASH CARDS

Some colleges and universities offer cash cards so that students do not have to carry a lot of money with them. A cash card works similarly to a debit card from a bank. Cash cards may be accepted at the campus bookstore, cafeteria, library, and copy centre, for example. You purchase a cash card in a certain amount, say $500, and each expenditure electronically reduces the available amount on the card until it is all spent. If your cash card works on a Personal Identification Number (PIN) system, be sure that you *never* let anyone know your PIN. Do not tell even your closest friend. Students have lost every cent to "friends" they trusted. Be cautious.

BUYING TEXTBOOKS

The biggest gripe that students today have about college and university life is the cost of textbooks. We have mentioned that it is not wise to sell your texts after each semester. Of course, you may have to do so because of financial concerns, and most schools purchase used texts from students at a reduced rate. This policy may be helpful to you, but it may also create a problem. Someone may see your books lying on the floor of the student centre and decide to take them and sell them to the bookstore. This could cost you upwards of $300 to $400. Guard your textbooks. Never leave them in your car overnight, in an unlocked residence room, or in a library study room.

Do not purchase a used textbook from a student until you have checked to see that the same book will be used in the course again. A professor may opt to use a new edition of the text or a different book altogether.

Also, do not buy a lab or workbook that has been used. If the assignments have been completed, then you do not have a chance to complete the assignment yourself, which may cause problems later on. Always buy new lab books and workbooks.

PARKING ON CAMPUS

The second biggest gripe on campuses is parking. Sometimes it seems as though there are 16,000 students, 750 employees, and 100 guests, but only 37 parking spots on campus! Although the situation is not really *that* bad, on almost every campus the parking situation *is* frustrating. We cannot create more parking spaces or valet park your car for you, but we can give you some advice learned by hard knocks about parking on campus.

- Purchase a parking decal if it is required. One ticket for not having a decal could probably have covered the cost of the sticker.

- If your sticker reads "Z Lot Only," *park in the Z lot only!* Parking in the wrong lot can cost you up to $50 per instance.

- Never, under *any* circumstances, park in a handicapped spot unless you have a decal that allows you to do so. Fines can range from $200 to $1000 for each violation. Also, by parking in a handicapped zone, you may be creating a hardship for someone who needs the space for more than mere convenience.

- Arrive early so that you have a slight chance of finding a parking space within an hour's hike of your classroom. The Z lot is usually in another county. Plan for this in your schedule.

- Pay your fines when you get them. Do not let them add up or you could quickly owe $100 to $500 in a semester. When you go to pay your tuition, your parking fines will be added to it, and you will not be allowed to register for classes until the fines are paid in full. (This is also true of library fines.)

- Do not park in a faculty member's parking place. The last thing you need is to be seen getting into your car in the faculty lot when the professor had to park in Timbuktu because you took that spot. Big mistake!

- Keep change in your car in case you have to park in a metered space owned by the college or the city. Meter fines can range from $5 to $50.

- If parking is restricted to students living in residence, drive on. Without a decal identifying you as a resident, the campus security will ticket or tow your car.

- Carpool when possible. You'll save money and your frustration level will decrease.

- Be polite to the traffic officer or the secretary in the transportation office. Do not use profanity; it will get you nowhere.

Glossary

A

ACADEMIC FREEDOM Academic freedom allows professors to conduct research and teach their findings, even if the subject matter is controversial. Academic freedom gives professors the right to teach certain materials that might not be allowed in high school.

ADDING Adding a class means enrolling in an additional class. The term is usually used during registration period or during the first week of a semester.

ADMINISTRATION The administration of a post-secondary institution is headed by the president and vice presidents and comprises the nonteaching personnel who handle all administrative aspects of running the institution. The structure of the administration varies at each college and university.

ADVISING An academic advisor may be assigned to each student on arrival on campus. It is the advisor's responsibility to guide students through their academic work, and to assist them when needed throughout the academic year. An advisor is most often a faculty member in the student's program who will work with the student through the student's entire academic career.

AIDS This acronym stands for **a**cquired **i**mmune **d**eficiency **s**yndrome, a disease that is transmitted sexually, intravenously, or from mother to fetus. There is currently no known cure for AIDS, but several medications, such as AZT, DDC, 3TC, DT4, Sequinavir, DDI, and Indinavir, help to slow the deterioration of the immune system. AIDS is the number one killer among people aged 25 to 44 years.

ALUMNA, ALUMNUS, ALUMNI These terms describe people who attended a post-secondary school. *Alumna* refers to a woman, *alumnus* refers to men, and *alumni* refers to more than one of either or both. The term *alumni* is the most often used.

ATTENDANCE Some colleges have an attendance policy, such as "any student who misses more than 20 percent of the total class hours will receive an F for the course." This policy is followed strictly by some professors and more leniently by others. Students should know the attendance policy of each professor with whom they are studying.

AUDITING Most colleges and universities offer the option of auditing a course. Whereas a student enrolled in a course pays a fee, must attend classes, takes exams, and receives credit, a student auditing a course usually pays a smaller fee, does not have to take exams, and does not receive credit. People who are having trouble in a subject or who simply want to gain more knowledge about a subject but don't need or want credit are the most likely candidates for auditing. Some colleges and universities charge full price for auditing a course.

B

BACCALAUREATE (BACHELOR DEGREE) The baccalaureate degree, more commonly called the bachelor's degree, is a degree awarded by a university after 3-4 years, upon completion of a program of studies. A student is an undergraduate during this time.

BOARD OF GOVERNORS The board of governors is the senior decision-making body of a post-secondary school. The board hires the president, approves financial budgets, and sets policies.

C

CALENDAR Each college and university publishes a catalogue outlining admission requirements for each program, and listing the courses and electives within each program.

CAMPUS The term *campus* refers to the physical plan of a university or college, including all buildings, fields, arenas, auditoriums, and other properties owned by the institution.

CAMPUS SECURITY All colleges and universities have a campus police or security office. Campus security helps students with problems ranging from physical danger to directions. Every student should know how to contact security in case of emergency.

CARREL A carrel is a booth or small room, often large enough to accommodate one person only, located in the library. Students and faculty can reserve a carrel for professional use by the semester or the week.

CERTIFICATE A certificate program is a series of courses, usually lasting one year, designed to educate and train an individual in a specific area, such as welding, automotive repair, medical transcription, tool and die, early childhood, physical therapy, and fashion merchandising. Although certified and detailed, these programs are not degree programs.

COMMUNICATIONS University curricula often mandate nine hours of communications, which commonly refers to English and speech (oral communication) courses. The mixture of courses is typically English 101 and 102 and Speech 101; the numbers vary from university to university.

COMPREHENSIVE EXAMS Exams that encompass materials from the entire course are comprehensive exams. That is, a comprehensive exam covers information from the first lecture through the last.

CONTINUING EDUCATION Continuing education or community education courses are designed to meet specific business and industry needs or to teach subjects of interest to the community. Many courses are not offered for credit, but continuing education units may be awarded. Continuing education courses range from small engine repair to flower arranging, from stained glass making to small-business management.

CO-OP/FIELD WORK This term refers to a relationship between a business or industry and the educational institution that allows a student to spend a semester in college or university and the next semester on the job. Co-ops may be structured variously, but the general idea of a co-op is always to gain on-the-job experience.

COREQUISITE A corequisite is a course that must be taken at the same time as another course. Science courses often carry a corequisite, for example, Biology 101 may have as a corequisite the lab course, Biology 101L.

COUNSELLING Most campuses have a counselling centre, staffed by counsellors trained to assist students with problems that might arise in their personal lives, with their study skills, and with their career aspirations. Counselling is different from advising—academic advisors are responsible for helping students with their academic progress. Some schools combine the two, but in most cases the counsellor and the advisor are two different people with two different job descriptions.

COURSE TITLE Every course has a course title. A schedule of classes may read: ENG 101, SPC 205, HIS 210, and so on. The course calendar defines what these terms mean. For example, ENG 101 usually stands for English 101, SPC could be the heading for speech, HIS could mean history. Headings and course titles vary.

CREDIT HOUR A credit hour is the amount of credit earned for a class. Most classes are worth three credit hours; science, foreign language, and some math courses that require labs are worth four credit hours. A class that carries three credit hours typically meets for three hours per week. This formula varies in summer sessions or midsessions.

CURRICULUM The curriculum is a set of classes that the student must take to earn a diploma or degree in an area of study.

D

DEAN *Dean* is the title given to the head of a division or area of study. The dean is the policy maker and usually the business manager and final decision maker for that area. A college or university might have a dean of applied arts, a dean of business, and a dean of technology. Deans usually report to a vice-president or provost.

DEAN'S LIST The dean's list is a listing of students who have achieved at least a 3.5 (B+) on a 4.0 scale (these numbers are defined under "GPA"). Although it varies, the dean's list generally comprises students in the top 5 percent of the institution.

DEGREE A student is awarded a degree for completing an approved course of study. The type of degree depends on the university, the number of credit hours in the program, and the field of study. A student who attends graduate school may receive a master's degree (after two to three years) and a doctorate (after three to ten years). Some universities offer postdoctorate degrees.

DIPLOMA A diploma is awarded upon completion of a two or three year college program that usually prepares the student to work in a specific career or industry.

DROPPING Students may elect to drop a class if they are not enjoying it or think that they will not be able to pass it because of grades or absenteeism. A course that has been dropped will no longer appear on the student's schedule or be calculated in the GPA. Rules and regulations governing dropping courses vary and are explained in the course calendar.

E

ELECTIVE An elective is a course that a student chooses to take outside his or her major field of study. An elective can be in an area of interest to the student or in an area that complements the student's major. For example, an English major might choose an elective in the field of theatre or history because these fields complement one another. An English major might also elect to take a course in medical terminology because of an interest in that area.

EMERITI This Latin term applies to retired personnel who have performed exemplary duties during their professional careers. A college or university president who procured funding for new buildings, enhanced curriculum programs, and increased the endowment might be named president emeritus (singular of emeriti) on retirement.

EVENING SCHOOL An evening school program is designed to allow students who have full-time jobs to enroll in classes that meet in the evening. Some colleges and universities offer an entire degree program in the evening; others offer only some courses in the evening.

F

FACULTY The faculty is the body of professionals who teach, conduct research, and perform community service. Faculty members prepare for many years to hold the responsibilities carried by the title. Some may have studied for many years or have extensive industry experience to obtain the knowledge and skill necessary to train students in their specific fields.

FEES Fees refer to the money charged by colleges and universities for specific items and services. Fees may be charged for tuition, meal plans, books, health care, and activities. Fees vary and are usually printed in the course calendar.

FINANCIAL AID Financial aid is money awarded to a student from the college or university, the provincial or federal government, or private sources on the basis of need or of merit. Any bursary, grant, loan, or scholarship is formally called financial aid.

FINE ARTS The fine arts encompass a variety of artistic forms, such as theater, dance, architecture, drawing, painting, sculpture, and music. Some universities also include literature in this category.

FIRST-YEAR STUDENT The term "first-year student" refers to a student who is enrolled in his/her first year of post-secondary studies.

FOREIGN LANGUAGE Many colleges offer courses in foreign languages, and some universities offer degrees in this area. Some of the many foreign languages offered are French, Spanish, Russian, Latin, German, Portuguese, Arabic, Japanese, Chinese, and Korean.

FRATERNITY A fraternity is an organization in the Greek system. Fraternities are open to male students only. Induction for each is different. Many fraternities have their own housing complexes off campus. Honorary fraternities, such as Phi Kappa Phi, are academic in nature and are open to men and women.

G

GPA The grade point average, GPA, is the numerical grading system used by many academic institutions in Canada. A student's GPA determines his or her eligibility for continued enrolment, financial aid, and honours. Most colleges and universities operate under a 4.0 system: an A is worth 4 quality points; a B, 3 points; a C, 2 points; a D, 1 point, and an F 0 points. To calculate a GPA, for each course the number of quality points earned is multiplied by the number of credit hours carried by the course; the numbers thus obtained for all courses are added together; finally, this total is divided by the total number of hours carried.

Example: A student is taking English 101, Speech 101, History 201, and Psychology 101, all of which carry three credit hours. If the student earns all A's, the GPA is 4.0; if the student earns all B's, the GPA is 3.0. However, if he or she had a variety of grades, you would calculate as such:

COURSE	GRADE	CREDIT HRS.	QUALITY POINTS	TOTAL POINTS
ENG 101	A	3 ×	4	= 12 points
SPC 101	C	3 ×	2	= 6 points
HIS 201	B	3 ×	3	= 9 points
PSY 101	D	3 ×	1	= 3 points

GPA = 30 points divided by 12 hours = 2.5 (C+)

GRADUATE TEACHING ASSISTANT In some universities, students working toward master's and doctorate degrees teach lower-level undergraduate classes under the direction of a senior professor in the department.

GRANT Usually a grant is money that goes toward tuition and books that does not have to be repaid. Grants are most often awarded by the government.

H

HIGHER EDUCATION This term applies to any level of education beyond high school; all colleges and universities are considered institutions of higher education.

HONOURS Academic honours are based on a student's GPA. Academic honors may include the dean's list, the president's list, and departmental honours.

HONOURS DEGREE An honours degree is usually a four-year degree, comprised of 20 credits, that may also require a certain GPA over the four years.

HUMANITIES The humanities are sometimes as misunderstood as the fine arts. Disciplines in the humanities include history, philosophy, religion, cultural studies, and sometimes literature, government and foreign languages. The course calendar defines what a university designates as humanities.

i

IDENTIFICATION CARDS A student identification (ID) card is an essential possession for any student. An ID card allows students to use the library, participate in activities, use physical fitness facilities, and often to attend events free of charge. ID cards can also be useful beyond the campus borders. Admission to movie theatres, museums, zoos, and cultural events usually costs less and is sometimes free for students with IDs. ID cards also allow access to most area library facilities with special privileges. Some colleges issue ID cards at no charge, and some charge a small fee. ID cards are usually validated each semester.

INDEPENDENT STUDY Many colleges and universities offer some independent study options. Independent study courses have no formal classes and no classroom teacher; students work independently to complete the course under the general guidelines of the department and with the assistance of an instructor. Often, students must maintain a minimum GPA in order to enroll in independent study classes.

INTERNET The Internet provides students with access to on-line magazines, software, live interactive services, and financial services. It can be one of the most informative and exciting learning tools for students today.

j

JOURNAL In many classes, such as English, orientation, literature, history, and psychology, students are required to keep a journal of thoughts, opinions, research, and class discussions. The journal often serves as a communication link between the student and the professor.

L

LECTURE The lecture is the lesson given by an instructor in a class. Some instructors use group discussions, peer tutoring, or multimedia presentations. The term *lecture* is usually used when the material is presented in a lecture format, that is, when the professor presents most of the information.

LIBERAL ARTS A liberal arts curriculum ensures that the students are exposed to a variety of disciplines and cultural experiences, that they take courses beyond those needed for a specific vocation or occupation. A student taking liberal arts at a university and majoring in biology would also have to take courses in areas such as fine arts, history, social sciences, math, hard sciences, for example.

LOAD The number of credit hours or classes that a student is taking is the student's load. The normal load is between 15 and 18 hours or five to six classes. In most colleges, 12 hours or 70% of the hours in a program is considered a full-time load, but a student can take up to 18 or 21 hours for the same tuition.

M

MAJOR A major is a university student's intended field of study. The term *major* indicates that the majority of the student's work will be completed in that field. Students are usually required to declare a major by the end of their second year.

MEAL PLAN A student purchases a meal plan at the beginning of a semester that allows the student to eat certain meals in the cafeteria or dining hall. These plans are regulated by a computer card or punch system. Meal plans can be purchased for three meals a day, breakfast only, lunch only, or a variety of other meal combinations.

MENTOR A mentor is someone who can help a student through troubled times, assist in decision making, and provide advice. A mentor can be a teacher, staff member, fellow classmate, or upper-level student. Mentors seldom volunteer. They usually fall into the role of mentor because they are easy to talk with, knowledgeable about the college and the community, and willing to lend a helping hand. Sometimes students are assigned mentors when they arrive on campus.

MINOR A university student's minor usually comprises six to eight courses in a specific field that complements the student's major area of study. A student majoring in engineering might minor in math or electronics, subjects that might help later in the workforce.

N

NATURAL SCIENCES The natural and physical sciences refer to a select group of courses from biology, chemistry, physical science, physics, anatomy, zoology, botany, geology, genetics, microbiology, physiology, and astronomy.

O

ORIENTATION All students are invited and many are required to attend an orientation session when they enter college or university. These sessions are extremely useful. They present important information about college life as well as details of the rules of the specific institution.

P

PLAGIARISM Plagiarism refers to the act of using another person's words or works as one's own without citing the original author. Penalties for plagiarism vary and can include asking the student to withdraw from the institution. Most institutions have strict guidelines for dealing with plagiarism. Penalties for plagiarism are usually listed in the student handbook.

PREFIX The code used by the Office of the Registrar to designate a certain area of study is called a prefix. Common prefixes are ENG for English, REL for Religion, THE for Theatre, and HIS for History. Prefix lettering varies at each institution.

PREPROFESSIONAL PROGRAMS Preprofessional programs usually refer to majors that *require* further study at the master's or doctoral level in order to be able to practise in the field. Such programs include law, medicine, dentistry, psychiatry, nursing, veterinary studies, and theology.

PREREQUISITE A prerequisite is a course that must be taken *before* another course. For example, students are required to take Business Communications I before taking Business Communications II. Prerequisites are listed in the course calendar.

PRESIDENT A president is the visionary leader of the institution. He or she is usually hired by the board of governors. The president's primary responsibilities include financial planning, fund-raising, developing community relations, and maintaining the academic integrity of the curriculum. Every employee at the institution is responsible to the president.

PRIOR LEARNING ASSESSMENT Prior learning assessment may allow a student to be awarded a credit for a given course if the student has practical experience and/or training equivalent to the course requirements.

PROBATION A student who has not performed well in his or her academic studies, usually manifested by a GPA below 2.0 in any given semester or quarter, may be placed on academic probation for one semester. If the student continues to perform below 2.0, he or she may be suspended. The rules for probation and suspension must be displayed in the course calendar.

PROFESSOR Not all teachers at the university level are professors. The system of promotion among university teachers is adjunct instructor, instructor, lecturer, assistant professor, associate professor, and full professor, or professor. A full professor is likely to have been in the profession for a long time and usually holds a doctorate degree.

PROVOST The provost is the primary policy maker with regard to academic standards. The provost usually reports directly to the president. Many institutions do not have provosts, but have instead a vice-president for academic affairs or a dean of instruction.

R

READMIT A student who has stopped out for a semester or two usually has to be readmitted to the college or university, but does not lose previously earned academic credit unless the credit carried a time limit. Some courses carry a five- or ten-year limit, which means that the course must be retaken if a diploma or degree is not awarded within that time period. Students who elect not to attend summer sessions do not need to be readmitted. There is typically no application fee for a readmit student.

REGISTRAR The registrar has one of the most difficult jobs on any campus, because the registrar is responsible for all student academic records as well as for entering all grades, recording all drops and adds, printing the schedules, and verifying all candidates for graduation. The Office of the Registrar is sometimes referred to as the records office.

RESIDENCE A residence is a facility on campus where students live. Residences can be single sex or coeducational. Many new students choose to live in residences because they are conveniently located and they provide a good way to meet new friends and to become involved in extracurricular activities. Each residence usually has a full-time supervisor and elects a student representative to the student council. In addition, a director of student housing oversees the residences.

RESIDENCY REQUIREMENT Many colleges and universities have a residency requirement, for example, they require that a student must be taking a full course load to be eligible for residence. All residency requirements are spelled out in the course calendar.

ROOM AND BOARD Students attending schools without residences often live off campus with a family, and pay a fee for room and board. Room and board refers to a place to stay and food to eat. Issues involving room and board are usually discussed during orientation.

S

SCHOLAR *Scholar* typically refers to a student who has performed in a superior manner in a certain field of study.

SECTION CODE When many sections of the same course are offered, a section code identifies the hour and instructor of the student's particular class. A schedule that includes section codes may look something like this:

English 101 01 MWF 8:00–8:50 Smith

English 101 02 MWF 8:00–8:50 Jones

English 101 03 T TH 8:00–9:15 McGee

The numbers 01, 02, 03, and so on refer to a specific section of 101.

SOCIAL SCIENCES The social sciences study society and people. Social science courses may include psychology, sociology, anthropology, political science, geography, economics, and international studies.

SORORITIES A sorority is an organization in the Greek system open to women only. Many sororities have off-campus housing complexes. Initiation into a sorority differs from organization to organization and from campus to campus.

STAFF College and university personnel are usually divided into three categories: administration, staff, and faculty. The staff is responsible for the day-to-day workings of the institution. People who work in admissions, financial aid, the bookstore, housing, student activities, and personnel, for example, usually hold staff titles, whereas the people who head these departments are usually in administration.

STUDENT GOVERNMENT ASSOCIATION One of the most powerful and visible organizations on campus, the Student Government Association (SGA) usually comprises students from all undergraduate classes. Officers are elected annually. The SGA is the student voice on campus and represents the entire student body before the administration of the college or university.

STUDENT LOAN A student loan is money that must be repaid. Student loans generally have a much lower rate of interest than bank loans, and the payment schedule for most student loans does not usually begin until six months after graduation. This delayed start is intended to allow the graduate to find a secure job and a steady income before having to make payments. If a student decides to return to school, the loan can be deferred, with additional interest, until the student's education is completed.

SUSPENSION Students may be suspended for a variety of reasons, but most suspensions are for academic reasons. Again, GPA requirements vary, but students are usually suspended if their GPA falls below 1.5 for two consecutive semesters. The course calendar lists the rules regarding suspension.

SYLLABUS A syllabus or course outline replaces the class outline of high school. A syllabus is a legally binding contract between the student and the professor; it contains the attendance policy, the grading scale, the required text, the professor's office hours and phone number(s), and important, relevant information about the course. Most professors include the class deadlines and important dates as a part of the syllabus. The syllabus is one of the most important documents that is issued in a class. Students should take the syllabus to class daily and keep it at least until the semester is over.

T

TENURE Tenure basically guarantees a university professor lifelong employment at an institution. Tenure is usually awarded to professors who have been with the university for many years in recognition of their successful efforts in research, their record of having books and articles published, and their community service.

TOEFL The Test of English as a Foreign Language, TOEFL, is used to certify that international students have the English skills necessary to succeed at the institution or to become a teaching assistant. Some colleges allow international students to use English to satisfy their foreign language requirement if they score high enough on the TOEFL.

TRANSCRIPT A transcript is a formal record of all work attempted and/or completed at a college or university. A student has a transcript for every school attended. Many institutions have a policy of listing all classes, completed or not, on the transcript. Some allow Ds and Fs to be removed if the student repeats the course and earns a better grade, but many others retain the original grade and continue to calculate it in the GPA. Rules regarding transcripts vary at each institution. Many employers now require that a prospective employee furnish a college or university transcript.

TRANSIENT A transient student is a student who is taking one or two courses at a college or university other than his or her home institution. For example, a student who enrolls in a college near home for the summer while maintaining student status at his or her chosen college is a transient student.

TRANSITIONAL STUDIES Many colleges and universities have an open admission policy, meaning that the door is open to any student, and colleges frequently offer a transitional studies or upgrading program to help students reach their educational goals. For example, a student who has not performed well in English, math, or reading may be required to attend a transitional studies class to upgrade basic skills in that area.

TRANSFER The term *transfer* can refer to course work as well as to students. A student who enrolls in one college and then moves to another is classified as a transfer student. The course work completed at the original college is called transfer work. Many institutions have rules regarding the number of credit hours that a student can transfer. Most institutions will not accept credit from another college if the grade on the course is lower than a C.

V

VICE-PRESIDENT Many colleges and universities have several vice-presidents who serve under the president. These are senior-level administrators who assist with the daily operations of the college and may include vice-presidents of academic affairs, financial affairs, and student affairs, among others.

VOLUMES A volume refers to a book or a piece of non-print material that assists students in their studies. If a college library has 70,000 volumes, it means that the library has 70,000 books *and* other pieces of media. Many colleges and universities have millions of volumes.

W

WOMEN'S STUDIES Some universities offer majors and minors in women's studies. The curriculum is centred on the major contributions of women in art, literature, medicine, history, law, architecture, and sciences.

References

Adler, R., Rosenfeld, L., and Towne, N. *Interplay. The Process of Interpersonal Communication.* New York: Holt, Rinehart and Winston, 1989.

Aggarwal, A. *Sexual Harassment: A Guide for Understanding and Prevention.* Toronto: Butterworths, 1992.

American College Testing Program. *National Drop Out Rates.* ACT Institutional Data File, Iowa City, 1995.

Astin, A. *Achieving Educational Excellence.* San Francisco: Jossey-Bass, 1985.

Beebe, S., and Beebe, S. *Public Speaking: An Audience Centered Approach.* 2d ed. Englewood Cliffs, NJ: Prentice Hall, 1994.

Benson, H. *The Relaxation Response.* New York: Carol Publishing Group, 1992.

Benson, H., and Stuart, E. *The Wellness Book: The Comprehensive Guide to Maintaining Health and Treating Stress-Related Illness.* New York: Birch Lane Press, 1992.

Berenblatt, M., and Berenblatt, A. *Make an Appointment with Yourself: Simple Steps to Positive Self-Esteem.* Deerfield Beach, FL: Health Communication, 1994.

Boyle, M., and Zyla, G. *Personal Nutrition.* St. Paul, MN: West Publishing, 1992.

Bozzi, V. "A Healthy Dose of Religion," *Psychology Today* (November 1988).

Buscaglia, L. *Living, Loving, and Learning.* New York: Ballantine, 1982.

Campbell, C. *Where the Jobs Are: Career Survival for Canadians in the New Global Economy.* Toronto: Macfarlane Walter & Ross, 1994.

Canadian Human Rights Commission Annual Report. Ottawa, 1995.

Chickering, A., and Schlossberg, N. *Getting the Most out of College.* Boston: Allyn and Bacon, 1995.

Chopra, D. *The Seven Spiritual Laws of Success.* San Rafael, CA: New World Library, 1994.

Christian, J., and Greger, J. *Nutrition for Living.* Redwood City, CA: Benjamin/Cummings Publishing, 1994.

The Chronicle of Higher Education, Almanac Edition. Vol XL, No. 1 (August 25, 1993).

Cooper, A. *Time Management for Unmanageable People.* New York: Bantam Books, 1993.

Cowan, D., and Weber, K. *Canadians All 4: Protraits of Our People.* Toronto: Methuen, 1983.

Crichlow, W. "Understanding the World of the Black Child." *ORBIT, OISE Journal,* Vol. 25 (1994).

Donatelle, R., and Davis, L. *Health: The Basics.* Englewood Cliffs, NJ: Prentice Hall, 1994.

Drugs in Ontario. Toronto: The Addiction Research Foundation, 1995.

Ellis, D., Lankowitz, S., Stupka, D., and Toft, D. *Career Planning.* Rapid City, SD: College Survival, Inc., 1990.

Elrich, M. "The Stereotype Within." *Educational Leadership* (April 1994), p. 12.

The Final Report of the Royal Commission on New Reproductive Technologies. 2 vols. Ottawa, 1993.

Foot, D. *Boom, Bust and Echo: How to Profit from the Coming Demographic Shift.* Toronto: Macfarlane Walter & Ross, 1996, p. 69.

Fulghum, R. *All I Really Need to Know, I Learned in Kindergarten.* New York: Ivy Books, 1988.

Gardenswartz, L., and Rowe, A. *Managing Diversity: A Complete Desk Reference and Planning Guide.* New York: Irwin/Pfeiffer, 1993.

Gardner, J., and Jewler, J. *Your College Experience.* Belmont, CA: Wadsworth, 1995

Grilly, D. *Drugs and Human Behavior.* Boston: Allyn and Bacon, 1994.

Gunthrie, H., and Picciano, M. *Human Nutrition.* Salem, MA: Mosby, 1995.

Hales, D. *Your Health.* Redwood City, CA: Benjamin/Cummings Publishing, 1991.

The Health of Canada's Youth. Ottawa: Health and Welfare Canada, 1992.

Lecky, P. *Self-Consistency: A Theory of Personality.* Garden City, NY: Anchor, 1951.

Legate, D. *Stephen Leacock, A Biography.* Toronto: Doubleday, 1970.

National Population Health Survey Overview 1994-95, Ottawa: Statistics Canada, 1995.

Nevid, J., Fichner-Rathus, L., and Rathus, S. *Human Sexuality in a World of Diversity.* Boston: Allyn and Bacon, 1995.

Olesen, E. *Mastering the Winds of Change.* New York: Harper Business, 1993.

Popenoe, D. *Sociology,* 9th ed. Englewood Cliffs, NJ: Prentice Hall, 1993.

Rathus, S., and Fichner-Rathus, L. *Making the Most out of College.* Englewood Cliffs, NJ: Prentice Hall, 1994.

Rogers, C. *On Becoming Partners: Marriage and Its Alternatives.* New York: Delacorte Press, 1972.

Romas, J., and Sharma, M. *Practical Stress Management.* Boston: Allyn and Bacon, 1995.

Schneller, J. *"Runaway Twain,"* Chatelaine (May 1996), p. 56.

Sciolino, E. World Drug Crop Up Sharply in 1989 Despite U.S. Effort. *New York Times,* March 2, 1990.

Shaffer, C., and Anundsen, K. *Creating Community Anywhere.* Los Angeles: Jeremy P. Tarcher Publishing, 1994.

University of California, Berkeley, Wellness Letter Editors. *Wellness Encyclopedia.* Boston: Houghton Mifflin, 1991.

Whitfield, C. *Healing the Child Within.* Deerfield Beach, FL: Health Communication, 1987.

Woolfolk, A. *Educational Psychology.* 6th ed. Boston: Allyn and Bacon, 1995.

Yale Study of Graduating Seniors. Yale University, New Haven, CT, 1953.

PHOTO CREDITS

Chapter 1
4 Chris Schwarz/Maclean's. 10 Robert Harbison. 11 Brian Smith. 16 Brian Smith. 25 Chris Schwarz/Maclean's. 26 P. Beringer/The Image Works.

Chapter 2
28 Canadian Olympic Association. 33 Canadian Space Agency. 34 Robert Achenbrenner/Stock Boston. 41 Wide World Photos. 44 North Wind Picture Archives. 47 Chrysler Corporation. 48 Anthony Neste.

Chapter 3
59 R. Sidney/The Image Works. 65 Will Faller. 66 Al Harvey. 72 Bachmann/The Image Works.

Chapter 4
84 C. J. Allen/Stock Boston. 89 Bob Daemmrich/Stock Boston. 104 Ellis Herwig/Stock Boston.

Chapter 5
110 Paula Lerner/Woodfin Camp & Associates. 115 (bottom left) Brian Smith. 115(right) Esbin–Anderson/The Image Works. 128 Anthony Neste.

Chapter 6
140 David H. Wells/The Image Bank. 144 Anthony Neste.

Chapter 7
164 Brian Smith. 167 Brian Smith. 174 Brian Smith.

Chapter 8
184 Brian Smith. 189 Brian Smith. 207 Robert Harbison.

Chapter 9
210 Bob Daemmrich/The Image Works.

Chapter 10
234 Francie Manning/The Picture Cube. 239 Sepp Seitz/Woodfin Camp & Associates. 249 Paula Lerner/Woodfin Camp & Associates

Chapter 11
264 Strauss/Curtis/Offshoot Stock. 274 Charles Gupton/Tony Stone Images.

Chapter 12
282 Phyllis Picard/Stock Boston. 293 Chris Schwarz/Maclean's. 295 Anthony Neste.

Chapter 13
298 Brian Smith. 303 PHC Archives. 310 Mark Walker/The Picture Cube. 312 Mark Antman/The Image Works.

Chapter 14
320 Richard Pasley/Stock Boston. 326 Bob Daemmrich/The Image Works. 332 William Johnson/Stock Boston.

Chapter 15
336 Spencer Grant/The Picture Cube. 340 Barbara Alper/Stock Boston. 342 Bob Daemmrich/Stock Boston. 355 Brian Smith.